ANSELM'S DOCTRINE
OF FREEDOM AND THE WILL

G. STANLEY KANE

Texts and Studies in Religion
Volume 10

The Edwin Mellen Press
New York and Toronto

Library of Congress Cataloging in Publication Data

Kane, G. Stanley,
    Anselm's doctrine of freedom and the will.

    (Texts and studies in religion ; v. 10)
    Bibliography: p.
    1. Free will and determinism. 2. Anselm, Saint,
Abp. of Canterbury, 1033-1109. I. Title. II. Series.
BJ1461.K36   123'.5   81-16939
ISBN 0-88946-914-8   AACR2

Texts and Studies in Religion ISBN 0-88946-976-8

Printed in the United States of America

CONTENTS

CONTENTS

ACKNOWLEDGMENTS

Some of the material included in this book has appeared in earlier versions elsewhere. In chapter one I have used material from my article, "'*Fides Quaerens Intellectum*' in Anselm's Thought," which appeared in *Scottish Journal of Theology*; in chapters one and five I have used material from "Anselm's Definition of Freedom," which appeared in *Religious Studies*; and in chapter four I have drawn on "Elements of Ethical Theory in the Thought of Saint Anselm," published in *Studies in Medieval Culture*. I am grateful to the editors of these journals for their permission to use this material.

Except where indicated otherwise, I have used the following translations. For *De Grammatico* and Anselm's Philosophical Fragments (*De Potestate et Impotentia, Possibilitate et Impossibilitate, Necessitate et Libertate*), I have used D. P. Henry's translation. For *Cur Deus Homo,* I have used E. R. Fairweather's translation. For all other treatises I have used the translations of Jasper Hopkins and Herbert Richardson. Occasionally I have slightly altered these translations.

Much of the final writing of this work was done during the Spring semester of 1980, while I was on leave from regular duties at Miami University. Acknowledgment is gratefully made for this leave.

I wish to convey special thanks to Bill Wortman, Humanities Librarian at Miami University's King Library, for his generous and proficient help in supplying bibliographic information and tracking down hard-to-locate sources.

CDH   *Cur Deus Homo*

DC   *De Concordia Praescientiae et Praedestinationis et Gratiae Dei cum Libero Arbitrio*

DCD   *De Casu Diaboli*

DCV   *De Conceptu Virginali et Originali Peccato*

DLA   *De Libertate Arbitrii*

DV   *De Veritate*

NUW   F. S. Schmitt's study and text of *Ein neues unvollendetes Werk des hl. Anselm von Canterbury: De Potestate et Impotentia, Possibilitate et Impossibilitate, Necessitate et Libertate*

CHAPTER ONE

INTRODUCTION

Anselm of Canterbury has for a long time been a major name in both philosophy and theology. Yet except among a rather small group of specialists he has been known primarily for only a small part of his intellectual work. Most students of philosophy and theology know of his *Monologion, Proslogion* (and the debate this occasioned with Gaunilo) and *Cur Deus Homo,* which are also the works of his that have been most frequently translated into the modern languages. And a considerable literature has grown up analyzing and interpreting the teachings of these treatises. Relatively few philosophers and theologians have been aware of what Anselm wrote in other treatises, in which he deals extensively with such major problems as truth, justice, the Trinity, the Incarnation, evil and free will. As a result Anselm has generally come to be identified primarily with only a few major points in his thinking: a doctrine of the nature and existence of God, including especially the ontological argument, grounded on the notion of God as the greatest conceivable being; a special concept of the relation of faith and reason in the apprehension of Christian truth; and a distinctive doctrine of the Atonement.

This situation has had some unfortunate effects. It has, in the first place, led to a partial and hence distorted understanding of Anselm's contribution to philosophical and theological thinking. In this respect he stands in sharp

1

contrast to medieval thinkers like Augustine and Thomas
Aquinas, who are widely recognized for dealing with a wide
range of philosophical, theological, and practical problems.
This is regrettable, not only because Anselm deals with many
of the same problems that vexed these men, but because his
treatment of them displays considerable power and subtlety
and so deserves more serious scholarly attention than much
of it has been given.

Secondly, a full and balanced understanding of even
some of the better known parts of Anselm's work requires an
acquaintance with what is taught in the lesser known parts.
Much, for example, has been written about Anselm's intellectual method and his program of *fides quaerens intellectum*. But
most of this concentrates on what he says and does in his
better known treatises, ignoring the fact that what he says
and does in some of his other works is also important and is
at points different from what comes through in his better
known works and statements.[1] Another example is the teaching of the *Cur Deus Homo*, where Anselm expressly states,
"There is another reason for thinking that we can hardly (if
at all) deal fully with this problem [the Atonement] now.
We should need to know about power and necessity and will
and several other things which are so closely connected that
no one of them can be fully considered without the others."[2]
Anselm here gives explicit warning that his soteriology cannot be fully understood without knowing his thinking about
matters he deals with elsewhere. Rather few interpreters,
however, have taken this warning to heart. The all-too-
frequent failure to consider Anselm's thinking in light of
the whole of his work has been so common that it has prompted
the comment from John McIntyre that "no major thinker has
suffered so much as St. Anselm from the hit-and-run tactics
of historians of theism and soteriology."[3]

The past few years have shown signs that this situation is beginning to change. As of the early 1970s, all of

Anselm's treatises had been translated into English,[4] with
the translation being based on a critical edition established
and edited several decades earlier by F. S. Schmitt.[5] An ex-
cellent general introduction to the entire body of Anselm's
thought was published in 1972 by Jasper Hopkins,[6] and a somewhat more specialized survey of his entire corpus has been
presented by G. R. Evans in *Anselm and Talking About God.*[7]
R. W. Southern gives an admirable account of both the life
and the thought of Anselm in *Saint Anselm and his Biographer.*[8]
In addition to these general works, special studies devoted
to particular aspects of Anselm's work have also appeared
recently. Most worthy of note are the rigorous investigations by D. P. Henry into Anselm's views on logic and language.[9] And since 1969, a periodical publication devoted to
the study and analysis of Anselm's thought, *Analecta Anselmiana,* has been appearing at various intervals.[10]

Much remains to be done, however, before the full scope
of Anselm's work is generally recognized among philosophers
and theologians. There are still major areas of his thought
that have not received much investigation and analysis. One
of these is the subject of the present inquiry, his doctrine
of the will and freedom. There has been no book-length study
of this subject published at any time in the English language
and only two or three in any modern language. Early in the
present century two small monographs appeared on the subject
in German.[11] These volumes, however, are not widely available in North America, and they are, of course, wholly inac-
cessible to those without a reading knowledge of German.

In addition to the difficulty of gaining access to
these works, they also suffer from flaws of analysis and interpretation. A common tendency among Anselm scholars generally has been to interpret him much more than is warranted
as strictly Augustinian in his thinking. The result has
been that the similarity between Anselm's thought and Augustine's has been much exaggerated. One scholar, writing

about Anselm's doctrine of freedom, went so far as to say,
"His whole doctrine is essentially a repetition of Augustinian thought."[12]   Though this is an extreme statement, many
scholars have endorsed a view very close to the one it
states.[13]   Both Lohmeyer and Baeumker, the authors of the
monographs just mentioned, fall prey to this tendency, though
in different ways.   Lohmeyer gives a Hegelian interpretation
of both Augustine and Anselm and indeed of all medieval philosophy.   He sees the entire sweep of medieval philosophy as
characterized by a series of overarching antitheses—univer-
sal vs. particular, abstract vs. concrete, unity vs. multi-
plicity, subjective vs. objective, internal vs. external relations, being vs. non-being, etc.—that in his view proceed
from Augustine and that determine the aims, the problems,
and the methods of all subsequent medieval philosophy.   Anselm's work, according to Lohmeyer, is a particular instance
of this general approach to the problems of thought.   His
monograph seeks to demonstrate that Anselm's work, though it
may not appear so on the surface, has "a deep intention,"[14]
namely, to address itself to the resolution of these antitheses.   In the process he interprets Anselm as having taken
over from Augustine his Neoplatonism, the fundamental psychological orientation of his metaphysics, and his general
method of intellectual inquiry, without making any essential
changes.

        Baeumker's work is much less speculative and more sober
than Lohmeyer's, sticking much more closely to what Anselm
actually had to say—doing so perhaps to a fault, for a major portion of the book is either a direct translation or a
close paraphrase of Anselm's own words.   Nevertheless, he
too fails to catch the spirit and the method of what Anselm
is doing, and again the reason seems to be that he fails to
appreciate the crucial differences between Anselm's work and
Augustine's.   He chastises Anselm, for example, for failure
to provide proof that man has free will,[15] not recognizing

that Anselm's aim and procedure, unlike Augustine's, make
the question of proof irrelevant. Proof is relevant when
one begins with a speculative definition, for then one must
face the task of showing that the definition applies to the
world of our actual experience. Anselm's approach, however,
is different from this. His investigation is grounded in
the recognition that the terms "freedom" and "will" do in
fact designate realities in our world, for they are used
in speaking about human beings and how they act. He sets
out accordingly to explore the meaning of these terms by examining how they are used and to clarify the features of experience which they pick out. Freedom, in Anselm's view, is
thus a part of the data of experience, so it does not require proof; instead it requires elucidation. His investigations and his search for definitions are attempts at such
elucidation.

Because the similarity of Anselm's doctrine to Augustine's is so constantly overdrawn, it might be useful at the
outset of our study to point out some of the significant differences between them. I have elsewhere done this in connection with some issues in Anselm's thought generally.[16] Here
I shall restrict myself to his thinking concerning the will
and freedom. Some of these points are elaborated more fully
within the body of this study. In the first place, Anselm's
view of the relation between the soul and the will marks a
departure from Augustine. As is well known, Augustine made
extensive use of psychological analogies for explicating the
doctrine of the Trinity. Just as the memory, the understanding, and the will are not three separate substances but the
same substance, the soul, considered in three different functions or relations, so Father, Son, and Holy Spirit are not
three separate beings but one God existing in three subsist-
ent relations. The will, then, in this view, is substantial-
ly identical with the soul itself. It is the soul, the whole
soul, insofar as it acts. Anselm employs some of Augustine's

psychological analogies in the *Monologion*, so it is clear
that at this early point in his career he held to the same
view that Augustine did concerning the relation of the soul
to the will and its other powers. But when he offers his
theory of freedom and the will, later in his career, he no
longer holds to the identity of the soul and its powers.
The will and the intellect are now powers *in* the soul, parts
of the soul, not the whole soul insofar as it is acting or
thinking.[17] At this time he no longer uses psychological
analogies for explicating the relations of the divine persons in the Trinity but employs different methods altogether.[18]

Secondly, Anselm offers quite a different definition
of freedom than Augustine does. This difference is not merely superficial and verbal, as many commentators have supposed, but represents significant differences in conception.
Anselm's definition reflects a different view of what the
free act consists in, of the relation of grace and freedom,
and of the connection between *liberum arbitrium* and *libertas*.
It is, moreover, set within the context of a moral theory
that grounds the end of human life and the duties of man
more on God and his will and less on the inherent nature of
man than Augustine's theory does.[19]

A third respect in which Anselm's work on free will
differs significantly from that of Augustine is his method
of investigation and analysis. This has already been mentioned briefly in discussing Lohmeyer's and Baeumker's works,
but it deserves further comment. Both Augustine and Anselm
subscribe to the dictum, "*Credo ut intelligam*." Both believe, that is, that one must first accept the truth of
Christian doctrine before one can genuinely understand it.
But the manner in which they put this principle into practice in their inquiries into free will differs quite strikingly.

Augustine employs a method which explains Christian
doctrine through concepts which are grounded fundamentally

in the personal experience of the soul. According to this
method, the account that best meets the requirements of
knowledge, and thus conveys the greatest understanding, is
the one which provides the greatest explanatory power for
the experiences which occur in the life of the soul. The
event in Augustine's life which was determinative for all
his thought and experience was his conversion. In meditating
on this experience, Augustine became unshakably convinced
that his conversion and the events surrounding it pointed up
not only the sovereign power and the grace of God but also
his own utter weakness and inability to do good by dint of
his own unaided will. Hence, the concepts of divine grace,
power, and election and the correlative concepts of human
sin and weakness became the leading explanatory principles
for an understanding of the nature of man and of his relation to God.

Human freedom, then, is interpreted in light of these
basic concepts. Augustine's method, therefore, in dealing
with the human will and its freedom is both speculative and
deductive. It is speculative in formulating and elaborating
the basic postulates which are to serve as the fundamental
categories for explaining human experience. And it is deductive in applying these categories when seeking an understanding of particular aspects of human experience, such as
voluntary actions. This deductive approach to freedom is
one which takes the basic postulates as the given framework
of knowledge and then seeks to produce a definition or conception of free will that fits harmoniously into the framework. If there is any conflict or contradiction found between one's conception of freedom and the basic postulates,
it is the conception of freedom that must be revised to
eliminate the conflict and achieve harmony.

In contrast to this, Anselm's procedure is more empirical, inductive, and dialectical. Anselm accepts just as completely as Augustine the doctrine of the Church concerning

the grace, the power, and the predestination of God, as he
does also those concerning the sin and the weakness of man,
but his procedure for developing a rational understanding of
human experience which is consonant with them is significantly different. Instead of first speculatively or dogmatically
defining these doctrines and then drawing out their implications for a theory of human choice and actions, Anselm starts
out by canvassing human experience in order, first, to determine the precise character of our experience, and then in
light of this, to interpret the received doctrine concerning
God's attributes and activities in a manner consonant with
the facts gathered from experience. In this Anselm's procedure is the opposite of Augustine's.

      The first step in Anselm's investigation of freedom is
the search for an adequate definition. The processes of
thought by which he arrives at the definition are recorded
in *DLA*, a short work which he requests be bound together between two other works, *DV* and *DCD*.[20] In *DV*, Anselm is also
engaged in a search for definition—the definitions of truth
and justice (justice being for Anselm a subspecies of truth).
Since the definition of freedom which Anselm gives employs
the notion of justice, the investigations of *DV* serve as a
preliminary to those of *DLA,* and the same principles and
methods are used in both. *DCD* begins a discussion, which is
continued in *DC*, of certain supposed problems in reconciling
human freedom and divine sovereignty.

      In his search for the definitions of truth, justice,
and freedom, Anselm engages in much preliminary investigation preparatory to the actual establishment of his definitions. The principal steps by which he moves toward a definition are as follows. First, he canvasses the various
statements that can ordinarily be made which use the term to
be defined. Then he examines the whole variety of things of
which the term is predicated in those statements and tries to
discern the element which all of them have in common and

which they share with nothing else. The element then constitutes the essential nature of that whose definition is
being sought. A clear expression of this element in terms
of genus and differentia will then be the definition.

The empirical and inductive character of this procedure can be seen from the deliberate and self-conscious attention paid to linguistic data, something that is found
wherever Anselm is looking for clarification or definition
of concepts. In his view such clarification can be best attained only by first considering the whole range of relevant
linguistic data. Before hazarding a definition, he consciously seeks to take into account all the ways he knows of
in which the term to be defined is used in ordinary discourse. At several points in *DV* (which, like *DLA*, is written as a dialogue between teacher and student), the teacher
stops to ask the student whether there are further sorts of
things which may be called true which they have not yet considered.[21] It is only after all these are examined and no
more can be thought of that Anselm proposes his definition.
The procedure in *DLA* differs slightly in actual practice but
in principle it is no different. The difference in practice
is due to the fact that there are not as many things we call
free as there are which we call true. Anselm is able, therefore, to suggest a definition of freedom much earlier in the
dialogue than he is with truth. But with freedom there is a
complication that is not found in dealing with truth. For
not only are certain beings said to be free, but they are
sometimes said to be free in certain situations but not in
others. The definition of freedom, then, must not only apply to such beings we call free as God and men but apply to
them only in those situations in which it is appropriate to
call them free. The situations in which a being may be free
present a rather bewildering variety. *DLA* thus devotes extensive space to an investigation of these situations. In
doing so it seeks to accomplish two things: (1) to vindicate

the proposed definition by showing that it does apply to all
the situations in which a person is thought to be free, and
(2) by showing how it applies in the various situations,
considerably to sharpen and clarify the meaning of the definition. Only when this is done does Anselm consider the
definition established. The important point to note here
about each of these cases, truth and freedom, is Anselm's
conscious point of departure in what is said in ordinary
language, and not just a random sample but as complete a
collection of specimen statements as he is able to gather.

The procedure is empirical in the further sense that
Anselm takes the language as he finds it and seeks to expli-
cate its meaning without imposing some preconceived structure on it. In this it differs strikingly from the speculative approach of Augustine. Anselm takes usages from every
level of experience and initially considers them all on the
same footing. There is no preliminary attempt to arrange
the various kinds of truth—the truth of thought, sense perception, things, actions—on a graded scale. If anything,
Anselm gives a certain methodological preference, because of
its pedagogical value, to truths which Augustine places near
the bottom of his graded hierarchy.

In order to avoid misunderstanding, it should here be
noted that when Anselm looks to language to supply him basic
data, he includes in his consideration not only what today
would be regarded as ordinary language but also statements
from the Christian faith based on the writings of Scripture
and the dogmatic formulations of the Church. This, of
course, fixes a great gulf between him and many contemporary
philosophical analysts in the Anglo-American world. And it
helps explain why, in spite of some shared methods of procedure, Anselm's conclusions differ so widely from those
reached by most of our own contemporaries.

Once the definition of freedom is secured, Anselm is
faced with the problem of how the fact of human freedom is

to be reconciled with God's sovereignty, reflected in his
foreknowledge, predestination, and grace. The problem is
resolved through a close and careful analysis of the concepts of foreknowledge, predestination, and grace and through
further analysis of the will and free choice. This analysis
yields an interpretation of foreknowledge, predestination,
and grace which takes nothing away from the sovereignty of
God but which at the same time is quite compatible with human freedom. Here, as at other points in the development of
his doctrine of freedom, Anselm's procedure is governed by
careful conceptual analysis and close attention to linguistic use, found both in ordinary language and accepted theological usage, and not by the kind of speculative hypothe-
sizing that Augustine does.

The widespread misconception that Anselm's doctrine of
free will merely echoes Augustine may help to account for
the fact that not more attention has been paid to it by
scholars of medieval thought. Even so, it is hard to understand the general neglect of this part of his thinking. In
the first place, he devotes a good deal of attention to it.
DLA and *DC* are wholly concerned with it, and major portions
of *DCD* and *DCV* as well as his philosophical fragments[22] have
to do with various aspects of this doctrine. Secondly, it
is the part of his work in which he develops most extensively
his theory of man. It thus provides an essential link between his earliest works with their primary interest in God
on the one hand, and the fundamental soteriological concern
of some of the most important of his later writings on the
other. It is a link, moreover, which is explicitly pointed
out by Anselm himself in *CDH*. The quotation given above
drawn from this work indicates clearly that in Anselm's mind
the teaching of *CDH* cannot be fully understood without understanding some of the important aspects of his doctrine of the
will and freedom. When one adds to these points the fact,
which I hope will be demonstrated in this study, that Anselm's

doctrine contains a great richness, power, and originality,
one can only hope that it will come to be more widely known
and appreciated.

       This study begins by looking at Anselm's theory of the
will. He teaches that the term "will" is used in three
quite different ways, one to indicate the basic faculty of
willing, a second to indicate what he calls the affections
of the will, and a third to indicate actual choices or volitions. The next three chapters, chapters two through four,
deal respectively with Anselm's thinking on these three sub-
jects. Chapters five and six turn to an examination of
freedom. Chapter five investigates the definition of freedom Anselm gives and some of the problems which arise in
trying to make sense of it. The sixth chapter takes up the
question of the relation of grace and freedom. The material
of this chapter is important not only for the question of
divine sovereignty and human freedom but also for the further
light it throws on the very nature of human freedom. The
book closes with a short chapter briefly discussing the historical significance of Anselm's understanding of free will.

CHAPTER TWO

WILL: THE BASIC FACULTY

The current literature on Anselm shows a tendency to regard his thought on the nature of the will as secondary to his concern with free choice. Franz Baeumker, for example, opens his study of Anselm's doctrine of free will with the observation that Anselm does not provide us with a well-developed theory of the nature of the will. This is because, as Baeumker tells us, Anselm's concern with the will focuses upon a single point, namely its freedom of choice. Baeumker concedes that what Anselm has to say about the nature of the will is considerable, but he claims that all of it is ancillary to the explication of free choice.[1]

It is certainly true that Anselm appears to be more interested in the nature and function of freedom than he is in the nature of the will. Free choice is a basic problem in two major treatises (*DLA* and *DC*) and is extensively discussed in two others (*DCD* and *DCV*). Furthermore, much of what Anselm teaches about the will is found in the writings on free choice and occurs therefore within the context of a systematic treatment of freedom.

Nevertheless, there are some very important factors which weigh against the view that Anselm's only interest in the will is a subordinate one, important only insofar as it casts light upon free choice. In the first place, there are important passages where the will is not discussed within the confines of a larger examination of free choice but where it is considered either for its own sake or because it

is directly relevant to some other important matter. The
most striking of these is the short and compendious *Liber de
Voluntate*.[2] But there are also others. The *NUW,* for instance, has a section entitled, *"Velle, Voluntas."*[3] And
then, of course, there is the well-known passage at the beginning of *CDH*, already quoted in the introductory chapter,
wherein Anselm states that, in order to deal fully with the
questions which arise concerning the God-man and his work of
redemption, "we should need to know about power and necessity and will...."[4] This passage indicates that the will has
importance for matters other than simply free choice.

        Moreover, certain of Anselm's basic philosophical prin-
ciples require one to understand his doctrine of the will
before one can understand the full impact of his doctrine of
freedom. In Anselm's view, one cannot understand the nature
of a thing unless one understands its purpose, for what a
thing is is inseparable from what it is for. The structure
and the purpose of a thing are perfectly co-ordinated. Whatever structure or properties a thing is endowed with fit it
to achieve its essential purpose. A definition, then, that
expresses the essential nature of a thing will also state
its essential purpose. Anselm also teaches that when something conforms to its essential purpose, it is true or upright. In his metaphysics, then, the concept of essence is
inextricably bound up with the concepts of purpose, truth,
and rectitude.[5] The will and freedom are particular examples of these general principles. Freedom is said by Anselm to be the power to keep justice, and justice is the
truth or rectitude of the will preserved for its own sake.[6]
Noteworthy here is the fact that both freedom and justice
are associated with the will. Freedom is a power of the
will, and justice is the rectitude of the will. The will,
in Anselm's doctrine, is the moving power in man which gov-
erns everything, including thinking, that he himself does
(as opposed to those things which happen to him that are not

subject to his control).[7] Thus the whole area of human
thought, action, and conduct fall under the domain of the
will. Anselm's investigation of freedom, then, is not one
that he undertakes for its own sake and to which he subordi-
nates other major interests. Rather he investigates freedom
as part of a wider investigation of the human will and more
generally still of the goals and purposes of human life.

A quick glance at Anselm's writing will make it appear
that he devotes much attention to freedom and rather little
to the will. This, however, is misleading. The careful
reader will find a great deal in Anselm's work concerning
the will, some of it quite subtle and suggestive. Indeed,
the full range and depth of his thought concerning the will
have yet to be appreciated. In the present study, this
chapter and the two following ones will explore his teachings on the will.

I.   THE THREEFOLD SENSE OF "WILL"

Anselm's analysis of the will takes its point of departure from the manner in which we customarily speak about
the will. On the basis of a consideration of our common talk
about the will, Anselm distinguishes several senses in which
we use the word "will" and picks out various aspects of the
faculty which we know and call by this name. He also shows
how the several aspects of the will thus distinguished fit
into and co-operate in the purpose for which God created
man.

In his survey of common usage, Anselm discovered three
distinct senses of "will" ("*voluntas*"). Unable to discern
any essential characteristic common to all three, he con-
cluded that "will seems to be used equivocally in three
ways."[8] The three senses in which the word is used are, in
Anselm's terminology, the instrument of willing (*instrumentum
volendi*), the affection of the instrument (*affectio instrumenti*), and the use of the instrument (*usus instrumenti*).[9]

Today we might feel more at home if these three senses
were spoken of respectively as (1) the faculty, or
capacity, or power, of willing, (2) the disposition, or inclination, to will, and (3) the act, or exercise, of the
power to will—the volition. It will be our task in this
chapter to indicate the general outlines of the distinction
which Anselm draws between the three senses of "will" and to
take a closer look at what he has to say about the basic
faculty of the will.

     We are referring to the basic faculty of the will when
we talk about directing our wills (or setting ourselves) to
willing various ordinary functions, such as walking, sitting,
etc.[10] Anselm conceives the nature of the will-as-instrument
on analogy with other instruments which man possesses. His
favorite analogy is with sight, but he also frequently draws
an analogy between will and reason.

> In our bodies we have five separate senses
> and also various members, each of which we
> use like instruments. Our members and our
> senses are all adapted to their own particu-
> lar uses. For example, our hands are suited
> for grasping, our feet for walking, our tongues
> for speaking, and our sight for seeing. In
> the same manner there are certain powers in
> the soul, which the soul uses as instruments
> for appropriate functions. There is, for
> instance, reason in the soul, which the soul
> uses as an instrument for reasoning; there is
> also will, which it uses for willing.... The
> instrument of willing is that power of the
> soul which we use for willing—just as reason
> is the instrument of reasoning which we use
> when we reason, and sight is the instrument
> of seeing which we use when we see.[11]

Anselm believes that every instrument, not just the
will, can be thought of in three different ways. "Every instrument has its nature, its aptitudes, and its uses."[12]
The aptitudes of a thing are those functions for which its
particular nature or structure makes it especially suited.
To cite examples given in the passage just quoted, human

hands have an aptitude for grasping while feet have an aptitude for walking. The aptitudes of the will are called
"*affectiones*" by Anselm. He uses this name because "the instrument of willing is obviously affected by its aptitudes.
For this reason, when the human soul strongly wills something, it is said to be affected to will that thing, or to
will that thing affectionally (*affectuose*)."[13]

Anselm tells us that a person is thinking of the will-
as-affection when he says such things as the following: "A
man always has the will for his own well-being," or "A saint
always possesses the will to live an upright life, even when
he is sleeping or is not thinking about it." For in each of
these cases what is called "will" is really an affection for
well-being or for the saintly life.[14] This usage of "will"
also shows up in cases where we compare two people and say
that one has a greater will for something than the other.

> When we say that one person has more of the
> will to live justly than another person, the
> only will we are referring to is the affec-
> tion of that instrument by which he wills to
> live justly. For the instrument is not
> greater in one person and less in another.[15]

The will-as-affection, then, is defined by Anselm as
"that by which the instrument is so disposed (*afficitur*) to
will something even when the person is not thinking of it,
that when this thing does come to mind he wills this thing
either immediately or for its own proper time."[16] For example, a person has an affection for good health. Whether
to seek good health is not a question on which one has to
deliberate and make up one's mind. A person always wants to
have good health whenever he thinks of it, and he wants it
right away, then and there. People also have an affection
for sleep. But here the situation is different in that we
do not necessarily want sleep right away every time we think
of it. But we do desire—and we always desire—to get our
sleep at its appropriate time and place. We never want

completely to forego all sleep. Nor do we ever want to be
ill.[17]

       If the will is thought of as an instrument like the
hands or feet, then a man always has will. But there is a
further sense in which a man may be said always to have will,
namely that he always has a will for some general sorts of
things. These general sorts of things are the objects of
his affections. In other words, not only does man always
possess the basic faculty of willing, but that faculty is
always directed toward some object or end.

       The third and final sense of "will" which Anselm expli-
cates is that of use. This refers to the actual and specific acts or volitions which the instrument consciously and
deliberately performs. This sense is found in such statements as "I now have the will for reading," or "I now have
the will for writing." These statements, Anselm tells us,
are equivalent respectively to "I now want to read," and "I
now want to write."[18] One of the most important characteristics of the will-as-use which distinguishes it from the
affections is that a volition in every instance involves
conscious thought of what is being willed. "The use of the
instrument is something which we have only when we reflect
upon the things we are willing."[19] The will-as-use, then,
is never found in a person who is asleep or unconscious.

       Anselm apparently thinks that the distinction between
will-as-instrument and the will-as-use is a fairly obvious
one, for beyond the points we have already noted he says
little more to make the distinction clear. One might object,
however, that the statements from ordinary language which he
draws upon as exemplifying these two senses are very similar,
so much so that it is not clear how they differ in essential
meaning. How—the objector might ask—is "will" being used
differently when we talk about (1) directing the will to
walking or sitting and (2) having the will for reading or
writing (the first having been used by Anselm to illustrate

the sense of "will" as instrument, and the second the sense
of "will" as use)? Surely there is no difference in the
meaning of "will" when one is said to be willing to read or
write and when one is said to be willing to walk or sit.
And "having the will for..." and "directing the will to..."
seem merely alternative ways of talking about applying the
will to its task of willing. The problem with this objection, however, is that it misses an extremely important
point in Anselm's analysis. When he speaks of directing the
will to something (*convertere voluntatem ad...*), he does not
speak of directing the will immediately to some kind of action such as walking or sitting (i.e. he does not speak of
convertere voluntatem ad ambulandum or *ad sedendum*). Rather
he speaks of directing the will *to willing* some kind of action. It is directed to *willing* to walk and *willing* to sit
(*convertere voluntatem ad volendum ambulare,* or *ad volendum
sedere*). But when he speaks of having the will to something
(*habere voluntatem...*), the object of this will is not the
act of willing but is some specific act of behavior such as
reading or writing (*habere voluntatem legendi, voluntatem
scribendi*). As Anselm explicitly tells us, having the will
to do something is the same as willing to do something
(*habeo voluntatem legendi = volo legendi*).[20] The distinction, then, that is being drawn here is between (1) that
which is directed—the will—and (2) that to which it is
directed—the act or volition.

   He believes, therefore, that the distinction between
instrument and use is fairly clear, but he devotes considerable effort to showing that the affection is a distinct sense of
"will." Even after he has defined the basic differences between the three senses and pointed out examples of their use,
he adduces added evidence for distinguishing the affections
from the instrument and the use. He points out, for instance, that while two people are both sleeping, it is possible to affirm that one has the will to live justly while

the other does not. He argues that what is here being af-
firmed of one is the same as that which is being denied of
the other. But this cannot be the instrument, for everyone
has the instrument of willing at all times, whether awake or
asleep. And it cannot be the will-as-use, for one never
performs specific acts of willing while he is asleep. Thus
it must be something which is different from both the instrument and its use.[21]

Anselm notes a further important difference among the
instrument, the affections and the use of the will. The instrument of willing is a single and unified power, whereas
the will-as-affection has a double aspect and the will-as-
use is manifold in nature.[22] In other words, in the human being there is only one instrument, but there are two affections and many volitions. This difference is tied to Anselm's basic philosophical perspective which sees the nature
of a thing in terms of its basic function or purpose. To
say that the instrument is a single and unified power is to
indicate that it has only one basic function or purpose,
namely willing. To say that there are two affections is to
say that there are two general kinds of objects or acts
which the instrument in its willing may will, and that the function of the affections is to dispose the instrument to will
them.[23] Finally, when Anselm says that the use is manifold,
he is indicating that the instrument in its actual, concrete
acts of willing may be engaged in willing any of a great
variety of specific acts.

We have noticed that Anselm thinks of the three senses
of "will" as equivocal. What he meant by "equivocal" was almost certainly determined by Aristotle's definition of the
term in his *Categories:*

> When things have only a name in common and
> the definition of being which corresponds
> to the name is different, they are called
> equivocal. Thus, for example, both a man
> and a picture are animals. These have

only a name in common and the definition of
being which corresponds to the name is different; for if one is to say what being an
animal is for each of them, one will give
two distinct definitions.[24]

In light of this, we might say that for Anselm the instrument of willing and the affections and the use of the
instrument have the name "will" in common but their definitions are different. Thus the term "will" is used equivocally. But we must notice that if this is all that is meant by
"equivocal," it does not rule out the possibility that the
things named equivocally by the term "will" have some important features in common.[25] And this is indeed the case with
"will," for each of the three aspects of the will which Anselm distinguishes has this much in common with the others:
each is related to the process of willing, and the three aspects are all necessary conditions for the actual occurrence
of specific acts of willing.

II. THE BASIC CHARACTER OF THE FACULTY

Several points in Anselm's characterization of the will
as a power of the soul which the soul uses as an instrument
for willing need clarification. First, there is a question
as to what precisely he means by the term "power" and what
exactly is included in the scope of this power; and secondly,
there is the knotty problem of the relation of this power to
the soul to which it belongs.

We will deal first with the question of the meaning of
"power." Anselm uses the terms *vis* and *potestas volendi* in
speaking of the instrument of willing. In this variation of
terminology, there is no discernible doctrinal difference, so
it is safe to conclude that *vis* and *potestas* are used synonymously. However, the use of the latter term is particularly significant in view of the fact that Anselm goes to some
trouble in *NUW* and *Liber de Voluntate* to define clearly what
he means by *potestas*.

   Potestas, he tells us, is an "*aptitudo ad faciendum.*"[26]
Immediately after giving this definition, he makes the point
that "*facere*" is a specimen verb which can be used to stand
for any other verb whatsoever. Any specific power or ability, then, is the aptitude for doing, or performing, that
particular kind of action which differentiates the ability
in question.[27] For instance, the ability to run is the
aptitude for actually running. Accordingly, the ability to
will (*potestas volendi*) is the aptitude for willing (*aptitudo
ad volendum*).

   This result should be noted carefully. The power of
willing which constitutes the will-as-instrument is an aptitude for willing and not for doing. There is, of course,
one sense in which it is an aptitude for doing—in the sense,
namely, that willing is a species of doing. But when it is
said that the power of willing is the aptitude for willing,
then willing as a species of doing is being differentiated
from all the other species of doing. In this sense, then
willing and doing are distinct. The reason this is important is that Anselm locates both justice and freedom in a
being's power to will, not in its power to do.

   This distinction between willing and doing is one
which in recent years has been subjected to vigorous criticism.[28] In view of such criticism, one might wonder what
sort of considerations can be brought in support of such a
distinction. In Anselm's eyes the maintaining of this distinction is not a particularly controversial matter. He
writes as if he expects everyone to accept the point as self-
evidently clear. Accordingly, he does not trouble to argue
the point as such. Nevertheless, remarks are scattered in
his writings which suggest the reasons he had for accepting
the distinction. All of these occur in contexts where he is
discussing major questions of moral philosophy—where, for
instance, he is inquiring into the nature of justice or of
duty, or where he is seeking to ascertain the conditions

which justify praise or blame.

In one such passage he suggests that it may not be possible in every circumstance for a man's *actions* to be conformed to the will of God, but he insists that his *will*
ought always to conform to the will of God.[29] He is no
doubt thinking of situations in which circumstances beyond
a man's control prevent him from doing the good work which
he wants (wills) to do and which he would do if the circumstances were different.[30] The principle underlying his
thought is that man is responsible only for what is in his
own control. In the sort of situation mentioned his actions
are not subject to his control. A man, therefore, may be
morally good even when his outward actions are not right actions. This requires that a distinction be made between
one's actions and one's willing.

Not only is it possible, in Anselm's view, for a man
to be upright when his actions are not, but conversely, it
is possible for his actions to be all that is required of
them in any given circumstance while the man himself is not
deserving of any praise. He gives several examples of this
kind of case. He asks us to consider, for instance, someone
who "willed to lock a door without knowing that there was a
man outside who wanted to enter the house in order to kill
someone inside."[31] In this situation the man's actions were
right. Nevertheless the man cannot be credited with fulfill-
ing his duty, because he did not realize that he was morally
obligated to do what he did, and hence he did not will what
he did as the act that was morally required in the circumstances. The fact that his action conformed to duty was
sheer accident. Examples like this show that making moral
appraisals requires a consideration of factors beyond what
the agent actually does. And these factors, we find, are
related to his willing. Once again we find it necessary to
make a distinction between a man's actions and his willing.

In the foregoing example, the necessary conditions for

meriting praise which were lacking to the agent were a knowledge of some of the critical circumstances in the situation
in which he was acting and thus also a knowledge of what
specific action was required in the circumstances. Besides
these factors, Anselm points out other conditions which must
also be fulfilled if the agent is rightly to be deemed
praiseworthy. The relevance of these conditions also supports the view that willing and acting are distinct operations, for these conditions pertain directly to a man's willing rather than to his acting. One such condition is acqui-
escence in one's duty. A man might meet all the conditions
mentioned so far, i.e., he might know what his duty is in a
given set of circumstances and he might will to do his duty,
but still not be praiseworthy because he resents having to
perform his duty.[32] Or a man might have a wrong motive. He
might do his duty to receive the applause of men rather than
for its own sake.[33]

Considerations such as these lead Anselm in *DV* to discuss not only justice, the truth of the will, but also the
truth of actions.[34] As we have just seen, the qualifications
for rightness in actions differ from those for rightness in
willing. We also find, however, that Anselm speaks not only
of the truth of actions but also of the justice of actions.[35]
This might lead to confusion unless we realize that in this
instance Anselm is not using the terms "truth" and "justice"
as equivalents. These terms are synonymous when they are
predicated of the will but they are not synonymous when
predicated of actions. For justice is the truth of the will
and is properly predicated only of the will. In ordinary
discourse it is sometimes predicated of actions, but when it
is, this usage is not strictly and technically correct. When
applied to actions, "justice" has an extended or analogical
sense that indicates that the action is one which follows
from a just will.[36] When, however, truth is predicated of
actions, this indicates that the action conforms to the

objective standards of right action (as opposed to right
willing). Thus every just action is a true action, but not
every true action is a just action. Justice and truth are
the same when thought of in connection with the will; they
are not the same when thought of in connection with actions.

There are important moral reasons, then, for making a
distinction between willing and acting. Because the moral
life takes place most fundamentally in the will, and because
one's actions are not always an accurate reflection of the
state of one's will, Anselm's focus in his discussion of the
moral life of man is on the will.

III.   SOUL AND WILL: HAS ANSELM A FACULTY PSYCHOLOGY?

Anselm shared with many other medieval thinkers the
view that the will is a power of the soul. We now need to
explore the question of how he conceived the relation between the soul and the will. This question was widely debated in the Middle Ages. Two major positions on the issue
were held. One, generally designated a medieval version of
faculty psychology, taught that there is a real (and not
just a mental or formal) distinction between the soul and
its powers and among the powers themselves. The theory also
holds that each power of the soul is situated in, and presupposes the existence of, an organ or faculty which has
some internal structure that makes it fit for the exercise
of that power. The other theory, which I shall call the
unitary soul theory, asserts the identity of the soul and
its powers. It acknowledges that for purposes of intellectual analysis mental distinctions can be made between the
powers of the soul, but it holds that these powers are all
attributes of the soul considered as a single, unitary entity and that in function they cooperate inseparably. They
cannot be traced back to independent organs or separate
parts within the soul. The most prominent representative of

this latter theory is Saint Augustine, whose trinitarian interpretation of the soul precludes a doctrine of separate
faculties, and the most prominent representative of the former is St. Thomas Aquinas.

Anselm's stance on this issue, like his thought in
general, has been widely interpreted as fundamentally Augustinian. I will cite just two examples of this. Robert
Pouchet has written that Anselm follows Augustine in teaching that the soul is a trinitarian structure.[37] And Charles
Filliatre holds that in Anselm's thought the soul and its
powers are conceived on the model of the divine psychology,
in which there is no real distinction of faculties or powers
from each other or from the very being of God.[38]

Whether or not this interpretation is ultimately found
to be correct, the case that these commentators make is, in
my estimation, fundamentally flawed. For they base their
entire case on what Anselm writes in *Monologion* and *Proslogion* and do not make reference to his later writings. This
is a serious oversight because, as I have argued elsewhere,[39]
a shift in perspective occurs in Anselm's thought between the
time he completed the writing of his *Reply to Gaunilo* and the
writing of his later works. One indication of this change is
that in this latter period he no longer talks of the soul in
trinitarian terms and he no longer explicates the doctrine of
the Trinity by means of psychological analogies. It does not
follow from this, of course, that he also abandons the unitary soul theory that he maintained earlier. But it means
that the evidence for attributing to him the unitary soul
theory which was clearly present in the early period is not
to be found in the later works. So if one is to ascribe the
theory to Anselm in his later thought, new evidence, drawn
from his later works, will have to be found. It is in his
investigations into the nature and freedom of the will that
the clearest clues to Anselm's thinking on this issue are
to be found.

Anselm's designation of the will as an instrument is
significant in relation to this issue. He also uses the
term of other powers which, as he puts it, we "use like instruments."[40] The closest parallel to the will is reason,
which is also a power and an instrument of the soul.[41] The
case of reason, however, does not advance our investigation
much, for he does not tell us very much that is specific
about the relation of reason to the soul. But he identifies
various members of the body also as instruments,[42] and he
applies the term to tools and implements like pens and axes.[43]
The most striking feature of all of *these* items is that each
of them has its own distinctive structure. Each sense organ,
for example, has its own physical structure that is different from the structure of each other sense organ, and though
each sense organ is a part of the body none is identical
with the body. The parallel, then, that Anselm draws between reason and the will as instruments of the soul and the
sense organs as instruments of the body suggests that he
thinks of reason and will as faculties having internal structures of their own distinct from that of the soul as a whole.

This conclusion is strengthened by a statement he
makes that "reason and will do not comprise the whole soul,
but each is something in the soul."[44]

Another statement that also points in the direction of
a faculty psychology is his contention that the will is not
a substance but nevertheless has an essential nature of its
own. As he puts it,

> I think that both the will and the turning
> of the will are something. For although
> they are not substances, nevertheless it
> cannot be denied that they are essential
> natures, since there are many essential
> natures besides those which are properly
> called substances.[45]

This statement presupposes a distinction between substance and accident. He gives an account of this distinction in *De Grammatico,* where he writes,

> We may take it that the name 'man' signifies
> directly, and as a single whole, the complete
> make-up of man. Of this, substance is the
> chief feature, as the ground and possessor of
> the others, and this not in the sense that it
> is incomplete without them, but rather that
> they are incomplete without it. After all,
> there is no characteristic of substance in
> the absence of which substance is also absent,
> whereas in the absence of substance no char-
> acteristics can exist.[46]

In line with this, the will would be one characteristic
included in the signification of the word "man," but it is a
characteristic which depends for its existence upon man and
belongs to the substance man. Anselm's point in saying that
the will, while not a substance, is an essential nature is
that even though the will is dependent for existence upon
some substance in which it inheres, it nevertheless has an
essential nature of its own.

This seems to confirm the view that Anselm thought of
the will as a psychic faculty, but we must be careful not to
read too much out of this passage. For while everything he
says in it is entirely congruous with a theory of psychic
faculties, we must also notice that everything he says about
the will itself in this passage is also applied to the act,
or turning, of the will. And no one would want to argue
that this exists in any way analogous to the way a faculty
exists. So, we have a passage which, taken by itself, is in-
conclusive with regard to our present problem. But taken together with the other passages cited so far, it forms a part
of a body of evidence in favor of interpreting his doctrine
as a faculty psychology that is quite impressive.

A problem arises, however, in that Anselm makes other
statements which seem to conflict with a faculty psychology.
These have to do mainly with the question of what is the most
basic and ultimate principle of willing in the rational creature—the will itself or the soul which possesses the will.
In some places he indicates that it is the will,[47] while in

other places he speaks of it as the soul, saying that when a
person wills it is the soul which does so through the will.[48]

It is not immediately evident that these two positions
are irreconcilable. But when we look at some possible sug-
gestions as to how a reconciliation might be achieved, we
find that the more obvious possibilities all run into difficulties. One could maintain, for instance, that when we
think of a bodily instrument like the hands and of their
acts, such as grasping, it makes perfectly good sense to say
either, "His hands reached out and grasped the railing," or
"He reached out and grasped the railing with his hands."
Similarly we can think of acts of willing as performed ultimately by the soul, but performed through the use of a special instrument, namely the will, which belongs to the soul
and which is peculiarly fitted for performing acts of willing.

A problem with this suggestion is that the two cases
referred to here, grasping and willing, are not really analogous. For in the case of grasping, we are already assuming
the existence of a basic principle that originates movement,
namely the will, and without this it would be impossible for
a man to move his hands or to use them for grasping something. But when our concern is with the first principle of
willing, we cannot assume there are already acts of will.[49]
So here we have a unique problem, and because it is unique,
there are no helpful analogies to be drawn from other forms
of human activity.

The difficulty in solving this unique problem is that
however we interpret the nature of the will, whether as a
special faculty of the soul or as a general capacity, problems remain. If we think of the will-instrument as having
its own structure or essential nature different from that of
the soul in the same way that the hands have a structure and
essential nature different from that of the body, we seem
unable to reconcile the two sets of statements which Anselm

makes concerning the basic principle of willing. For if the
soul and the will are distinct, then we have two principles,
and they cannot both be the ultimate principle of willing,
for obviously there can be only one *ultimate* principle. It
seems that the only way out of this difficulty is to think
of the power of willing as a general capacity of the soul.
Then we could say that the soul is the first principle of
willing, i.e., that the only structured thing which does any
willing is the soul. The term "will" would then be the name
of this capacity, and the will-instrument would just be the
soul in its capacity for willing. In this case, it would be
a matter of indifference whether one spoke of the soul willing or whether one spoke of the instrument willing, for
whichever locution were used, the basic referent would be
the soul.

This suggestion, however, is not without problems of
its own, for it requires us to take the term "instrument" in
an extremely loose sense when used of the powers of the soul
as distinct from when it is used of the powers of the body.
It is not at all clear from the close analogies which Anselm
draws between the instruments of the soul and those of the
body that he would accept this, especially when we consider
that he shows extreme care and precision in the use of language. Moreover, he speaks of the will as an instrument in
more than just an isolated passage or two. It is used widely
in works that cover a period of around thirty years.

Perhaps our problem is that in thinking of the will as
a faculty of the soul, we are making too much of a distinction between the soul and its powers. It might be suggested,
for instance, that while we do not want to say that the immediate structural basis for willing is the whole soul, we
do not want to go to the other extreme and hold that there
is a very sharp distinction between the soul and the will.
But this makes sense only if a *via media* can be found which
squares with all of Anselm's various statements. Can such a

a middle ground be found?

Joseph Fischer has proposed that in Anselm the relation
of the soul to its powers is conceived along the lines of the
relation of the body to its members.[50] Now this may seem no
different from the suggestion already discussed and criticized. There is, however, at least one critical difference.
The earlier suggestion was that an analogy be drawn between a
body and the hands grasping and the soul and the will willing.
That is to say, the analogy was drawn between a man and his
use of a bodily power and the soul and its *use* of the will.
The present suggestion is that an analogy be drawn between the
body and its members and senses (i.e., its instruments) on the
one hand and the soul and its powers on the other. Accordingly, just as the body is made up of its members and senses, and
just as these members and senses together constitute the or-
ganic unity, or substance, of the body, so also the soul is
made up of its powers, which together constitute the substance
of the soul. Because the analogue is now the body and its
powers rather than the body and the use of its powers, we avoid
the difficulty encountered earlier concerning the principle or
ultimate source of movement for the bodily instruments. According to the view we are now considering, the body is not something above and beyond the totality and unity of its members and
senses, and yet it cannot be identified with any one or several
of its members or senses taken in separation from the others.
Similarly, the soul is not some principle which is above and beyond the totality and unity of its powers, and yet, it too cannot be identified with any single power or set of powers belonging to it taken apart from the others. The powers of the soul,
then, are all essential to the nature of the soul, just as the
instruments of the body are all essential to the nature of the
body.

This provides us with a way of thinking which allows us
to say either that the soul or that the will-instrument is
the ultimate principle of willing, yet without being forced

to adopt the view that the will-instrument is merely a general capacity of the soul. We may still think of the will-instrument as a power that is really distinct from other powers of the soul. Here again the analogy with the body is helpful. When a man grasps a handrail, he does it with his hands. Nevertheless we recognize this as a bodily action, an action performed by the body. But we do not think of the ability to grasp handrails as a general capacity of the body as such, but rather as a specific capacity of one clearly defined part of the body, the hands. Similarly with the soul and acts of will. Even though willing is properly an act performed by the will-instrument, we can say that willing is an act of the soul, because the will is a part of the soul. But this does not mean that the power of willing is a general capacity of the soul any more than the fact that grasping is a bodily action means that the ability to grasp is a general power of the body. The power of will is a specific power of one clearly defined part of the soul.

This solution preserves the view that the will has a distinctive nature and structure which is not identical with that of the soul as such, yet does so without differentiating the will from the soul so completely that there is a conflict in saying at one time that the soul, and at another time that the will, is the first and basic principle of willing.

Fischer's proposal, then, seems to offer a promising solution to our difficulties. Nevertheless, it is not entirely free of problems. The most important of these is that Anselm mentions only two powers of the soul, namely reason and will, and says of them that "reason and will do not comprise the whole soul, but each is something in the soul."[51] If Fischer's interpretation is correct, we would have to construe this statement as meaning that there are powers other than reason and will which belong to and go to make up the soul. But outside of this statement Anselm gives no indication whatsoever that he recognizes any such

powers. This is so striking that commentators have been led,
with some justification, to conclude that for Anselm the
soul has only two functions, knowing and willing.[52] This,
of course, does not demonstrate that Fischer's solution is
wrong. It does, however, show that the evidence for it in
Anselm's writings is not conclusive.

The upshot of our examination of this question, nevertheless, is that the most reasonable interpretation of Anselm's conception of the relation of the soul and the will
is the one suggested by Fischer. That the evidence for this
is not conclusive is due, I think, to the fact that Anselm
was not particularly troubled by the kind of theoretical
question we have been considering. He was much more concerned with practical problems about the operation of the
will than with strictly theoretical questions.[53]

If the above conclusion about Anselm's doctrine is correct, it is clear that the claim that Anselm's thought is
basically Augustinian cannot be sustained with respect to
the psychology of his later period. In this later period
Anselm rejects the identity of the soul and its powers found
in Augustine. Moreover, he draws an important distinction
not found in Augustine between the powers of the soul and
the use or exercise of these powers. This distinction came
later to be viewed as a specific instance of the broader
distinction between act and potency. And together these
distinctions undergirded the development of a full-blown
medieval faculty psychology. It would be a mistake, of
course, to assimilate Anselm's psychology to the highly
elaborated faculty psychology of Thomas Aquinas and his fol-
lowers, which recognizes a whole panoply of powers in the
soul and arranged them into a clearly defined hierarchical
order. Nevertheless it has more in common with it than with
the Augustinian view, and in the history of medieval psychology it is one of the first important steps in its direction.

A feature of Anselm's doctrine which has been clearly

evident in what has been said so far but which has not been
singled out for special attention is his contention that the
will is a power *of the soul*. In a few places Anselm gives
indications that he thinks that man is to be identified with
more than simply his soul, that man is a composite being
made up essentially of both soul and body. The strongest
statement of the intrinsic unity of soul and body in man is
an *obiter dictum* dropped to illustrate the intimate unity of
the two natures, divine and human, in the God-Man.

> Thus, while it is necessary to find a God-
> Man in whom the integrity of both natures
> is preserved, it is no less necessary for
> these two complete natures to meet in one
> person—just as body and rational soul
> meet in one man—for otherwise the same
> person could not be perfect God and perfect
> man.[54]

Along with this, Anselm also indicates that both soul and
body are included in God's ultimate purposes for man.

> If man had persevered in justice, he would
> have been eternally blessed in his entire
> being, soul and body. Thus we can conceive
> nothing more just and appropriate than for
> him to be eternally and entirely miserable
> in soul and body, if he persists in injustice.[55]

    In spite of these statements, however, the great weight
of Anselm's teaching concerning man and the soul clearly in-
dictates that the unity of soul and body is not one of equally fundamental principles. All the most important activities
of man, particularly knowing and willing, are operations not
of the soul and the body combined, but of the soul alone.
Even sensation, in which there is clearly bodily involve-
ment, is essentially an activity of the soul. "The members
and the senses will nothing through themselves. . . . It
is really the soul . . . which feels and acts in those
senses and members."[56] The senses, then, are merely instruments of the soul, and they remain passive in the activities
of the soul. What is true here of the senses is true also
of the body generally. Its essential character as part of

the human composite is to be an instrument of the soul. It
is the soul, then, which is the center of all life and consciousness for man. But not only is it the center, it is
the whole life and consciousness for man. A man's entire
history could be written in terms of the events and activities of his soul.

Anselm's debt to Augustine on this point is clearly
evident. Augustine had defined man as "a rational soul
using a body."[57] Commenting on this definition, Etienne
Gilson writes, "Taken literally, this formula would mean
that a man is essentially his soul. Augustine himself never
took it quite literally, but, rather, as a forcible expression of the transcendent superiority of the soul over the
body."[58] Anselm takes over Augustine's view of the nature
of man and of the relation of soul and body in man without
essential change, for every account that he gives of the
operations and activities of the human being reflects Augustine's definition. But because, like Augustine, he too
wants to make room for the body in the essential nature of
man and in the ultimate purposes of God for man, the remark
which Gilson makes concerning Augustine's doctrine applies
equally to Anselm: he never takes the definition completely
literally but his agreement with it indicates his strong
belief in the overwhelming superiority of the soul over the
body.

This provides us further explanation of why, in his
study of morality and freedom, Anselm's attention is focused
so exclusively upon the soul and its internal acts of willing rather than upon the observable man and his actual behavior. The external actions of a man which make up his observable behavior are the result of something more fundamental, namely activity in the soul.

This leads us naturally to the question of the general
function and purpose of the will as an instrument of the
soul.

IV. THE GENERAL FUNCTION AND
PURPOSE OF THE WILL

We have seen that in Anselm's thought it is not possible to distinguish the nature of a thing from the purpose
or function it fulfills. Up to now we have concentrated
our attention on the general character of the will and on
its relation to the soul. Now we must turn to a consideration of the purpose or function it fulfills. Our treatment
of the function of the will will be divided into two sec-
tions. The first of these will deal with its immediate
function in human action, while the second will place its
operation within the wider context of the final end of man.

A. Its Immediate Function. The basic function of the
will is to serve as the moving principle of all action. All
that a person does, as opposed to that which happens to him
and over which he has no control, is subordinate to his will.
As Anselm himself states it,

> The instrument of will moves all the other
> instruments which we freely move—both those
> instruments which are a part of us (such as
> our hands, our tongue, our sight) and those
> that are independent of us (such as a pen or
> an axe). Furthermore, it causes all our
> voluntary movements.[59]

Anselm's views on reason and on sensation fall
right into line with this. The use of reason is governed by
the will,[60] and in sensation it is the soul which actually
does the perceiving and not the senses—the soul uses the
senses as its instruments. It is also true that "whatever
the members and senses do must be imputed entirely to the
will."[61] It follows, therefore, that when the soul is active
in sensation or other activities, it is the will by which it
is active. Anselm carries this point to what may seem an
extreme position, for he seems to believe that whatever the
body sees, feels, and experiences, is really seen, felt and
experienced by the will. He says, for instance, that when
the senses are delighted or tormented, it is really the will

which is delighted or tormented.[62] But be that as it may,
he clearly holds that whatever is within the power of a rational being to do is under the control and direction of the
will.

He brings out the point in another way when he says
(to render it literally), "All power follows the will."[63]
D. P. Henry translates this a little more freely: "The exercise of every personal capacity is dependent on the will."[64]
This simply means that rational agents are not able to perform any activities of their own unless they first will to
do so. Anselm explains,

> When I say that I can speak or walk, it is
> implicitly understood that I can do these
> things only if I will to do so. If willing-
> ness is not implicitly understood in this
> fashion, then it is no longer a matter of
> power, but rather of necessity.[65]

Thus, when there occurs in a person some behavior
which he himself has not willed, then this behavior, strictly speaking, is not his action at all, because he did not
will it. It is the result of some other force acting on him.

The doctrine that all power follows the will has
several important consequences. One of these is that even
though a person is completely fitted in every way to do some
particular thing, so that all that is needed for him to do
it is to will it, yet at the same time he is for some reason unable to will it, there is a categorical sense in which
he is unable and lacks the power to do it. A clear example
of this is seen in the case of the God-Man, who, says Anselm,
wholly lacks the power to sin even though he has the subjective capacity to say or do things that in certain contexts
would be sinful.

> How shall we say that he could not have
> lied, though this is always a sin? For
> when he says to the Jews concerning the
> Father, "If I shall say that I know him
> not, I shall be like you, a liar," and
> in the midst of this sentence pronounces

> the words, "I know him not," who will
> say that he could not have spoken these
> words and no others, so as to say simply,
> "I know him not"? But if he did this,
> as he himself says, he would be a liar,
> that is, a sinner. Therefore, since he
> could have done this, he could have sinned.[66]

Anselm's answer to this query applies the principle that all
power follows the will.

> We can say of Christ that he could tell
> a lie, provided that it is implicitly
> understood that he could do so only if
> he willed so to do. And since he could
> not tell a lie without being willing to
> do so, but at the same time could not be
> willing to do so, he can equally properly
> be said to have been unable to tell a lie.
> In this way, then, he both could and could
> not tell a lie.[67]

A second consequence of the doctrine that all power
follows the will is that in order for one to be justified in
holding a person responsible for a deed or action, that deed
must be something that the person willed to do. If a person
does not will an action, it is not his action at all, and it
would be wrong to hold him responsible for it. Anselm is so
insistent upon this that he maintains that all who share the
guilt of original sin and experience the moral weakness
which comes as a result of it are in some sense responsible
for it, and responsible for it *through the will*.[68] Because
the will is the focal point of all a person's own activity,
it is also the ultimate bearer of moral responsibility.

This ties in with Anselm's claim that moral duty—
justice—is to preserve the rectitude *of the will* for its
own sake.[69] Sin, or injustice, is the failure *of the will*
to preserve rectitude; it is therefore the lack of justice
where justice ought to be, *namely in the will*.[70] In Anselm's
doctrine, all the basic moral categories and predicates apply directly to the will; indeed, in the strictest sense,
they apply only to the will.[71] Hence everything for which
a man merits moral praise or blame is something which he

wills to do.

The contrast between Anselm's doctrine of will and
power and Augustine's is striking. Unlike Anselm, Augustine
makes a sharp distinction between *voluntas* and *potestas*.

> There are then two faculties—the exercise
> of the will and the exercise of power—and
> not everyone that has the will has the
> power also, nor has everyone that possesses
> the power got the will in immediate control;
> for as we sometimes will what we cannot do,
> so also we sometimes can do what we do not
> will.[72]

For Augustine, will and power are often independent of
each other. They are not ordered, as they are for Anselm, so
that power is always subordinate to the will. In Augustine's
view, the will does not always have the efficacy to carry
out its decisions or to put its good intentions into practice. This impotence of the will constitutes one of the
greatest moral and theological problems for Augustine. In
his thinking it was one of the distinguishing characteristics of the state of sin, and it was the condition which
made the state of sin so utterly hopeless for man apart
from the grace of God. In the *Confessions* Augustine tells
of his own experience of this condition when he was struggling to become free from his sin and to give himself to God.

> But I was mad that I might be whole, and
> dying that I might have life, knowing what
> evil thing I was, but not knowing what good
> thing I was shortly to become.... I was dis-
> quieted in spirit, being most impatient
> with myself that I entered not into thy
> will and covenant, O my God, which all my
> bones cried out to me to enter, extolling
> it to the skies. And we enter not therein
> by ships, or chariots, or feet, no, nor by
> going so far as I had come from the house
> to that place where we were sitting. For
> not to go only, but to enter there, was
> nought else but to will to go, but to will
> it resolutely and thoroughly; not to stag-
> ger and sway about this way and that, a
> changeable and half-wounded will, wrestling
> with one part falling as another rose.[73]

Augustine is here echoing the experience which the Apostle
Paul records in the famous and anguished cry of his, "For to
will is present with me, but how to perform that which is
good, I know not."[74] Not surprisingly, this is a verse
which Augustine frequently quotes.[75]

It must be carefully noted that Augustine's problem is
not primarily that of executing decisions that have already
been made. It is something deeper than that; it is the
problem of how to bring oneself to will effectively something which we readily recognize and concede to be right
and which in some sense we already sincerely desire to will.

> So many things, then, I did, when to have
> the will was not to have the power, and I
> did not that which both with an unequalled
> desire I longed more to do, and which
> shortly when I should will, I should will
> thoroughly. For in such things the power
> was one with the will, and to will was to
> do, and yet it was not done; and more
> readily did the body obey the slightest
> wish of the soul in moving its limbs at
> the order of the mind, than the soul
> obeyed itself to accomplish in the will
> alone this its great will.... The mind
> commands the body, and it obeys forth-
> with; the mind commands itself and is re-
> sisted.... The mind commands the mind to
> will, and yet, though it be itself, it
> obeys not. Whence this monstrous thing?
> and why is it? I repeat, it commands it-
> self to will, and would not give the com-
> mand unless it willed; yet is not that
> done which it commands.[76]

Augustine's experience here is of a will divided
against itself. On the one hand, it has a sincere desire
to do what is right; on the other hand, the desire is not
strong enough to yield a resolute and effective decision.
The sort of thing described here is starkly illustrated in
the famous prayer of Augustine's youth: "Give me chastity
and continency, but not yet."[77]

Now Anselm does not deny that there are times when a
person is not able actually to do what he wills to do. But

the only cases of this sort which he considers are those
where a person is prevented from carrying out his will because of external circumstances beyond his control. This,
however, is clearly not the kind of case that troubles
Augustine, who is just as quick as Anselm to recognize that
external circumstances beyond one's control do not affect
one's moral standing.[78] The kind of inability which torments Augustine is caused by some kind of internal force or
inertia within one's own soul, something within which prevents us, as we might say, from following our better judgment. As common as the experience of this kind of inability
may be, Anselm's thought makes no room for it. In his view,
if a person wills anything in his power, i.e., anything within
the range of his *aptitudines*, then barring only the interfer-
ence of external circumstances, he is able, in an absolute
and categorical sense, to carry it out.

There are several possible misconceptions which might
be drawn from this which we should avoid. First, Anselm's
doctrine of the relation of power to will does not mean that
the will never experiences any impotence or inability. Anselm insists just as strongly as Augustine that the will
does not have the same kind of power after it has sinned
that it had before. But for Anselm this inability is precisely an inability to will rather than an inability to will
strongly or efficaciously. In his view the will either has
the ability to will or it does not. There is no *tertium quid*
where the will has only a weak, partial, or ineffectual ability to will. When the will through sin loses its ability to
will what is right, the only way it can be restored is by
grace. Grace plays just as central a role in human salvation for Anselm as for Augustine. But Anselm is not as
alive as Augustine to the subtleties, complexities, and ambiguities in man's struggle to find redemption. In contrast
to Augustine's sensitive and penetrating portrayal of the
search for God, Anselm roundly declares, "Those who say,

'Convert us, O Lord,' are already in some sense converted."[79]
In other words, the desire, or will, of these people for
conversion is an efficacious will. Not once in any of his
extant writings, including his letters, prayers, and medita-
tions, does Anselm ever quote Romans 7:18, the verse that
was so significant for Augustine: "To will is present with
me, but how to perform that which is good I know not."[80]
This is not surprising, for it is hard to see what he could
have made of such a statement.

   This is not to suggest—and this is the second misconception we should avoid—that there cannot be any moral
struggle. It is quite possible for one to be deeply torn
between moral alternatives. At a number of points Anselm
asks us to imagine a situation in which a person is forced
to make a decision between telling a lie or losing his life,
and he offers this case as an example of a particularly difficult moral choice.[81] He thus recognizes the occurrence of
difficult moral conflicts. The point, though, of his doctrine of will and power is that however difficult the choice
between alternatives may be, if we are able to will any of
the alternatives facing us, then we are able to will them
efficaciously.

   A third possible misconception is one which would see
Anselm as denying that a person can be hesitant or vacil-
lating in what he wills. The doctrine that all power follows the will pertains primarily to the ability, or power, a
person has to will and not to his actual volitions. A decision which is made with hesitation or vacillation is a
particular act of willing, and these properties of the act
should not be ascribed to the basic ability to will. If I
have the ability to will something then I *can* will it reso-
lutely and effectively. This does not mean that I always
will do this.

   The dictum that all power follows the will is an extremely important point in Anselm's doctrine, because freedom

in his view, is defined in terms of power. "All freedom,"
he tells us, "is power."[82] It is the power to preserve the
rectitude of the will for its own sake.[83] The nature of
freedom, then, must be understood in light of the nature of
the will, and the exercise of freedom depends upon the ability to will.

There is a second immediate function of the will,
closely related to the one we have just been looking at.
Once it is established that the will moves all the other
powers an agent has, there is still the question of what
moves the will. Anselm's answer is that the will moves itself; as he puts it, the will is a "self-moving instrument."[84]
This function of the will is logically prior to the other one:
before the will can move any of the other powers it must
first move itself.

There are at least two possible ways in which self-
movement in the will can be understood. The will can be
thought to be self-moving in the sense that it is autonomous
and acts in a contra-causal way. This means that the choices
of the will are not caused or brought about by some external
force, but that the will itself is the sole sufficient cause
of its actions. On the other hand, the will may be thought
of as self-moving in the sense that the will moves or wills
itself to will. This is not incompatible with the first
sense but it adds a further ingredient, namely, that it *is*
possible to find causes of a volition in prior volitions, or
second-order volitions. A second-order volition or decision
is a decision to decide, or a will to will. There is an obvious problem with this view, for it leads to an infinite
regress of ever-higher order volitions.

How does Anselm conceive the self-movement of the will?
This question is not easy to answer, for there are some passages which seem at first sight to favor the first meaning
given above, while there are others which seem to support
the second. Examples of the latter are: "A man cannot will

against his will because he cannot will unwillingly to will.
For everyone willingly wills himself to will;"[85] and "It is
wrong to say that a man wills to lie against his will, since
he only wills this willingly. For just as he wills to lie
when he lies, so he wills to will when he wills to lie."[86]
These passages strongly suggest that Anselm's view is the
one which generates the infinite regress.

        Yet we also find statements that seem to show he avoid-
ed the infinite regress. When the student-interlocutor in
DCD raises the question about Satan, "Why did he will what
he was not supposed to will?" the master replies, "No cause
preceded this will except his mere ability to will." But
assuming that different effects cannot have identical causes,
he amends this by saying that there must be some other cause
than the mere ability to will, for the good angel had the
same ability to will but did not sin. The student thereupon
presses the question, "Why, then, did he will?" to which the
master answers, "Only because he willed. For there was no
other cause by which his will was in any way driven or drawn;
but his own will was both its own efficient cause and its
own effect—if such a thing can be said."[87] Another passage
shows that Anselm clearly recognizes that an infinite regress is fatal to the theory of the will as self-moving.
When the teacher asks "Why do you say that you did not will
to persevere in the willing?" the following exchange takes
place.

> S. Again, I might reply that I did will to
> persevere, but that I did not persevere in
> this willing to persevere; but then the ar-
> gument would continue to infinity, with you
> always asking the same question and me always
> giving the same answer.
>
> T. Then you should not say, "I did not will
> to persevere in the willing because I did
> not will to persevere in the willing of this
> willing to persevere." But rather, when you
> are first asked why you did not persevere in
> any activity in which you were willing and

> able to persevere, you should answer,
> "Because I didn't persevere in willing."
> But if you are asked again why you
> didn't persevere in willing, you must
> not answer that you did not persevere
> in willing to will to persevere, but
> you must give another reason which ex-
> plains the failure of the will. For
> unless you give this other reason, you
> merely repeat the question in your reply,
> i.e., that you haven't persevered in will-
> ing to persevere in the action.[88]

But if Anselm specifically recognizes the force of
the objection concerning infinite regress, how are the passages to be interpreted which seem to commit him to it?
The best answer is to read these passages not as postulating higher-order causes in the process of willing but as
making a logical point about the very concept of willing.
The contexts in which we find the statements quoted above
support this interpretation. The whole paragraph in which
the first quotation appears is as follows.

> No one deserts rectitude except by willing
> to desert it. If "against one's will" means
> "unwillingly," then no one deserts rectitude
> against his will. A man can be bound against
> his will because he can be bound unwillingly;
> a man can be tortured against his will be-
> cause he can be tortured unwillingly; a man
> can be killed against his will because he can
> be killed unwillingly. But a man cannot will
> against his will because he cannot will un-
> willingly to will. For everyone willingly
> wills himself to will.[89]

Anselm thus is not saying that there is always a second-
order decision prior to the first-order decision to do
something, but simply that it is logically incoherent to
say that one can will something against one's will. If one
wills something, he is doing it with his will, so he cannot
be doing it unwillingly.[90]

The second of the two statements cited above as seeming to commit Anselm to an infinite regress is also susceptible to this interpretation. It deals with the same

general problem—how the will can sin; and it makes the same
general point—one cannot sin, i.e., will something wrong,
against one's will. We can safely conclude, then, that
Anselm thought of the will itself as the sole sufficient
cause of the will's own acts, thus avoiding an infinite
series of acts of willing before every act.

    Though infinite regress is avoided, there still re-
mains the question of how this self-movement is possible.
If *all* movement of the will is self-movement, then the tran-
sition in the will from a state in which it is not acting to
a state in which it is must be a work of the will. But how
can the will, in a state of non-action, bring itself to act?
The very phrase "bring itself to act" suggests that there is
already some activity in the will before it acts, which of
course is logically impossible. This difficulty is clearly
seen by Anselm. In *DCD* the master asks, "Can you tell me how
someone moves himself from not-willing to willing? Does he
will to move?" and the student answers, "If I should say
that someone is moved, but not by his own willing, then the
consequences would be that he was not moved by himself, but
by something else." The master then suggests, "Therefore,
you should say that whoever moves himself to willing any particular thing must first will that he move.... But whoever
is not willing anything at all can in no way move himself to
willing."[91]

    It might be possible to avoid the problems by saying
that the first movement of the will is completely spontan-
eous, that no action precedes it, but that it simply happens.
But this will not do either, for if this is how the first
movement of the will takes place, it is something entirely
random and wholly inexplicable. The question, then, which
we are considering, seems to resolve itself into a dilemma,
the horns of which are either logical impossibility or ir-
rationality.

    Anselm's answer to this dilemma is found in his theory

of the affections of the will. He tells us that "the instrument of the will...moves itself by its affections."[92]
We find, therefore, that a close examination of the nature
of the will-as-instrument leads into the subject of the
will-as-affections. Before we can fully answer the questions which arise about the will-as-instrument, we must investigate the affections. We will undertake this investigation in the next chapter. At this point we will turn to
the question of the ultimate purpose of the will.

      B. Its Ultimate Purpose. Since the will is a power
which belongs to man, the ultimate purpose of the will is
subordinate to the ultimate purpose of man. The will is the
power of man which controls all that he does, hence it is
the primary power which enables him to fulfill his basic
purpose. The ultimate purpose of the will, then, is not
only subordinate to but actually identical with the ultimate
purpose of man. The purpose of all his other powers and capacities is to serve as the instruments of the will in pursuing this ultimate purpose.

      We are here talking about the will of men. Human be-
ings, however, are not the only ones endowed with will. All
rational beings are. Besides men, this includes God and the
angels, both the good angels and the bad. God, of course,
is unique and presents a special case. But men and angels
are alike in being rational *creatures,* and they possess in
common all the same essential features of will. The only
differences between the wills of men and those of angels
pertain to the mode in which they possess or do not possess
the same characteristics. Both good angels and good men
possess rectitude of will, while evil angels and evil men
do not. The good angels differ from the good men still
living in that the latter can lose their rectitude while the
former cannot. The evil angels differ from the evil men
still living by virtue of the fact that the latter may still
have rectitude restored to them in grace while the former

cannot. The fundamental similarity of humans and angels is
further seen in the fact that men were created by God to
fill in the gap left in the ranks of the good angels when
the evil angels fell,[93] and they would not be able to do this
unless they were of the same nature.[94] The ultimate purpose,
then, of men and the angels, and therefore of the human and
angelic wills, is the same.[95]

Anselm speaks of the end of men in different terms in
different places. A shift in his thinking on this topic
takes place between his earliest writings and his later
ones.[96] Since he explicates his doctrines of the will and
freedom in the later writings, we will confine our attention
here to his thinking in this later period. But even in his
later period, he describes the end of man in a variety of
ways.

One of his leading statements on the subject is, "We
should not doubt that the rational nature was created just
by God, so that it might be blessed in the enjoyment of
him."[97] The word here translated "blessed" is "*beata*,"
which could also be translated "happy." This term is quite
in keeping with the Christian tradition that the ultimate
end of man is the beatific vision of God. So is the term
"enjoyment" ("*fruendo*"). Besides these words, Anselm uses
others which also fall into line with the tradition. He
talks of blessedness, for instance, as a state in which people engage in the "contemplation of God;"[98] and he uses the
term "sight" ("*species*") to characterize redeemed man's
final state.[99]

But he also discusses the final end of man in much
more moralistic terms. He writes that man is created with
the ultimate purpose of living a life of rectitude. "To
keep rectitude of the will for its own sake is, for whoever
keeps it, to will what God wills him to will."[100] Man has
been endowed with reason, we are told, in order for him to
know what is right, and he has been given free will in order

for him to do what is right.[101] Sin is a willful defection
from the standard of rectitude,[102] and its result is the
complete loss of rectitude. This leaves the will incapable,
apart from God's grace, of ever willing rectitude again.[103]
The grace of God, however, can restore the lost rectitude to
the will.[104] If this happens, the final reward in the next
life for a righteous life in the present one will be elevation of the will to a status in which it is no longer able
to abandon rectitude but will be confirmed in righteousness.

This way of describing man's ultimate end sounds very
different from enjoying the contemplation and vision of God.
We must therefore consider how the life of rectitude is related to the contemplation of God in man's ultimate end.

The basic principle underlying Anselm's thought on
this matter is that every one of the basic powers and quali-
ties with which man was created was given to him in order to
make it possible for him to achieve his ultimate purpose.
The two basic powers with which the human soul is endowed
are reason and will. Both have been given to man for a
moral purpose. Reason has been given "for the very purpose
of distinguishing the just from the unjust, and good from
evil, and the greater good from the lesser good."[105] The
power of moral discrimination is thus at the very heart and
essence of reason. But reason has been given not simply for
the sake of knowing right from wrong, but to make it possible for a person intelligently and freely to choose the
just and reject the unjust.

> It can be proved that it [the rational
> nature] received the power of discern-
> ment so that it might hate and shun evil,
> and love and choose good.... For otherwise
> God would have given it the power of dis-
> cernment in vain, since it would distin-
> guish in vain if it did not love and avoid
> in the light of its discrimination.... Thus
> it is certain that the rational nature was
> created to love and choose the supreme good
> above all other things, not for the sake of
> another good, but for its own sake.[106]

Only if a man goes beyond knowing the good to choosing it is reason wholly fulfilled. But a power beyond reason is needed for choosing the good, and this, of course, is the will, which then shares the same overall moral purpose.

This makes it sound as though reason is subordinate to will. The most important thing in life is to *choose* the good, and one's rational knowledge is of value only insofar as it both makes this possible and actually leads into good choices. But though it may sound that way, what we have seen so far does not entail that reason is subordinate in an absolute sense, for it might be that Anselm thinks of choosing the good in this life as merely the means by which one attains a fuller rational contemplation of God in the next life. To put the point a little differently, we have to concede that for Anselm, as far as morality is concerned, reason is subordinate to the will; however, morality may not be the final good but only an instrumental good leading to an entirely different kind of life and existence. The ultimate good—the *summum bonum*—is, Anselm tells us, God himself.[107] And God might be apprehended and clung to by reason just as well as, if not better than, by will, especially after one has been released from the conditions of this earthly, material existence. If that were to be the case, in the final analysis will would be subordinate to reason rather than vice versa.

Is this in fact the way Anselm sees the issue? An argument that it is could be made on the grounds that he never really says in so many words that the ultimate purpose of man is purely and simply to live justly but he does explicitly state that redeemed man's final state will be characterized by contemplation and sight. But there are strong considerations against taking this as his belief. In the first place, he writes that man was created "to love and choose the supreme good above all things...*for its own sake*."[108]

Taken literally, this means that loving and choosing God
must not be done to achieve something else (e.g., the contemplation of God), for there is no more ultimate goal than
doing this. One could argue, however, that choosing the supreme good for its own sake does not mean that the manner in
which we cling to it is primarily or ultimately through the
will. The claim here may be only that there is no greater
or more ultimate *object* to be sought, not that the highest
way in which it can be *subjectively apprehended* is through
the will. It would then make sense to say that we choose
and love the supreme good in this life, i.e., we make the
supreme good the object of will, in order that in the next
life we might have the supreme good as the object of contemplation.

There are problems, however, with accepting this as
Anselm's view. One is that it seems at odds with other
claims he makes about the end of man. There is only one
place in his later writings where he uses "contemplation" in
speaking of the final end of man. It is the one already
quoted in which he says of "the rational nature" that it
"either is or is going to be blessed in the contemplation of
God."[109] But there are other places where he uses different
terms to characterize man's final end. As we have already
seen, one of these is "happiness," which he sometimes ex-
pands to "happiness in the enjoyment of God."[110] This suggests that "contemplation" and "happiness" are simply alter-
nate ways of saying the same thing. But does this square
with what Anselm says about happiness, about its nature and
the conditions leading to it? In the passages in which "happiness" occurs there is no intimation that the conditions of
happiness in man's final state will be any different from
the conditions of happiness in this life. This is significant because Anselm provides considerable information on the
conditions of happiness in this life. There is in fact only
one necessary condition for happiness, namely justice.

"Unless it [the rational nature] is just, it cannot love the
supreme good.... The rational nature, then, was created just,
so that it might be happy in the enjoyment of the highest
good, that is, God."[111] Since justice is the rectitude *of
the will* preserved for its own sake, it follows that an activity of the will, namely justice, is a component of happiness—a component of happiness and not just a means to it.
Happiness thus is not found wholly in an activity of reason;
it is not merely rational contemplation.

But is happiness constituted only in part by justice,
or is justice the whole of happiness? Is it the only component of happiness, or are there others? There are strong
indications that Anselm thinks of justice as the whole of
happiness. Writing of the two affections of the will, he
says, "It is clear that...the affection for willing justice
is in every way superior and to be preferred. Everyone who is
just is just through this will, and without it a person cannot be happy."[112] This passage makes it clear that justice
is not ordered to happiness as to something larger and more
desirable than itself. Justice is the most desirable end of
all. When one is just one is also happy, and happiness is a
feature of justice which persists only as long as justice itself is maintained. Happiness is thus not a state that encompasses justice as a part of itself.

But if happiness consists simply of justice, what are we
to make of Anselm's claim that the end of man is the enjoyment of God? The answer to this is that knowing and loving,
and thus enjoying, God are things that human beings ought to
do. They are, in fact, their highest obligations.[113] Loving
God, of course, means obeying his will. Accordingly, happine
in the enjoyment of God consists in knowing what God requires
of us and doing it, which is merely another way of saying it
consists in preserving the rectitude of the will for its own
sake. In short, we will be happy in the enjoyment of God because enjoying God is what justice requires of us.

A number of other points in Anselm's writing support
this interpretation. He tells us, for instance, that man
was created happy and just so that he could keep these quali-
ties and *thereby* fulfill God's plan for him. But when he
elaborates this point, the emphasis always falls on justice.
He teaches, for example, that man's original state, in Adam,
was one in which he conformed to the purposes of God for
him, and that Adam could have maintained himself in this
purpose by keeping the justice, and thereby the happiness,
in which he had been created. He did this for a while, but
then he sinned and fell from his original state of perfection. The first and foremost loss that Adam suffered when
he sinned was justice. And having lost justice, he also
lost happiness.[114] By the same token, the work of grace is
to restore justice.[115] Furthermore, the reward of the good
angels, who persevered in keeping the justice which was
originally given to them, was not fundamentally admission
into a state of happiness or contemplation but rather confirmation of their righteousness such that it became impossible for them ever to lose justice. They were transferred
from a state in which it was possible for them not to sin
(*posse non peccare*) to a state in which it was not possible
for them to sin (*non posse peccare*).[116] The future reward
of redeemed men will also be elevation to this state, where
they will live as equals with the angels.[117] It is not immediately apparent that these points fit in with the supposition that man's ultimate end is contemplation, but they
create no difficulty for the view that his ultimate end is
justice.

We may feel justified, therefore, in affirming that
Anselm thinks of the state of happiness as identical with
the state of justice. This still leaves unsettled the
question of how he views the relation of happiness and
justice on the one hand to contemplation on the other. What
launched us into our exploration of the relation of happiness

and justice was his apparent identification of happiness and
contemplation in the final end of man. If happiness and
contemplation are in fact identical, the conclusions we have
reached so far would force us to the further conclusion that
justice and contemplation are also identical. But does Anselm in fact equate justice and contemplation?

One difficulty that stands in the way of making such
an identification is that justice is an activity of the will
while contemplation is an activity of the intellect. Perhaps an investigation of Anselm's doctrine of the respective
roles of reason and will in attaining man's ultimate end
will shed some light on his understanding of the relation of
justice and contemplation.

We have seen that reason is an essential part of the
process of willing justice, for the will cannot will justly
unless it knows what it is willing. But this is compatible
with three quite different views of the relation of reason
and will in determining our choices. One possibility is that
the apprehensions of reason determine the acts of the will.
Another is that the choices of the will determine the apprehensions of reason. A third possibility is that on some occasions the causal determination runs from will to intellect
while on other occasions it runs in the opposite direction.

Anselm's position on this question is a complex one.
In speaking of how one comes to a knowledge of God and a life
of justice, he states that a minimal understanding is a
necessary but not a sufficient condition.[118] Reason, insofar
as it possesses this minimal understanding, does not determine the will to believe and to act justly, for this understanding of the truth is quite different from the will to believe it and the will to act on it.[119] Nor does the intellect determine the will when it acts unjustly and sins. Sin,
like justice, has an intellectual aspect; but this intellectual change
results from sin, it is not its cause. In the process of coming
to God, then, the activities of the will and the intellect

are separate, and it is the activity of the will which is
causally determinative of a human being's standing vis-à-vis
God and justice.

Within the life of one who already believes, the situation is more complicated. For believing is an act of commit-
ment (will) which leads a person to seek and sometimes to
gain deeper understanding. So while minimal understanding
is a necessary condition for belief, belief is a necessary
condition for more complete understanding. There is thus a
complex interplay of reason and will in the life of the
Christian believer.[120] But even so, it is still the will
that is fundamentally determinative of the quality of a person's life and action and of the depth of his understanding.
For a person's understanding never reaches the point in this
life where it makes it impossible for the will to defect
from God and justice. Anselm acknowledges that there are
items of knowledge which are incompatible with the free exercise of will in created beings,[121] but he teaches that
precisely because they are incompatible with free will, God
saw to it that men and angels do not have them at any time
before they are confirmed in righteousness or sin. In this
life the will always has the capacity, which it can exercise
at any time, however advanced one's moral standing and understanding of God are, to act unjustly and contrary to the
will of God.[122]

Anselm's view of the will and intellect as separate
and independent powers may seem to spell trouble for the notion that justice and contemplation are somehow identical.
But we need to be careful here. The doctrine of the relation of will and intellect so far spelled out has to do
with the situation of the present life, as man is in the
process of attaining (or failing to attain) his ultimate
end. The idea, however, that justice and contemplation are
identical pertains to the state of affairs in the next life,
where the ultimate end has (for the redeemed) been achieved,

and where, therefore, it is something that is enjoyed rather
than sought. There is clearly no inconsistency in holding
that the relation of the will and intellect in the present
life differs from their relation in the next life. And this,
it is reasonable to think, is precisely what Anselm believed.
In the next life there will be no possibility for the redeemed to act unjustly or to turn away from God. Intellect
and will will no longer be independent powers with the capacity to focus on different objects and to divide the soul.
They will be united in a common devotion to God, in which
desire for God will be one with knowledge of God. The
knowledge of God will be supported by a supreme desire for
God, and the desire for God will be sustained by the knowledge of God's supreme goodness and reality. Since this is
the ultimate end of man, that which every human being *ought*
to gain, i.e., that which justice requires, the attainment of
this end will be both perfect contemplation and perfect
justice. The perfection of the intellect in contemplation
will *ipso facto* be the perfection of the will in justice.
The disorders and conflicts that trouble the soul in the
present life, between intellect and will and between the
pursuit of happiness and the pursuit of justice, will be
wholly overcome. Justice, happiness, and contemplation will
coincide.

     As we see more and more clearly what is involved in
Anselm's view of the ultimate end of man, it becomes evident that he considers the purpose of man to be the same
both in this life and in the next, though the degree to
which it can be achieved is not the same. Man was originally made for justice and happiness. This is still his purpose after the entry of sin into human experience. And it
continues to be his purpose after he passes into the next
life. There is no distinction between a natural and a supernatural purpose for man. At whatever stage of a person's histor
if justice is to be achieved both free will and grace are

necessary. The possibility of achieving justice is not
postponed to the next life. It can be gained now, though
there is an important difference between having it now and
having it in the next life. If justice is achieved in this
life it can be lost again, something which cannot happen in
the next life. But though there are significant differences
between the life now and that hereafter, there is no difference of ultimate purpose.

A major debate that has occurred among Anselm scholars
concerns the question whether he should be classified an intellectualist or a voluntarist. The preceding discussion on
the relation of will and reason is relevant to that debate.
One of the most emphatic champions of the theory that Anselm
is an intellectualist is Filliatre. He thinks that the basic inspiration for Anselm's thought as a whole is Neopla-
tonic, and in discussing Anselm's theory of the will he
writes that Anselm is "haunted too much by his metaphysical
theory of ideas not to subordinate the will itself to his
intellectualistic system."[123] Filliatre concedes that Anselm tried valiantly, toward the end of his career when he
turned mainly to theological and moral problems, to work into his system a theory that gives more scope and importance
to will and action. But he concludes that the effort was
unsuccessful because such a theory is fundamentally at odds
with the metaphysical principles developed earlier in Anselm's career and never relinquished or modified to any important extent.[124] Other scholars have interpreted him to
hold that the final end of man is achieved pre-eminently
through the use of the intellect. Robert Pouchet thinks
that Anselm believes that the fundamental gift of grace is
faith, which may grow until ultimately it gives way to direct vision and contemplation.[125] J. Bayart holds much the
same view.[126] Other commentators, however, think of Anselm's
thought as voluntaristic. Pierre Mandonnet specifically
calls him a voluntarist.[127] Gilson writes that Anselm's

doctrine is strongly marked with some of the same features
as that of Duns Scotus, a leading voluntarist.[128] Joseph
Fischer, though writing that Anselm is a deeply mystical
thinker who puts great emphasis upon contemplation, believes
that Anselm values the will more highly than the intellect.[129]

One of the problems in this dispute is that the terms
"intellectualist" and "voluntarist" are seldom defined with
much precision. Sometimes they are used to designate positions taken on the question whether the will or the intellect is the "higher" ("*altior*") faculty.[130] Sometimes the
dispute revolves around the question whether the intellect
or the will is the power by which man primarily clings to
God and fulfills the basic purpose of his existence.[131] This
question is not necessarily independent of the one just
noted, but neither is it necessarily linked. A third sense
in which the terms are sometimes taken is as indicating alternative views as to which power, reason or will, is the
basic cause of the free act.[132]

If the terms are understood in the first sense, then
the question whether Anselm is an intellectualist or voluntarist is anachronistic, for the question whether the will
or the intellect is a higher power did not arise as a serious issue until later in the Middle Ages. Anselm does not
deal with it. If the terms are understood in the second
sense, we get different answers to whether Anselm is an intellectualist or a voluntarist as we view different parts of
his doctrine. If we focus on his understanding of the final
state of righteousness as one in which reason and will are
both involved and neither has priority over the other, we
have to say either that he is neither a voluntarist nor an
intellectualist or that he is both. If, on the other hand,
we look at his claim that the will rather than reason determines (in cooperation with grace) whether we act justly and
enter the final state of righteousness, we are forced to say
he is a voluntarist.

If the terms are understood in the third sense, we ar-
rive at an even more complex result than the one just noted,
and for some of the same reasons. Does Anselm regard reason
or will as the basic cause of the free act? Once again, we
have to make distinctions, this time among types of free
acts. Anselm holds that any just act, whether it be one in
which justice is restored to a will which has lost it or
one in which justice is kept in a will which possesses it,
is performed freely. So the distinction above, between just
acts performed in the final state of righteousness and those
performed in this life, applies here also. With respect to
the former we have to say again that Anselm is either both
an intellectualist and a voluntarist or neither, while with
respect to the latter he is a voluntarist. But now we have
a further complication, for Anselm teaches that unjust acts
are also performed freely. So we have to consider whether
he believes that the cause of these acts is the intellect or
the will. This gets into issues we have not examined yet,
but a brief comment can be made in anticipation of material
that will be developed in the next chapter. There can be
little doubt that Anselm regards the will as the basic determining cause of unjust acts. This is certainly the case
with the unjust act of a man who has theretofore been just.
It is also the case with an unjust man who, because he is unjust, continues to act unjustly. To be sure, this man's
reason is unable to grasp the truth with any clarity and
depth, but this is a result of his disordered will, not its
cause.

A simple classification of Anselm as an intellectualist
or voluntarist is thus inadequate and misleading. It glosses
over ambiguities in the terms themselves and overlooks subtleties and complexities in his thought. Scholarly discussion could be measurably improved by avoiding disputes over
such classifications and by concentrating on the precise con-
tours of a thinker's thought.

CHAPTER THREE

THE AFFECTIONS OF THE WILL

As we saw in the previous chapter, Anselm believes
that the will has its basic nature, its fundamental *apti-*
tudines, and its diverse uses. *"Affectiones"* is the name
which he gives to the basic *aptitudines* of the will-instrument. Basically, an affection is an innate disposition to
will.[1] The will-instrument has two such basic affections:
the affection for justice (*affectio ad justitiam*) and the
affection for what is useful or beneficial (*affectio ad*
commodum, sometimes also referred to as *affectio ad commodi-*
tatem).[2] Everything that we will falls without exception
under one or both of these two drives: it is either something just or something we will for our own benefit. "The
will as instrument wills nothing except rectitude or what is
beneficial. Whatever else it wills, it wills for the sake
of one of these."[3] Thus, the affection by which we will
something gives that act of will its basic character and
its motivation. Because of this, the affections are the basis upon which a man's choices are found to be deserving of
praise or of blame and on which, therefore, they (the
choices) are determined as good or evil.[4]

Because of the importance of the affections as the basis of the moral quality of a man's choices and because of
their role in the operation of the will, Anselm's account of
them is the critical center of his doctrine of the will, and
this makes them important also for his doctrine of freedom.

It is important, therefore, that we get just as clear as we possibly can about them. It is not easy to do this, however, for Anselm really says rather little about them, and what he says is at times quite cryptic. The only systematic treatment is found in *DCD*, III, xi-xiii. There are scattered other passages which, though not specifically naming the affections, shed light upon them. An especially significant example of such a passage is *DCD*, XII-XIV. Though what Anselm says regarding the affections is not quantitatively great, nevertheless it is loaded with significance and repays careful study. In our examination of the affections, we will concentrate on the passages from *DC* and *DCD* and draw upon the scattered other passages where they prove helpful.

I.   THE NATURE OF THE AFFECTIONS

A. As Aptitudines. One of the striking things about Anselm's account of the affections is that one of the words he uses in describing what they are is "*aptitudo*," the same word he uses of the will-instrument. We saw earlier that the will-instrument is basically an *aptitudo* for willing. But each of the affections is also an *aptitudo* for willing. This might lead us to ask what the differences between them are. An important difference is that the will-instrument is an *aptitudo* of the soul, whereas the affections are *aptitudines* not of the soul but of the will.

It is not immediately clear, however, that this kind of distinction makes sense. We will recall that *aptitudo ad faciendum*, of which the *aptitudo ad volendum* is a particular instance, is the definition for power (*potestas*). But if the instrument of willing is defined as an *aptitudo ad volendum*, and if its affections are also thought of as *aptitudines ad volendum*, it seems that the affections are the power of a power—an extremely odd if not unintelligible notion.[5] This difficulty can be avoided, however, if we

think of the affections as representing not powers which are
distinct and separate from the general power of willing
which constitutes the instrument, but as specifications of
that general power which delimit it and make it more determinate. In other words, the fact that the instrument of
willing has two basic affections means that it is not an in-
discriminate power of willing just anything, but it is a determinate power which can will in only two broad sorts of
ways. The basic *aptitudo ad volendum* is really then an
aptitudo either *ad volendum justitiam* or *ad volendum commodum*—nothing more.

The possession of affections is absolutely essential
to the will-instrument, for one could not be said to have
the ability of willing if he did not have the ability to
will something. The affections specify the sorts of things
which can be the object of willing.

B. As Dispositions to Will. There is more to the affections, however, than the mere specification of the types
of objects that the instrument can will. The fact that the
instrument has the two affections means that whenever we
will we choose one or both of these two things, but in Anselm's thought it also means that there is an inherent tendency in the instrument to will these things. In fact, this
tendency is the most important aspect of an affection. The
character of the affections as tendencies to action comes
through most clearly in Anselm's description of an affection
as "that by which the instrument is so disposed to will
something even when a person is not thinking of it, that
when this thing comes to mind, he wills it either immediately or for its own proper time."[6] By describing an affection
in hypothetical terms, Anselm is characterizing it in the
same way that contemporary philosophers characterize a disposition. Both are tendencies to act, describable in terms
of how one *would* act *if* the appropriate circumstances arose.
There is a difference, however. A disposition may be either

an innate or an acquired tendency to act. The affections
are innate tendencies in the will. They belong to all rational wills (though not always in the same sense) as long
as they continue to exist.

Dispositions have a law-like character. "[A disposi-
tion] is to psychology what a law is to physical science...."[7]
Physical laws, like dispositions, can also be stated in
hypothetical propositions. The law, for instance, that
water freezes at 32°F can be expressed by saying that if the
temperature falls to 32°F then water will freeze. Such law
admits of no exception. If a verified negative instance is
found, then the law is modified and to that extent over-
thrown, but if it is a law, there is no exception to it.
This property of unexceptionability is also a feature of an
affection.[8] If a person has an affection for something,
then given the requisite conditions, he will will it. The
affections, then, are principles which introduce a lawlike
order into the voluntary acts of rational beings.

This similarity of the affections to physical laws
raises the question of whether Anselm is a determinist. Do
the affections imply determinism? If they operate with law-
like regularity, it seems they would leave no room for a
person to exercise his own individual influence over the
choices he makes. Anselm himself holds that in the case of
any created being, what follows from the nature of that being does not occur of that being's own accord.[9] What comes
about *naturaliter* is always contrary to what comes about
sponte.[10] The affections are part of the natural equipment
of human beings; it is not within a man's power to have them
or not to have them. Thus if they determine what a man
wills, it is not within his own power to determine what he
wills.

A solution to this problem depends upon distinguishing
kinds of dispositions. Dispositions can be classified according to genus and species. "Some dispositional words are

highly generic and determinable, while others are highly
specific or determinate."[11] Generic or determinable dispositions are "abilities, tendencies or pronenesses to do, not
things of one unique kind, but things of lots of different
kinds,"[12] whereas a completely determinate disposition would
be a tendency to do something of one unique kind. The obvious way to solve the present problem is to hold that the
affections are dispositions of a determinable kind, and that
therefore there are many different determinate acts which
can be willed in accordance with each of them. Thus, while
the will always by natural necessity wills in accordance
with the affections, nevertheless it has it within its power
to decide which of the large number of determinate acts open
to it within these limits it will perform.

        This may be an obvious solution to the problem, but it
is not immediately clear from what Anselm says in explaining
the affections that this solution is open to him, for it is
not unambiguously clear that he thinks of the affections as
highly determinable dispositions. On the one hand he states
that whenever we will anything we will it *for the sake of*
either justice or the beneficial. This suggests that the
affections are dispositions to will with certain general
ends in mind. If they are, there is no problem with viewing
them as determinable dispositions, for there are many different actions which can serve justice and the beneficial as
ends. On the other hand, in illustrating what it means to
will in accordance with the affections, Anselm gives specific
examples which seem to indicate that they are quite determinate dispositions. In illustrating what it means to will in
accordance with the affection *ad commoditatem* he cites the
example of willing sleep. "The instrument of willing is so
disposed to will sleep that when it comes to mind, even if
the person does not reflect upon it, he wills it for its own
proper time."[13] There is no intimation here that sleep is
willed for anything but its own sake, or that there are other

means for achieving whatever it might be that we want to
achieve through sleep. "Never is the instrument of willing
disposed...to will never to sleep."[14] What are we to make
of this apparent discrepancy in Anselm's account of the affections?

     The answer to this question can be found by looking at
the ultimate purpose of the affections (of which more will
be said later). Their purpose is to make possible the
achievement of man's ultimate end, which, as we have seen,
combines justice and happiness. The affection for justice
is obviously what enables the will-instrument to will justice. And the affection for the beneficial enables it to
will happiness. Justice and happiness are clearly ultimate
ends of human willing, both of which can be achieved in a
variety of ways. This doctrine of the ultimate purpose of
the affections, then, makes it clear that the affections
are determinable dispositions that may under different circumstances take different determinate forms. The affection
ad commodum is the disposition to will the general end happiness, to which there is a great variety of possible means.
The affection for justice is also a highly determinable disposition, not in the sense that in any given situation there
are many different choices which all might be right but in
the sense that the specific act which justice requires varies
from situation to situation, with the consequence that there
are many different acts which can be done in keeping with
justice.

     But if happiness and justice are determinable rather
than determinate dispositions, we need to ask why Anselm so
often calls the affection for happiness the affection *ad*
commodum, i.e., the affection for the beneficial thing, and
why he illustrates it with his example of sleep. For both
the name and the example suggest a much more determinate
type of disposition. Part of the reason is found in his
view that happiness is not something that can be willed and

possessed directly in and of itself alone but is something
which can be willed and possessed only through various means.

> By common consent, happiness is understood
> to include a sufficient degree of beneficial
> things, without there being any want for
> more. And this is true whether one is
> thinking of the happiness of the angels or
> of the happiness of Adam in Paradise.[15]

Willing happiness thus means willing the things that promote
happiness. The things which promote happiness are "*commoda*."
So the affection for happiness includes an affection for
beneficial things.

This explains why Anselm so often calls the disposition
to will happiness the *affectio ad commodum,* but we need something further to explain the example of sleep in illustrating
the *affectio ad commoda.* For his presentation of the example
indicated that sleep is willed just as inexorably as happiness itself. To say that willing happiness necessarily involves willing beneficial things does not entail that willing
happiness necessarily involves the willing of some one particular beneficial thing. Nonetheless, if there are particular beneficial things which are normally necessary for happiness, then the affection for happiness would lead a rational
being to will it. Sleep is obviously necessary for happiness,
since it is necessary for good health. Because the connection between end and means here is so strong and so obvious,
a person does not have to stop and deliberate about whether
he wants to sleep (at the appropriate time), but rather wills
it automatically as soon as he happens to think about it, and
wills it with the same inevitability and law-like regularity
as that with which he wills happiness.

There are, then, things which a rational being is determined to will. They include the two general ends indicated in the affections and whatever else one believes is
necessary to the achievement of those ends. The only exceptions to this occur in cases of moral conflict, in which it
is possible for the will to avoid willing even those things

which are necessary to one or other of the two general
ends. For these are circumstances where one is forced to
choose between the affections themselves. In the situation,
for example, in which a person is forced either to tell a
lie or to lose his life, he may choose either the *commodum*—
self-preservation, life, survival—or the justice of telling
the truth. He is forced to choose between alternatives,
both of which, in circumstances other than those of moral
conflict, he would will necessarily.

The situation of moral conflict, then, is an area
where the will is able to exercise its own power. When
there is a fundamental conflict between the affections, the
will is not determined to will according to either one of
them. It may choose in favor of the just act or in favor of
a *commodum* which conflicts with justice. It is entirely up
to the will.

It might be useful at this point to summarize our findings on the question of whether and to what extent the will
is determined. The only willing which is always determined
is the willing of the most general ends of human conduct,
justice and happiness. In some situations, things which
are means to these ends are also determined, but they are
not determined in every situation. Since one loses justice
if he sins, even willing justice is not always and invariably necessary for the will. The only kind of willing,
therefore, which is wholly inescapable is willing happiness.
Correspondingly, the areas in which the will has the power
to determine its own course are (1) choosing the means for
achieving the basic ends given in the affections in those
cases where the particular means chosen are not (believed)
absolutely necessary to the end but where (it is believed
that) the end could be achieved by a different means, and
(2) choosing in the situations of moral conflict between
justice and particular *commoda* which conflict with it. By
far the most important of these areas in Anselm's mind is,

of course, the latter. Virtually all that he writes about
the affections—indeed, about the will in general—is written with a view to explaining choice in the moral situation.
He says almost nothing about choice of the other kind.

A few of Anselm's commentators have written that he regards the will as a faculty of desire or concupiscence.[16]
He states, "What I am saying about the will can just as well
be said about desire and concupiscence, since the will is
desire and concupiscence."[17] This statement could not refer
to the will either as instrument or as use, so it obviously
refers to the affections. The affections, then, are desires
for their respective general ends[18] as well as dispositions
to will those ends. Dispositions and desires are not the
same, though a disposition may be grounded in a desire.
Both dispositions and desires, however, are tendencies to
action, and both will result in the actions to which they
tend unless there are stronger conflicting desires or dispositions or other countervailing forces.

Now that we have seen the general character of the affections, let us turn to an investigation of their function
and purpose.

II. GENERAL FUNCTION AND PURPOSE

In explaining the general function and purpose of the
affections, we will first look at their immediate function
in the life of the soul and then consider their ultimate
purpose.

A. Immediate Function. In discussing the self-movement of the will-instrument in the previous chapter, we
noted that there is a problem with the notion of self-movement in the will. How can the will, if it is originally not
acting, move itself to act? Before the will acts it is not
acting. But if it is not acting, how can it move itself to
act? It would seem that the only way in which something

that is not acting can be brought into action is through
something else acting upon it. Anselm solves this problem
with his doctrine of the affections, for the immediate function of the affections is to be the basic principle of movement or activity in the will.

One place where Anselm develops this notion is in *DCD*,
in a passage in which teacher and student discuss various
elements in an act of will. The inquiry is undertaken in
order to discover which elements are in the control of the
creature and which are not. The reason for looking into
this issue is to see whether God is responsible for man's
sin or man is. The discussion is conducted with reference
to Satan, but since the will of the angels is not essentially different from the will of men, the discussion applies
also to humans. The first question the teacher raises is
the following.

> Let us suppose that God created Satan step
> by step, and not all at once; and that God
> wished to make him happy. And let us sup-
> pose that Satan had been created up to the
> point of being suited to have a will, but
> without yet having willed anything.... Do
> you suppose that Satan, in this condition,
> could will anything through himself?[19]

Two points should be noted about this question. One is that
we are to suppose that Satan has only the instrument of
willing; he does not yet have the affections, and he has
not yet made any actual volitions. The other is that we
are to suppose that God has created Satan with the purpose
that he should be happy. Nothing is said here about the
other part of the ultimate end of rational creatures, justice. The question, then, is whether under these conditions
Satan would by himself (*per se*) be able to perform any act
of will, or do something, that would contribute to his happiness. Anselm explains that anything a person can do with
the powers he has and without outside help is something he
can do *per se*.

The student replies that if Satan had the instrument
of willing and lacked only the actual use thereof, then he
was able to will *per se*. The teacher points out that the
problem is one of how the will moves itself from a state of
non-willing to willing, and asks pointedly, "Does it will to
move?"[20]   The student sees that if he says that the will is
moved from without, he would have to admit that the will is
not moved by its own power. He suggests, therefore, that
the first movement of the will might be one which occurs
instinctively as a reaction to some outside stimulus. "A
person might suddenly blink when he sees a blow coming, or
might be forced by some pain or other, to will something he
previously was not willing. But I don't know whether in
such a case he first wills to move to this willing."[21]   The
teacher responds that no one reacts instinctively to external stimuli unless there is some general tendency within
the will to act that way in the presence of such stimuli.

> No one is forced by fear or a feeling of
> pain (*incommodi*), nor attracted by love
> of any pleasure (*commodi*), to will any
> particular thing, unless he first has the
> natural inclination (*voluntatem*) to avoid
> pain and to enjoy pleasure. By this
> natural inclination he moves himself to
> other willings.[22]

Before there can be any particular act of will, there has to
be an inclination within the will. But this inclination is
also a kind of willing, and so it is ruled out by the hy-
pothesis on which the whole discussion is predicated. Hence,
the final conclusion on this question is that, "It turns out
that Satan, at the time when he was created with a capacity
for having a will, but had not yet willed anything, couldn't
have had his first willing from himself" (i.e., *per se*).[23]

Though Anselm does not explicitly say so, the "natural
inclination" (*naturalis voluntas*) spoken of here is clearly
the affection for happiness. Both the inclination and the
affection are directed toward happiness and *commoda*. And

both are principles which, just as much as the instrument,
engage in willing.

What this question about Satan's will reveals is that
the instrument of willing alone does not have the power to
fulfill its own proper and distinctive function. To do this
it needs the affections. The basic function of the affections, then, is to make it possible for the instrument to
fulfill its function. The affections thus belong to the
will necessarily. They do not merely provide the instrument
an enabling condition for the exercise of a power that it
already has. For it has no power to will unless it has the
affections. Rather, the affections give the instrument a
power which it does not and cannot have without them. Since
the function of a thing is essential to its very nature,
without the affections the instrument is not a genuine instrument at all, i.e., not a real capacity or power for
willing.

This, however, does not mean that the instrument is
reduced to its affections, obliterating any distinction between them. Though the power which constitutes the instrument is activated by the affections and is absent without
them, still the power of the instrument, namely the power to
make determinate choices in accordance with the affections,
is something quite different from the natural tendencies to
seek certain goals that constitute the affections.

The need of the instrument for the affections is a re-
ciprocal one. As the instrument cannot be itself or fulfill
its proper function without the affections, so the affections
cannot be effective in the actual life and choices of a person unless they belong to an instrument that can choose particular acts to fulfill the general ends to which the affections are directed. Moreover, for the affections to be effective, not only must there be an instrument which is *able*
to make those choices, there must be actual choices made.
Thus the three elements of the will which Anselm identifies—

the instrument, the affections and the use—mutually imply
one other.

It is not yet clear, however, that the problem concerning the self-movement of the will has been solved. The
problem is how the will can bring about its own first movement, and the answer that we have found is that the first
movement of the will is given to it in the affections. But
the affections are part of the natural endowment of the will;
they have been bestowed upon it by God. The first movement
of the will, then, is not something that the will itself
brings about. It seems mistaken, therefore, to think of
this first movement as a case of self-movement.

We can resolve this difficulty by distinguishing types
of movement in the will. Movement in the will may be either
a tendency or an act. When Anselm thinks of the affections
as the first movements of the will, he is clearly thinking
of tendencies. The view that the basic tendencies of the
will are given to it by God is quite compatible with the
claim that the first act of the will is something it performs on its own. Anselm's question whether Satan could
will anything *per se* if he had been given the instrument of
the will without the affections had to do with acts of will,
with volitions. And by acting *per se* he means acting solely
through the use of one's own powers, unaided by anything
outside oneself.[24] His answer is that Satan could act *per
se* so long as he had all the essential features of the will,
including affections. Obviously, a finite creature cannot
give a will to himself. But once endowed with will, he has
all that is needed to perform volitions on his own power.
The will, then, is a self-moving principle in the sense that
it has the power to act *per se*. Self-movement in the will,
then, pertains to acts, not basic tendencies or affections.

We must not read more into Anselm's claim than is warranted. One of the major points he is making when he asserts
the self-movement of the will is that there is a basic con-

trast between the will and other instruments, like the
senses and reason or the hands and feet. These instruments
are not self-moving, for their power has to be activated by
a power external to themselves, the will. Such is not the
case with the will. By virtue of its affections, the will
is endowed in its very nature with its own activating principle. The objection stated earlier, then, is correct. It
is a mistake to think of the movement of the affections as a
case of self-movement in the will. The objection is wrong
only insofar as it is taken as a point against Anselm, for
Anselm's doctrine is that the first *act* of the will is self-
moved.

A final aspect of the immediate function of the affections should be noted before we move on to an examination of
their ultimate purpose. As the basic dispositions of the
will they establish the ultimate purposes or goals of all
human action. Different people, of course, have a great
many different ways of seeking these goals, but all these
ways are directed toward the same general ends, which are
those established by God as the ultimate ends of human life.
This aspect of the affections is implied in their function
as the basic dispositions of the will. For an affection is
both a *desire* for something and a desire *for something*. As
desires or dispositions the affections are alike. Their
differences, which as we shall see are considerable, stem
from the different ends toward which they are directed.

B. Ultimate Purpose. The ultimate purpose of the affections is to play an essential role in the attainment of
the ultimate purpose of man. As we have just seen, their
immediate function is to provide the will-instrument with
the impetus that gives it the power to perform acts of will.
But in doing this their ultimate purpose is also fulfilled,
for the impetus they provide is toward the two ultimate ends
of human life, happiness and justice.[25]

Human beings, Anselm teaches, were created not only

with the basic desire for happiness and justice but in full
possession of these goods.

> So then, God created man happy and in
> need of nothing. Rational nature re-
> ceived at once the will for happiness,
> and happiness; the will for justice (i.e.,
> it received rectitude, which is justice);
> and free choice, without which it could
> not keep justice.[26]

God created man perfect, lacking nothing needed for achieving his purpose. Man's task was simply to use his powers
to maintain himself in the state of perfection.

It is worth emphasizing that justice was a part of the
original nature of man, for there have been scholars who
have written that Anselm viewed justice as a supernatural
gift given by God to man as something extra added to his
nature. E. R. Fairweather, for example, states, "In such
works as *De casu diaboli* and *De concordia*, where ethics and
dogma are so closely interwoven, it is made clear that Anselm sees *rectitudo* as a supernatural gift of God, separable
from the essence of man."[27]

Now Anselm does speak in places as though justice were
something added to the will after the creation of human nature had been completed.[28] He also asserts, "Justice is
not a natural possession, but in the beginning it was something separable in both the angels in heaven and man in
paradise."[29] Furthermore, one could argue that the fact
that justice is not only separable from the will but is in
fact separated from it in a great many men, shows that it
is not natural to man, for what is truly natural to man cannot be lost without destroying man's nature.

Nevertheless, there are very strong reasons for rejecting Fairweather's interpretation. In the first place,
there are passages in Anselm's writings which *prima facie*
go contrary to those just cited. I have already quoted one
three paragraphs back. To this one could add Anselm's remark that "To have had justice and to owe justice are

evidence of a natural dignity."[30] Moreover, in *DCD*, XVI,
where Anselm talks as if justice were something added on to
an otherwise complete will, he is still making the same kind
of supposition that we saw him making in *DCD*, XII, where he
was discussing the problem of the first movement of the will.
That is, he is supposing, in an effort to get clear on the
role of various elements in the will, that the will was created in stages. His talk, then, of justice as something
added onto the will, is a result of the supposition he is
making, not an indication that the will really received justice some time after it was created.

As for the argument that justice cannot be natural to
man because he does not always possess it, that argument is
based on a doctrine of natural essences that is quite different from Anselm's. As we have seen, Anselm defines the essential nature of a thing in terms of what it ought to be,
not in terms of the attributes which it always possesses.
Man was created to be just. The fact that he sometimes
fails to achieve this purpose makes no difference to what
he ought to be. If at some moment a person does not possess
justice, his essential nature is not affected, only his moral
standing. He becomes unjust, he does not become unhuman.

But what are we to make of Anselm's statement that justice is not a natural possession? The answer to this question is found in the way he completes the sentence in which
he makes the statement:

> Justice is not a natural possession, but
> in the beginning it was something separable
> in both the angels in heaven and man in
> paradise; and even now in this life it is
> separable not by necessity but by the proper
> willing of those who possess it.[31]

"Not natural" here is being used synonymously with "separable." But, it might be objected, this shows that Anselm is
using "natural" in the usual sense to describe those attributes which are invariably present in a thing. He uses the

word "natural," however, in different senses. The sense in
which justice is natural to the will is the sense of "natural" found in his definition of "essential nature," according to which what is essential to a thing is whatever belongs to its ultimate purpose or to what it ought to be.[32]
The sense in which justice is not natural to the will is
that in which what is natural to a thing is always present
in it. For Anselm, the former is by far the more important
sense ontologically and morally. We may safely conclude,
then, that when he said that justice is not a natural possession because it is separable, he did not mean to deny
that it belongs to man's essential nature, as essential nature is defined in *DV*.

Fairweather's interpretation also depends on a dichotomy of natural and supernatural which is quite foreign to
Anselm's thought. Anselm does think of justice as a gift of
God which he gives in his grace,[33] and he extols it as a
gift of the highest order, constituting "such a lofty
grace."[34] However, he thinks of all of human nature as a
gift of God, not just justice. This is particularly significant in the case of happiness, for the affection for happiness is something that stays with man as long as he lives.
He cannot lose it. On the non-Anselmian view of what is
natural, then, the affection for happiness would belong to
man by nature. But the affection for happiness is described
by Anselm as a gift bestowed by grace.[35] So the fact that
justice is referred to as a special gift of God is no argument in support of the theory that justice is not natural to
man.

We have seen now that man is endowed at creation with
a desire for each of the two basic ends for which he was
made and a drive to will those things that will achieve
these ends. We must be careful, however, not to misconstrue
the relation between man's natural inclinations, the affections, and his ultimate end. Many medieval thinkers develop

their moral theories on the basis of their theories of human
nature. They understand human duties in terms of the basic
human drives. According to this view, human beings are obligated to do what is best suited to achieve these ends.
Morality and psychology are thus closely related, but psychology is fundamental and morality is dependent on psychology. Anselm agrees with these thinkers that there is a cor-
relation between ethics and psychology, but he understands
their order of dependence differently. For him duty is
fundamental and psychology is dependent. Human beings have
been given the affections they have because of the duty they
have, and without the affections they would be unable to do
their duty. We see here the specific application to man of
Anselm's general ontological principle that the essential
nature of anything is determined by the purpose for which it
exists, i.e., by what it ought to be. While many medieval
philosophers hold a natural law theory of morals, Anselm
holds what we might call a moral law theory of nature.

    Another way in which Anselm's doctrine of man differs
from that of many others is in postulating two basic drives
or affections. A great many thinkers have held that there
is only a single basic drive in man, and they have thought
it possible to develop an adequate moral psychology on this
basis. We might ask, therefore, why Anselm thought it necessary to postulate two basic drives. He teaches, of course,
that the end of man includes both justice and happiness,
and he claims that it is impossible to be just or happy
without the will for justice and happiness. But this does
not explain why there should be two different drives, one
for happiness and the other for justice. It would make just
as good sense, it seems, to say that happiness is found in
being just, hence all that a person needs to be both just
and happy is a single affection for justice which leads him
to act justly. One could even find some support for saying
this in Anselm's doctrines. "Justice" is his blanket-word

for all that a rational being ought to be. As an ultimate
end happiness is part of what human beings ought to be; happiness therefore is a part of justice.

There is, then, serious question why two affections
are needed. But the problem is actually more acute than so
far indicated. For Anselm holds that not only do we need
one affection each for happiness and justice, but that both
affections are needed to achieve each of these ends. That
is to say, we need both affections just to achieve justice
and both just to achieve happiness. Is there a way to make
sense of these claims?

DCD, XIV gives an argument for the claim that both affections are needed in order to achieve justice. But this
argument presupposes a discussion in earlier chapters of *DCD*
of the achievement of happiness. To lay the groundwork,
therefore, for examining the argument concerning justice, we
need to look at the argument concerning happiness.

In this argument the question is raised whether Satan,
if he had been given only the affection for happiness, could
will anything other than happiness. The answer given is, "I
can't see how he could move himself to will something other
than happiness when he didn't want anything else. For if he
willed to move himself to some other willing, then he wanted
something else."[36] But this prompts an objection: what if
he should think something would promote his happiness which
really did not: would he not be able to will this through
the affection for happiness? This question seems to lead to
a dilemma.

> I am in doubt about what to answer. For if
> he could not, then I don't see how he would
> will happiness—for he could not will that
> by which he thought he could acquire happi-
> ness. But if he could, then I don't under-
> stand why he could not will something other
> than happiness.[37]

The dilemma is resolved by the principle that the basic
character of an action is specified by its end. Hence,

however mistaken a person may be in his judgment that what
he wills is something that will lead to happiness, his willing it for the sake of happiness means that he is willing
happiness. Thus, the conclusion is secured that with only
an affection for happiness a person could not will anything
but happiness.

But this suggests further questions. Granted that the
will for happiness is not able to will anything other than
happiness, would it be able to stop willing happiness? "I
am asking whether he could desert this will and move himself
from willing happiness to not willing it."[38] The answer is
no; for if he did so willingly, i.e., if he willed to stop
happiness, then he would be willing something other than
happiness, which he cannot do.

Now, if he cannot stop himself from willing happiness,
would it be possible for him to choose something which he
knew would bring less happiness than an alternative equally
possible for him to choose? Again the answer is no. "The
more he could understand that there was a happiness higher
than his own, the happier he willed to be."[39]

In this series of questions Anselm shows not merely
that someone with only the affection for happiness could not
choose anything other than happiness, he shows also that
such a person is not free, for he wills whatever he wills
as a direct consequence of his psychological make-up——he
cannot help willing what he wills. Moreover, in these circumstances Satan's sin would have been inevitable, for he
would necessarily have willed to be like God, since as an
angel he would know that God's happiness was higher than
his.[40] The implication here is that a person is able to
will a lesser happiness when he sees a greater happiness
only if there is some entirely different kind of good for
the sake of which he chooses the lesser good. He could, of
course, choose a lesser happiness if he knew no higher one,
but he could not refrain from willing the highest happiness

he knows if he has only the affection for happiness.

This is exactly the situation of the animals. They
pursue beastly pleasures and do so necessarily.[41] It is also the situation of rational beings who have lost their affection for justice through sin. When the rational will
sins, it is "made a slave to its own affection for what is
beneficial, for once justice is taken away, a man can only
will what this affection wills."[42] This means that a man
"falls into the likeness of brute animals and becomes subject with them to corruption and to the appetites."[43] The
will of such a man becomes "fervent with desire for benefits
it cannot now keep from willing because it cannot now have
those true, but lost, benefits which are suitable for rational nature."[44] Thus, what was said earlier to show that the
possession of affections does not determine one's actions
must be understood as applying to beings which have more
than a single affection.

A significant feature of this line of reasoning is
that it is taken over completely and applied to the (imag-
ined) case where Satan has only the single affection for
justice.

> In this case too, he would have a will
> which could be neither just nor unjust.
> For even as the will for happiness would
> not be unjust if it willed unseemly things
> which it could not keep from willing, so
> this will for justice would not be just
> if it willed seemly things, since it had
> received no ability to do anything else.[45]

In this passage Anselm is noting some parallels and
symmetries between the two affections. But there is a significant asymmetry which he slides over, which is perhaps
more important than the symmetries. Let us grant to Anselm
that if a person has only a single affection then his
choices are determined. This, Anselm maintains, results in
the same consequences for one's actions, regardless of which
affection one has: these actions cannot be just or unjust

because the individual could not help willing what he did.
There is a sense, however, in which the consequences are
quite different for the two affections. When the affection
is that for happiness, the fact that the person's choices
are determined does not prevent them from being made in accordance with the affection for happiness or from being
fully in keeping with the pursuit of happiness. When, however, the affection is that for justice, the fact that a
person's choices are determined means that they are not in
accord with the pursuit of justice. (Actually, what Anselm
says here is that these choices are not just, but since he
teaches that justice and the affection for justice are one
and the same,[46] it follows that these choices are not in accord with the affection for justice and therefore do not
follow from a true affection for justice.)

The problem here can be looked at from a different
angle. When a person has two affections, he can freely
choose between acts motivated by the one and acts motivated
by the other, and these choices, of course, are not determined. If a person has both an affection for justice and
another affection, then any just choice he makes is both
(a) not determined and (b) fully just. But why should the
presence of another affection change the moral quality of
the act performed under the impetus of the affection for
justice? In both cases, the act is done from the same impulse, with the same goal, and for the same motive. But the
act is just if the person has a second affection, unjust if
not. Why should the presence or absence of a second affection make this difference?

One thing it seems clear Anselm is not saying is that
will-acts done by a person having only an affection for justice are not in accord with some kind of purely objective or
behavioral standard of justice. Anselm sets forth both objective and subjective criteria for an act being a just act.[47]
Not only must an act conform to an objective law, but it must

also be done solely for the sake of justice. There is no
reason for thinking that an act performed by a person who
had only the affection for justice could not be in accordance with an objective law. Neither is there reason to
think that such an act could not conform to the criterion of
intention, for if an individual had only the one affection
for justice, it would be impossible for him to will for the
sake of anything else. Hence, Anselm must have some other
criterion of justice in mind when he denies that such an act
could properly be called just.

What is this criterion? The answer to this question
comes out most clearly in his treatment of how the good angels merited their reward of confirmation in goodness and
why they deserve praise for their present inability to sin.
That treatment shows that what makes these angels praiseworthy is that in some sense they have their goodness (justice) *from themselves (a se)*. "Angels are not to be praised
for their justice because they were able to sin [and did not
do so], but because as a result of this ability they possess
their present inability to sin from themselves."[48] The underlying principle here is that in order for a person *himself* to be just his justice must come from himself. What
this means is explained in the following way.

> When an angel could have deprived himself
> of justice and did not, and could have made
> himself unjust and did not, it is correct
> to say that he gave himself justice and
> made himself just. In this way, then, he
> possesses the justice from himself...and
> for that reason he is to be praised for
> his justice.[49]

A person, then, has a just act from himself when he has both
the ability to do what is just and the ability to do what is
unjust, and when, faced with a choice between something just
and something unjust, he chooses the just act. There must
be genuine moral alternatives from which to choose before a
man's just choices can be worthy of praise and thus be fully

just. A determinism which makes it impossible to choose between moral alternatives prevents one from acting *a se*. It
is precisely this sort of determinism which obtains when a
person has only a single affection, even when that affection
is the affection for justice.

Anselm's thought is that a person with a single affection would be no more praiseworthy for performing an objectively good act than, say, a surgical knife is for saving
the life of a dying patient. The fact that the knife is an
instrument for good stems from the one who makes it and the
one who uses it. The fact that an individual with only the
affection for justice acts in a manner that is objectively
just stems from the one who made him.

The doctrine that for a person's acts to be just they
must proceed *a se* makes sense of two closely related points.
First, it shows why the affection for happiness is necessary
not only so a person can achieve happiness but also so he
can achieve justice. Second, it makes clear why these must
be *different* affections which sometimes incline people in
morally different directions.

Though it is clear now why Anselm believes there must
be two affections, there still remains a serious question
about how the affections fulfill the role he sees them playing. The very nature of a rational moral creature requires
that it have the two affections. Both are essential to the
fulfillment of the ultimate end of man, for their co-exist-
ence makes it possible for human beings to sin and therefore
also possible for them to be just. It is not clear, however,
that this idea is coherent with other parts of his thought.
Both the affections are essential constituents of human nature, but the affection for happiness is restricted by the
requirements of justice. It is difficult to see how this
fits in with Anselm's metaphysics and psychology of morals.
For justice, as he conceives it, is perfectly co-ordinated
with human nature. But how can something which is an

essential part of human nature require restriction by a principle that is co-ordinated with human nature? If the affection for happiness is part of our essential nature and purpose, it would seem impossible for it to be, or to lead to,
something that is inappropriate or excessive for our nature.

One could say, of course, that it is simply human nature to want more than one can ever possibly achieve. But
this will not help Anselm. In the first place, he teaches
that human nature was created in a morally perfect condition,
one in which man did not originally will more than what was
right for him to will. Secondly, he tells us, "By common
consent, happiness is understood to include a sufficient degree of beneficial things, without there being any need for
more,"[50] and "God created man happy and in need of nothing."[51]
Now if in his original state man's happiness was complete and
he lacked nothing, it is hard to see how he could want anything more. Even if, as Anselm teaches, there was a greater
happiness than man's, the very fact that he is completely
satisfied with his own more limited happiness seems to rule
out the possibility that he could desire anything more, for
there is nothing to motivate a desire for something more.

One might seek to rescue Anselm by invoking the concept of order. This is a leading Augustinian category,
which some interpreters have used extensively in explicating
Anselm.[52] And it is a concept which Anselm himself employs
in speaking of the relation between the two affections.[53]
We might say, then, that while human nature includes both
affections, the affection for happiness is subordinate to
the affection for justice. Justice is the overarching moral
category which encompasses the moral rules that apply to the
pursuit of happiness. On this view, happiness would be included in justice but the two would be distinct enough to
allow for the possibility of sin. One could sin by seeking
the happiness that one already possesses but seeking it for
its own sake rather than for the sake of justice, thus over-

overturning the proper order of human nature.

This might answer the difficulties as they have so far
been posed. Unfortunately, it does not fit what Anselm has
to say about the occurrence of the first sin. (The first
sin, of course, is that of Satan, but as we have seen, there
is no essential difference between original angelic nature
and original human nature.) "Satan sinned," Anselm writes,
"by willing something beneficial, which he neither possessed
nor was supposed to will at that time.... He extended his
will beyond justice by a disordered willing of something
that was more than he had received."[54] Satan's sin, then,
did not consist in willing with the wrong motive something
that he already had; it consisted in willing something he
did not have but wanted. We are thus back with the problem
of how one who is completely happy can want something which
he does not need.

As far as I can see, Anselm never satisfactorily explains how the interplay of the two affections in beings
created perfect can develop into a full-fledged moral conflict between them. In order to make sense of moral conflict and the experience of temptation, he resorts to two
expedients, both of which are inconsistent with certain basic principles of his. These two expedients are not clearly
distinguished; they are, in fact, combined in the same explanation. On the one hand, he holds that Satan's affection
for happiness did exceed the limits appropriate to his nature and did cause him actually to desire something he should
not have. He wanted something which belonged properly only
to God.[55] On the other hand, he implies that when God placed
upon man the moral obligations binding upon him, he included
certain arbitrary restrictions upon the free expression of
his natural being. He says that "Satan sinned by willing
something beneficial, which he neither possessed nor was
supposed to will at that time, even though it was able to
increase his happiness."[56] Satan was supposed to will only

what God allowed him to will at any given time, even though
what was restricted by God's will was something which would
have genuinely increased his happiness had there been no restriction on it when he willed it. Thus, what prevented
Satan from willing and enjoying the added happiness was not
that it was something inappropriate to his nature, but that
it was something God had forbidden him to have. Far from
being inappropriate to his nature, this happiness, Anselm
tells us, would have been given to him later if he had not
willed it at this time. The doctrine here is, apparently,
that God places arbitrary restrictions upon the angelic nature simply to make possible the conflict between an angel's
duty and his natural inclination which makes for temptation
and the possibility of sin.

Each of these explanations is inconsistent with other
doctrines of Anselm. The first is inconsistent with his
teaching that man was created completely just, for it holds
that his will was characterized by a desire that goes beyond
and thus violates the rules of justice. The second is at
odds with the notion that justice and human nature are perfectly co-ordinated, for it sees man's duty as imposing certain prohibitions on the free expression of his essential
nature.

Anselm, it seems, correctly senses that if justice
must involve making a choice between genuine moral alternatives, there must be some tension within the will between
what one wants to will and what one ought to will. The
problem, however, is to conceive how such a tension is possible within a system of thought which combines Anselm's
notion of justice with (a) an ontology that holds that the
essential nature of man is justice and (b) a theology which
maintains that human beings were created completely just.
For such a system of thought leads to paradox. It entails
that if a being is to be created perfectly just he must be
created partly unjust. For in order that a person be

completely just, there must be some element in his will
which is not completely subordinated to justice. Otherwise
choice is impossible and so is justice.

The paradox can be set out in somewhat different terms
by making a distinction between two kinds of justice, one a
justice of the affections, the other a justice of volitions.
Justice of the affections consists in a complete subordina-
tion of the affection for happiness to the affection for
justice, while justice in volitions consists in making actual right choices and making them rightly (which includes
making them a se). The paradox is that if human beings were
created with the justice of the affections, the justice of
volitions is impossible, while if the justice of volitions
is possible, human beings could not have been created with
the justice of the affections. Whichever the case, God
could not have created rational beings completely just, just
both in the affections and in volitions.

Even if Anselm is unable to resolve this paradox, the
concerns which lead him into it are clear. He thinks that
the human will must include the power of self-determination
—the ability to choose, contradeterministically, between
moral alternatives. The doctrine that there are two affections in the will is part of the attempt to spell out the
psychological conditions necessary if human beings are to
have such a power. And all of this grows out of the teaching that the highest end of man is justice.

It is the fundamental orientation to justice which
marks off the rational will and rational beings from lower
orders of being and will. Anselm holds that there is will
in animals, but animal will is characterized by only the
single affection ad commodum.[57] What essentially differentiates man from the animals, then, is the affection for justice. This is significant, because in Anselm's day it had
long been customary to regard the quality which differentiated man most fundamentally from the animals as reason.

Anselm agrees that reason is one of the differentiating features, and he goes along with the convention of identifying
human nature with rational nature. But for him reason is
not the most fundamental differentiating characteristic, for
reason is subordinate to justice. Man has reason because he
must have it to be just. The animals do not need reason because their end is not justice. Once again we see the supreme role played by morality in Anselm's metaphysics.

       In rational beings the requirements of justice deter-
mine their entire nature and thus the structure of their
wills. As we have seen, in rational beings will is the
power of self-determination. So far we have concentrated
on the form which this power took originally in men and angels. But this power takes different forms in different
beings; it even takes different forms at different stages
in the lives of these beings. The present form of this
power in the angels, for example, is quite different from
the form it had for them originally. Originally the angels
had the ability to make choices between moral alternatives.
Now they do not. The good angels have been confirmed in
righteousness and no longer have the ability to do anything
unjust, while the wicked angels have been confirmed in injustice and have no ability to do what is just.[58] The good
angels' acts are causally determined by the affection for
justice, while the wicked angels' acts are causally determined by the affection for happiness. We might ask, therefore, whether it makes sense to ascribe self-determination
to these beings and so whether it makes sense to ascribe
justice to the good angels and injustice to the wicked.

       Anselm maintains that the just acts which the good
angels perform are truly just, because their present inability to do anything unjust is a result of a choice they
made earlier between what is just and what is unjust. Thus,
even though they are unable to do anything unjust, their
just acts are something they have from themselves. "So then,

when an angel could have deprived himself of justice and did
not, and could have made himself unjust and did not, it is
correct to say that he gave himself justice and made himself
just. In this way, then, he possesses justice from himself."[59] The same sort of reasoning shows that the evil angels have their injustice from themselves. The will of the
angels, whether good or bad angels, whether in their original state or their present condition, is a power of self-
determination. Before the angels became confirmed in righteousness or wickedness, this power was a power of choice between moral alternatives. But the ability to choose between
moral alternatives disappears once the angels have been confirmed. This, however, does not destroy their power of
self-determination. For the choices they now make are those
they determined earlier are the ones they should make. They
are now doing exactly what they wanted to be doing.

     God, too, has the power of self-determination without
the ability to choose between moral alternatives. He differs from the angels, however, in that he never had the
ability to choose between moral alternatives. God has always chosen according to the standard of justice, and it is
impossible that he should ever do anything else. Nonetheless, God's actions are self-determined, for everything he
does proceeds *a se* and is solely the expression of his own
nature.[60] In God self-determination is compatible with the
inability ever to do anything unjust, for God is uncreated
and has his entire being from himself. Nothing other than
God himself determines what he does. In creatures, however,
self-determination is incompatible with the inability ever
to do anything unjust. For creatures have their being from
God, not from themselves. Hence anything they do as a result of being determined by their nature does not come from
themselves but from God. Self-determination in created
beings exists only in those who have, or have had, the
ability to choose what is right when they could have chosen

what is wrong.

We may now bring this section on the ultimate purpose
of the affections to a close by drawing three general conclusions. First, what constitutes the praiseworthiness of
any being's justice is that the being has it from himself.
Secondly, as a consequence, what constitutes will in any
rational being, i.e., any being whose ultimate end is justice,
is the power of self-determination. Third, the ultimate
purpose of the affections in man is to provide the will with
the conditions which make human self-determination possible.

III. THE TWO AFFECTIONS

In discussing the nature, function and purpose of the
affections, we have been concentrating primarily on features
they have in common. In this section we shall be looking
at some of the major differences between them and at how
they are related to each other in achieving man's ultimate
end.

A. Their Differences. One of the most important ways
in which the affections differ is that the affection for
happiness is a permanent feature of all wills and linked to
them inseparably, whereas the affection for justice is not
inseparable from every will. It is, of course, a permanent
feature of the will of God and now of the good angels, but
it is not a permanent feature of the will of the evil angels
or of human beings who are living at the present time.[61] The
affection for justice becomes actually separated from the
will when a person sins. The separability of justice, then,
indicates the possibility of sin, and correspondingly, the
inseparability of justice indicates the impossibility of
sin. With the angels, once the affection for justice is
lost, it can never be retrieved. With men in the present
life, however, when the affection for justice is lost, there
is still the possibility of recovering it. But the recovery

is not something which can be accomplished by the one who
does not have justice. It must be effected by grace.

     Unlike the affection for justice, the affection for
happiness cannot be lost, even when a person sins. It does,
however, change its character when a person sins. Before
sin, the affection for happiness is subordinate to the affection for justice. In this condition, the *commoda* which
it wills are truly beneficial to the person who wills them,
and they genuinely minister to his happiness. But when a
person sins, not only is justice lost, but so is true happiness. In the first place, the *commodum* which was willed
contrary to justice is not obtained. And secondly, the happiness which one had before sin is now lost.

> The angels who preferred what God had not
> willed to give them, rather than preferring
> to remain upright in the justice in which
> they were made, received the judgment of
> justice; not only did they fail to obtain
> what they preferred to justice and what
> made them despise justice, but they even
> lost the good which they had.[62]

But though happiness itself was lost, the affection
continues to operate. And since justice is gone, the affection *ad commoda* becomes the dominating principle. Without
the guidance of justice, however, it drives men to will all
sorts of bogus *commoda*. In this condition the will turns
itself to "the false benefits sought by brute animals at
the urging of their appetites."[63] "In such a state [the
will] is driven by various appetites until it precipitates
itself and all the various members subordinated to it into
manifold evils."[64] This is all part of the punishment of
the sinner. Because he elects to follow the affection for
happiness rather than the affection for justice, he is given
over to the affection for happiness. He continues to will
happiness but now never achieves it. Thus the continued
possession of the affection for happiness after a person
sins leads only to misery. Though a person who sins rejects

justice, the fact that he suffers as a result of it is it-self just. "If one should forsake justice...the will for happiness would still remain, so that through a need of the good things which he had lost, he would be justly punished with dire misery."[65]

On the other hand, the final reward of justice is the complete satisfaction of one's desire for happiness. This does not occur in this life for people who remain just. Final reward and final punishment for men will come in the next life. The present conditions, therefore, of human life are somewhat mixed. But the pure conditions may be seen in the case of the angels. The good angels were immediately given their reward once they persevered in justice when the evil angels did not. As their reward God gave them every-thing they could possibly desire through their affection for happiness.

> The angels who preferred the justice which
> they had to that thing [i.e., the *commodum*]
> which they did not have, have received,
> through the reward of this very justice
> the good which they, on account of their
> choosing justice, had seemed to lose; and
> they also remained eternally secure in the
> justice which they had. For this reason,
> they were raised to honor, so that they
> obtained whatever they were able to will,
> and they no longer saw anything to will
> which exceeded what they already had.[66]

We see now that the affection for happiness is not only a condition which makes temptation possible for a creature whose end is justice, it is also a condition which makes reward and punishment possible.

There are, however, serious problems with this picture of the reward that is granted for justice. The reward af-fects both affections. The affection for justice is made inseparable from the will, while the affection for happiness is supplied with all the benefits it can desire. It appears that not only does the reward affect both affections but

that each affection enjoys a separate reward: the affection
for justice is strengthened so that one can never again
place anything else before justice, and the affection for
happiness is granted all it desires. But this is not the
case. There is no strengthening of the affection for justice. It is the added satisfactions one enjoys which now
make it impossible ever to will anything unjust. Confirmation in righteousness, which appears to represent a state of
great moral virtue, consists merely in the absence of tempta
tion and opportunity to sin. Instead of being a condition
of moral strength, marked by the power to overcome in moral
conflicts, it is a condition in which there are no moral
conflicts at all. Anselm himself puts it very clearly.
"The good angel's inability to sin glorified him, since because of the merit of persevering he was elevated so that
he could no longer see anything more he was able to will
than what he already had."[67]

We have already seen that Anselm regards anyone who has
been confirmed in righteousness as praiseworthy. This is
because such a person's inability to sin comes *a se*. But
the praise that is due him is not primarily for something
which he has or does now, but for something which he did in
the past. Anselm apparently believes that a person should
continue receiving praise indefinitely for this kind of past
act even though he never does anything similar again.

Such confirmation and such praise would perhaps be un-
derstandable if the act they reward represented a great
triumph over a powerful evil which, once defeated, can no
longer rise to trouble moral beings. But one can hardly
speak of the act of the good angels in such grandiloquent
terms. For the reward that God gives is precisely the good
thing which he initially forbade the angels to will. God
deliberately withheld this from them so that they could
prove themselves by obeying him in refusing to will it. We
saw earlier that Anselm is forced by the logic of his posi-

tion to the expedient of postulating an arbitrary command of
God in order to account for the moral experience of temptation. We now see the consequences of this in his view of
the act of the good angels and of the confirmation they receive as its reward. And we see the implications of it for
a theory of the nature of evil. The just act of the good
angels turns out to be nothing more than obedience to the
arbitrary ruling of a God jealously guarding his own honor
(the affection for justice, Anselm tells us, is given to us
by God for his own honor),[68] sin is the desire for something
which would have been given anyway if it had not been desired,
and the reward is the giving of this thing because it was
not desired.

A second major question arises in connection with the
doctrine that the affection for justice is separable from
the will. If the affection for justice can be lost suddenly
and completely the moment an individual sins, is it proper
to call it a basic, even an essential, disposition of the
will? This problem is accentuated when considered in relation to man in this life. For man can presently lose justice and regain it any number of times. Now, if a person
has it one day and not the next, and regains it the third
day only to lose it again on the fourth, and if this process
can go on indefinitely as long as the person is alive, what
sense does it make to call this a disposition? A disposition is more stable and permanent than this, is it not? We
have already examined the sense in which the affection for
justice is an essential characteristic of human nature: it
is something a human being ought always to have.[69] But that
is quite different from calling it a disposition which a man
has in his present situation. Even if he has this affection,
how can it be a *disposition,* if it is something he can lose
completely tomorrow?

This is not a question Anselm directly answers. But
he makes some points that are relevant to it. He holds,

for instance, that as long as a person has an affection for
justice it shows the characteristics that typify a disposition. As long as one has justice, he consistently desires
to be just, even when he is asleep or not thinking about it.
Justice is not confined to volitions which are just; it is a
tendency in one's will that prompts one to perform just
volitions.[70]

But if the affection for justice is indeed a disposition, it is difficult to see how one can lose it instantan-
eously. An answer to this depends on claims that Anselm
makes in elaborating the second major difference he sees between the two affections. We will therefore turn to an examination of this second difference and then return to this
problem afterward.

Anselm describes the second difference in the following terms.

> These affections also differ in that the
> will which is the affection for willing
> what is beneficial is not itself the ob-
> ject that it wills [non est hoc quod ipsa
> vult], whereas the will which is the af-
> fection for willing rectitude is rectitude.[71]

It is not easy to understand what it means to say that an
affection is not its own object or that an affection for
something is that very thing. However, Anselm does shed
further light upon this puzzling claim. Immediately after
the sentence quoted above, he adds, "For certainly no one
wills rectitude unless he possesses rectitude; and no one
can will rectitude except by means of rectitude."[72] The
point of this statement lies in the implied comparison with
the affection for happiness. One can will rectitude only
if one already possesses rectitude, but one can and does
will happiness at any time, whether one actually possesses
happiness or not. As Anselm puts it in another passage,
"The will for justice is itself justice; but the will for
happiness is not itself happiness."[73] The claim that one

one can desire happiness even when one does not have it
seems true enough. But there is still obscurity in the notion that the disposition for justice is justice itself.

We can begin to make sense of this claim, I believe, by em-
ploying a distinction that is sometimes made between two ways
in which an action may be directed towards a purpose or may
bring about a result that it aims at. A purpose or goal
might be quite distinct from the actions which aim at it.
Such is the case when students attend classes, take notes,
write papers, read books, work in laboratories, etc., with
the aim of getting a college degree or a well-paying job.
On the other hand, a purpose or goal may be a pattern or
kind of activity which is exemplified in the actions and
which cannot exist apart from them. Such is the case when
an individual reads newspapers, attends political rallies,
contributes time and money to qualified candidates for pub-
lic office, votes regularly, etc., in order to be a good
citizen. Acquiring a college degree or getting a well-paying job is different from reading books, taking notes and
other activities which are the means thereto. Being a good
citizen, however, just is voting regularly, keeping socially
and politically informed, etc.

If my understanding of Anselm is correct, part of what
he means by saying that the affection for justice is justice
itself is that the kind of goal aimed at in the actions
brought about by this affection is the kind that is exemplified in the actions themselves. In contrast, the affection
for happiness is an affection which is directed toward an
end-condition that is separate from the actions directed toward it.

This, however, is not all he means by saying that the
affection for justice is justice itself, for he holds that
one must possess justice before he can perform just acts.
If justice were merely the performing of deeds which exemplify a pattern or conform to a standard, one could never act

justly because it would be impossible to possess justice before one acted justly. The performance of just deeds presupposes a desire to act justly. On the other hand, it is
the nature of a desire to lead to the desired action unless
there are countervailing factors. So the desire for justice
will lead one to act justly unless something interferes.
Justice, then, is both the desire to act justly, i.e., the
affection for justice, and the performance of just volitions,
volitions which conform to the standard of justice. Thus,
when Anselm states that the affection for justice is its own
object, he is drawing on the distinction between these two
aspects of justice, the desire and the volitions, and he is
saying that a person cannot have one without the other. A
person cannot perform just volitions without possessing an
affection for justice, and he cannot have an affection for
justice which does not lead to just volitions. And since,
as we saw above, the end toward which just volitions are
directed is one that is exemplified in those volitions themselves, the affection for justice is justice—it is its own
object.

     In summary, the points I believe Anselm is making
when he holds that the affection for justice is justice and
is its own object are (1) the goal toward which the affection is directed is the kind of goal which is immanent in
the actions that aim at it, (2) the actions which aim at
and exemplify the goal of justice presuppose a desire for
them, and (3) this desire must be manifested in such actions.

     We may now return to the problem that we left hanging
a short while back, the problem of how a disposition for
justice may be lost suddenly and completely the moment a
person sins. The answer depends upon understanding both
that justice must be the supreme principle in a person's
life, else it is not justice, and that the affection for
justice is its own object in the sense just explained. If
justice is supreme, then a person must always be disposed

to do just deeds, for the only thing that can prevent a desire from manifesting itself in the appropriate deeds is
another desire contravening it. But as soon as another desire contravenes the affection for justice, a person is no
longer just, for he has failed to will the just deed over
one that serves the competing desire. But since justice and
the affection for justice are identical and the desire and
the deeds are inseparable aspects of the same thing, this
means that one no longer has the affection for justice either. And so, not only is justice lost when a person sins,
but so is the affection for justice.

     B. Their Relation. We have seen already that there
are serious problems in conceiving how, given Anselm's moral
and metaphysical doctrines, happiness and justice can really
be distinct. But there is no doubt that he actually thinks
that in some sense or other they are distinct. This, then,
raises the question as to what relation they have to each
other as ends or motives of human action.

     Both happiness and justice, according to Anselm, are
ends of human action. That is, every action is motivated
by either a desire to achieve justice or a desire to obtain
happiness or perhaps by both. In this section I wish to explore the two following questions: Is it possible for a single act of will to be done both for the sake of happiness
and for the sake of justice? And if so, how are the two
motives properly ordered or related?

     Not a great deal has been written on this problem in
the interpretation of Anselm, but a few writers have expressed their views on it in passing. The diversity of
opinion among these writers is an indication of the complex-
ity and trickiness of the problem. Filliatre states that in
accord with all of Christian ethics, especially that of
Saint Augustine, the will's ultimate end for Anselm is happiness.[74] On the other hand, John McIntyre notes the non-

utilitarian character of happiness for Anselm and concludes
that happiness is nothing more than simply justice.   "In
fact, this blessedness is *itself* right discerning, loving
and following the *summum bonum*."[75]   Jean Rohmer interprets
Anselm at this point dualistically, suggesting justice and
happiness are different kinds of perfection and drawing a
parallel between Anselm's doctrine of justice and Kant's
doctrine of the good will.[76]   Vernon Bourke seems to agree
basically with Rohmer. He writes that the *affectio ad
commoditatem* is a "willful inclination toward personal happiness and satisfaction in man's life on earth," while the
affection for justice is "an inclination to desire something
simply because it is right and just."[77]   E. R. Fairweather
takes issue with Rohmer and argues, "Anselm does not mean
to relate the two affections in a merely external way....
The rational creature's capacity for *justitia* means that it
can freely choose the due ordering of its desire for beati-
tude to the transcendent and perfect good."[78]

      One reason for this diversity of opinion is that An-
selm says things which seem to point in opposite directions.
The definition of justice as the rectitude of the will preserved *for its own sake* seems to indicate that there can be
no other motive for our just acts than simply justice itself. Yet he also asserts that happiness is part of the
ultimate purpose of man, and writes that the human will has
an affection for happiness separate from the affection for
justice. As we have seen, his teaching that this affection,
unlike the affection for justice, is inseparable from the
will indicates that we can never avoid willing happiness. He
even seems to suggest that the hope of future happiness and
the fear of future torment are legitimate motives for doing
what is just. This can be seen in his case study of a man
who finds himself in a situation where he must either tell a
lie or surrender his life. He comments that,

            If he had a vivid sense of the eternal

glory which he would immediately attain
upon choosing the truth, and if he had
the same vivid sense of the torments of
hell to which he would be delivered without any delay after lying, then, without
any doubt, we would see that he had sufficient strength to hold to the truth.[79]

The thrust of this seems to be contradicted, however,
in a passage in DCD, in which Anselm is dealing with possible motives Satan might have had for keeping the justice in
which he was created, the possible motives being the love
of justice for its own sake and the fear of punishment. He
says, "If [Satan] had refrained from sinning because of this
fear, he would not have been just."[80] Is there any way to
resolve the seeming discrepancy in these various teachings?

Let us begin our effort to answer this question by
looking at what Anselm says in those passages where he
specifically deals with the ordering of the two affections
to each other. There are two such passages, one in DCD,
XIV, the other in DC, III, xiii. Neither is more than a
few sentences long, so I shall quote them in full.

It was necessary for God to make both wills
[affections] agree in him [Satan], so that
he could both will to be happy and will
this justly. To the degree that justice
was added, it would so temper the will for
happiness that its excesses could be cur-
tailed and yet its ability to transgress
not be destroyed. Because Satan willed
happiness, he could exceed the standard;
and yet because he willed justly, he would
not want to exceed it. So, having a just
will for happiness, Satan could and should
be happy.[81]

God has so ordained the two wills, or affections, that the instrument of the will
should use the affection for justice to
order and govern one's choices under the
guidance of the spirit, which is also
called mind, or reason; and that it should
use the other affection to will obedience
without any disadvantage [sine omni incom-
moditate].... Indeed, God gave happiness to

man (not to mention the angels) for his
benefit [ad commodum eius], but he gave
man justice for his own honor.[82]

From these two passages, at least this should be clear: the
motives for justice and happiness are not mutually exclusive. It is possible in the same act both to will happiness
and to will justly. Thus the phrase "for its own sake" in
the definition of justice should not be interpreted so as to
exclude the possibility of willing what is right with one's
own well-being or happiness also in mind.

But precisely how can or how should the desires for
happiness and justice be adjusted in one's willing? One
clue is the doctrine that the affection for happiness is inseparable from the human will. From this we can infer that
happiness is included in justice, since justice, as we have
noted, is perfectly proportioned to human nature. Justice,
however, sets certain controls on how far one can will happiness, i.e., on the types of things which one may legitimate-
ly seek for the sake of happiness (cf. the first passage
quoted above).

Still, how can a person that wills happiness, even
when doing so within proper moral limits, be willing justice
simply for the sake of justice? A possible answer is that
one is seeking justice for the sake of justice when he sub-
ordinates his desire for happiness to the principle of justice. Acting justly does not preclude seeking happiness.
Nonetheless there is a definite order which must be maintained. Justice is the fundamental value and must take
precedence over happiness. Accordingly, when one's desire
for happiness conflicts with the standards of justice, the
desire for happiness must defer to the requirements of justice. When a person's desire for happiness is subordinated
to the standards of justice, he is seeking justice for the
sake of justice. If the only reason a person places restrictions on his pursuit of happiness is that it is right

or just to do so, then he is being just for the sake of justice.

It may still be wondered, however, just how pure a person's motive for justice is when he seeks to obtain happiness even in this restricted way. The problem is accentuated by the fact that Anselm maintains that perfect justice brings perfect happiness. Even if one curbs his pursuit of happiness to keep it within the bounds of justice, it would still seem that what the person is after is happiness. After all, pursuing happiness within the bounds of justice is still pursuing happiness. Indeed, to pursue happiness in this way may be only a more shrewd and calculating way of going about it, undertaken in the recognition that it is worthwhile to sacrifice some desired benefits now so as to achieve a higher happiness later. When one is aware of such a great reward for justice, it becomes extremely difficult to put it out of mind and curb a present desire for happiness *solely* because it is right and just to do so.

Anselm himself seems to agree. In a passage in which he discusses the original moral situation of the angels, he indicates that the angels did not have knowledge either of the reward that was to be given if they acted justly or of the punishment that was to be inflicted if they sinned, because if they had had this knowledge they would not have been able to act in a properly just way.[83] It looks, therefore, as though he is endorsing the view that such knowledge is withheld from the angels because, if they had had it, their motive for gaining happiness and avoiding unhappiness would have been so strong that they could not have the motive of doing what is right solely for the sake of justice.

The appearance, however, is deceiving, for a careful reading will show that in this passage Anselm is making a different point. He is not dealing with the issue of the compatibility or incompatibility of motives at all. He is not saying that, given the kind of knowledge in question,

the angels' motive for happiness would be so strong as to
overwhelm any motive they might have for justice. Instead
he is saying that such knowledge would determine the will
to act justly and thus deprive it of freedom and self-determination. Since acting freely is a necessary condition of
acting justly, anything that destroys freedom also makes
justice impossible. What Anselm is arguing against, then,
is not something that would make it impossible to will with
the right motive; he is arguing against determinism, something that would make it impossible to act freely.

If this passage about the angels does not help us,
perhaps something Anselm says about man will. He tells us
that man's situation, as far as knowledge of the consequences
of just and unjust actions is concerned, is quite different
from that of the angels. As a result of what happened to
the angels (something disclosed in revelation), human beings
can be fully aware of the kind of reward and punishment
which await the just and the unjust. This information, however, does not ruin self-determination for men. Anselm is
quite specific about this.[84] Since this knowledge is gained
through revelation and grounded on faith and hope, the degree of subjective certainty that any man has concerning it
may vary quite widely, and in no case is the knowledge so
strong and unshakeable that it prevents one from willing
something that is not right. One factor that tends to di-
minish one's assurance about such knowledge is temptation;
accordingly, steadfastness in the faith and hope with which
such knowledge is held is just and meritorious.[85] This last
point is an important one. For it indicates that part of
what we ought to believe, and therefore what it is just to
believe, is that we shall be rewarded in the next life if
we are just in this one.

Does not this, however, open up the possibility of
willing what is just precisely in order to receive the happiness that one believes will follow as its reward in the

next life? It certainly does. The crucial question, however, for evaluating the coherence of Anselm's doctrine is
whether this is compatible with willing what is just for
its own sake.

Anselm apparently thinks so, and supplies hints of how
one can make sense of this view. His thinking is best interpreted, I believe, along the following lines. Willing
eternal happiness as an end means willing according to a
scale of values which judges the various kinds of happiness
according to their moral correctness. This scale of values
is such that if one wills for the sake of the happiness
which is to be given as the reward of justice he will curb
his desire for other, wrong or unjust forms of happiness.
When Anselm defines justice as the rectitude of the will
kept for its own sake, he does not mean to rule out as unjust the individual who does what is just with the motive of
achieving the happiness that God has promised as a reward
for justice. What he is ruling out is the case where a person does what is objectively just (i.e., what externally conforms to the standard of justice) but does it in order to
achieve some benefit which is not in keeping with justice.
He gives an example of this in *DV*, XIII. "Consider the case
of someone who feeds a poor, hungry man for the sake of his
own hunger for glory.... His rectitude must not be praised;
and so it is not to be equated with the justice we are seeking." The desire of a human being for his own glory is an
unworthy one. Such glory is an inferior benefit and one,
therefore, which is unjust.

Would the man's charity have been fully just if his
motive had been to gain eternal happiness instead of personal glory? Anselm does not directly address this question,
but we can make a reasonable guess at what he would say.
We have already noted his view that a man cannot help willing happiness in whatever he does. Willing happiness, then,
cannot in itself be wrong. But there are certain kinds of

happiness which it is wrong to seek. If someone were to ask
a man why he wills happiness, it would be enough to say that
he cannot help willing it. But if someone were to ask why
he wills a particular kind of happiness, then he can say (if
he knows or thinks it to be the case) that he wills it because it is the right kind of happiness to will. Consider
again the man who feeds the hungry, but let us suppose now
that he does it not for glory but to accumulate merit that
will earn for him eternal happiness. In this case he has
brought his affection for happiness into conformity with the
principles of justice. He is willing the particular happiness he wills because it is the right one for him to will.
In doing so he is both acting justly and doing so for the
sake of justice.

We are now in a position to summarize our conclusions.
In Anselm's thinking, happiness and justice are perfectly
balanced in man's ultimate end and in his final reward.[86]
Before the final end is reached, however, human beings are
in a situation where it is possible for them to will certain
kinds of beneficial things, or pleasures if you will, which
are outside the bounds of justice. Hence, a person must
bring his affection for happiness into line with the demands
of justice. This does not require the complete renunciation
or suppression of the desire for and the pursuit of happiness; that is a psychological impossibility. It requires
seeking only those benefits or pleasures which it is right
to seek. Since ultimate happiness is included in man's
final end established by God, it is quite legitimate for a
person to do his duty with the achievement of this eternal
happiness as an ultimate goal and motive. But in all of
this, justice is the supreme principle while happiness is
subordinate. Hence Anselm is fully consistent in thinking
that one can act so as to do one's duty for the sake of duty
while at the same time acting for one's own highest happiness.

Anselm's doctrine here is significantly different from
some of the better known ethical theories of the Middle Ages.
To highlight the distinctiveness of his contribution, it
will be useful to briefly compare his theory with some of
these others.

Our examination has shown that Anselm allows great
play to the desire for happiness, but unlike Augustine and
Thomas Aquinas and other leading medieval thinkers, he does
not make it the basis of his morality or of his theory of
obligation.[87] Both Augustine and Thomas are eudaemonistic
in their moral theory, for in their doctrines moral duty is
made to serve man's natural desire for happiness. For them,
duty is the obligation to perform those acts or kinds of
acts which are best suited to achieving the highest happiness for oneself. Anselm agrees with these thinkers that
man was made to enjoy complete happiness. He also agrees
that man cannot but will happiness. But he does not think
of this psychological fact as having fundamental importance
for morality. In the final analysis, this fact is irrelevant to the establishment of the basic moral principles.
For, in his view, there is something of more fundamental
importance for morality than that man seeks his own happiness, and that is that God created man for his (God's)
glory. Human duty, therefore, is determined ultimately by
what brings honor to God rather than by what brings happiness to man. Accordingly, the affection for justice was
given to enable men to do that which brings honor to God.
The affection for happiness was given so that (among other
reasons) men could be happy as well as just in performing
their duty and bringing honor to God. Happiness is thus
also included in God's ultimate purpose for man, but not as
that which provides the basis for duty. The affection for
happiness is given so that human beings can be happy in doing their duty but not so that they should seek happiness
as their duty. As Anselm puts it, "God gave happiness to

man...for his [man's] benefit, but he gave man justice for his [God's] own honor."[88]

Grounded in justice rather than happiness, Anselm's moral theory is God-centered rather than man-centered. Duty consists most fundamentally in doing what *God* has established that human beings should do, not what will bring *man* happiness, satisfaction or peace. The moral life requires a man to focus his attention primarily on God, not himself. Duty is determined by an objective *telos* placed on man by God rather than by an internal *eros* found within man.

A further significant way in which Anselm's theory differs from that of Thomas Aquinas and others is that in Anselm's view even the ultimate end of a man's actions is something which a man is free to adopt for himself. In Thomas' doctrine, the end of a man's actions, happiness, is determined by nature. Both Anselm and Thomas agree that man is necessitated to will happiness. But in Anselm's doctrine, though the pursuit of happiness is something we cannot avoid, there is the need and the opportunity for determining for oneself whether one will seek happiness in the right way or the wrong way. That is to say, each one must determine for himself the kind of happiness that will be his ultimate goal. In contrast, in a theory like Thomas's, which founds morality upon the fact that man necessarily seeks happiness and which makes this pursuit man's primary obligation, the only possibility of moral self-determination occurs in selecting the means for achieving happiness. The scope and importance of self-determination is significantly reduced in comparison with a theory like Anselm's, in which both duty and self-determination pertain to both the ends and the means of one's actions.

CHAPTER FOUR

VOLITIONS

In earlier chapters investigating the will and
its affections, we had occasion to see some of the important characteristics of volitions or, as Anselm dubs them,
uses of the will. We have seen, for example, that the ability to perform volitions, i.e., to make choices and to set
ourselves to do things, depends on the existence of a basic
power of willing, which must be equipped with at least one
affection. We have also seen that for a man to be able to
perform the most important kind of volition, namely, an act
of moral choice, his will must have two affections. Further, we have seen that a volition occurs only when an individual is thinking of what he is doing. Volitions, in other
words, are conscious acts. And finally, we have seen that
the making of a moral choice and the performance of a just
volition must be something that a being performs *a se,*
through self-determination. In created beings, this means
that such a volition is not determined—it has no efficient
cause sufficient to bring it about.

There is a further point at which it will be worth
our while to look. Anselm teaches that there are four main
ways in which one may be said to will something. He calls
these modes of *velle* the efficient, approving, conceding,
and permitting senses of the term. He explains these senses
clearly. "'Wills' is sometimes used in the sense that he

who is willing to do something performs or achieves the object of his willing, if he can do so, and if he cannot,
would still do it if he could (e.g., the sick man wills to
get well)."[1] Willing in this way is willing in the efficient sense. Willing in the approving sense occurs when "he
who is willing wills something within his capacity, yet
does not perform it. Thus a beggar who lacks clothes cannot accuse me of willingly allowing him to lack clothes,
since although I do nothing about his plight, I still approve the action of someone who clothes him."[2]

     An example of willing in the conceding sense occurs
"when a creditor is willing to excuse a debt of corn, and
to accept barley in its place. He would prefer the corn
but allows the return of the barley on account of the pov-
erty of the debtor."[3]

     Finally, a person is said to will in the permitting
sense when it is "in his power to prevent that which he is
said to will. Thus, should a ruler abstain from taking
measures against thieves and robbers in his kingdom, he
could be said to be willing that they should do evil because
he is willing to permit it, notwithstanding the displeasure
which it causes him."[4]

     These senses of "velle" are not mutually exclusive.
Willing efficiently encompasses all three of the other ways
of willing also. Willing in the approving sense includes
willing in the conceding and permitting senses. One who
wills concedingly also wills permittingly. Permissive willing is the only kind of willing which does not include any
of the other kinds of willing within itself.[5]

     Anselm correlates these senses of "velle" with some of the
senses of "facere" which he also distinguishes. It will be
useful, therefore, at this point, briefly to present some
of his tabulation of the senses of "facere" and the ration-
ale behind it. This is relevant not only to an understanding of volitions but also to questions we will be

considering later concerning the relation of grace and freedom.

   In a set of fragments that Anselm left dealing with
matters of logic and language, he provides a full-scale tabulation of the senses of "*facere*."[6] This systematic treatment of the various ways in which one may be said to do
something is part of a general approach that Anselm takes
to language. At many places throughout his writings he offers analyses of linguistic expressions that people commonly
use. He does so because he is convinced that "many things
are said according to grammatical form which are not said
according to actual fact."[7] When a statement employs a
grammatical form that does not conform to the structure of
the reality it is used to describe, Anselm speaks of it as
using language improperly (*improrie*). Language is used
properly only when a statement has a grammatical form which
accurately reflects the objective state of affairs it pur-
ports to describe. The distinction between proper and improper usage is also found in the distinction which Anselm
draws between "*significatio per se*" and "*significatio per
aliud,*" which can be translated respectively "direct signification" and "indirect signification."[8] Anselm makes it
clear that to gain any kind of scientific understanding of
things, it is necessary to penetrate behind the superficial-
ities of ordinary language. When the student in *DCD* objects
to one of the teachings of the master by saying "our common
way of speaking does not agree with this [*usus loquendi non
consentit*]," the unmistakable answer is: "That's not surprising. For we say many things improperly in our ordinary
way of speaking. But when we wish to come to the heart of
a matter, it is necessary to analyze, as far as the subject
matter allows, the improper usage which is troubling us."[9]
At another point in the same dialogue Anselm asserts, "But
we shouldn't so much cling to inappropriate words which
conceal the truth, as we should seek to discover the genuine

truth which is hidden under the many types of expression."[10]
As Anselm sees it, the major problem with ordinary language
is that a single sentence while retaining the same grammatical form may be used to refer to a variety of different objective situations. The remedy for this is the construction
of a somewhat artificial language which will have grammatical forms that accurately reflect the objective states of
affairs.

Anselm examines *"facere"* as a way of analyzing the
logic of verbs, for *"facere"* is a word that can stand for
any verb whatsoever. He sets forth the various ways in
which the term may be used properly, and then for each of
these he catalogues the variety of improper uses to which
it may be put in ordinary language. Once the tabulation of
usages has been made, it can serve as a guide in translating
the improper statements of ordinary language into their
logically correct (i.e., their proper) forms.

Anselm gives four basic sentence forms in which *"facere"*
appears in ordinary language, two of which are affirmative
and two negative. For each of the four basic forms, he
teaches that there are six different "modes" (or logical
forms) which may all be expressed by the basic form. The
affirmative forms are *"facere esse"* and *"facere non esse"*;
the negative forms are *"non facere esse"* and *"non facere
non esse."* Using "X does so that p" and "X does so that
not-q" as the translation of *"facere esse"* and *"facere non
esse"* respectively,[11] the following is a tabulation of
"facere" for each of the affirmative forms.[12]

```
a:  X does so that p
b:  X does not so that not-p
c:  X does other than doing so that p
d:  X does not so that other-than-p
e:  X does so that not-other-than-p
f:  X does not so that not-other-than-p

a': X does so that not-q
b': X does not so that q
```

```
c':   X does other than doing so that not-q
d':   X does not so that other-than-q
e':   X does so that not-other-than-q
f':   X does not so that not-other-than-q
```

These tabulations are made clearer by the examples which
Anselm provides for illustration. He shows how each of
these varieties of "doing" may be understood when the doing
in question is the act of killing somebody. The six modes
then, are as follows:[13]

```
a":   X kills A directly by stabbing him.
b":   X fails to do what he can to make it so that A
      is not dead. The only example that Anselm can
      think of here is the failure of someone who has
      the power, to raise A to life from the dead.
c":   X orders that A be killed, or provides B with a
      sword which he uses to kill A, or brings accu-
      sation against A.
d":   X fails to provide A with weapons for self-
      defense, or fails to restrain the killer.
e":   X takes away A's weapons, causing him to be
      unarmed and unable to defend himself.
f":   X does not take away the weapons of the killer,
      i.e., he does not so that the killer is not armed.
```

If, following a suggestion made by Henry, "p" in the original tabulation is replaced by "A is dead" and "q" by "A is
alive," then this single set of examples will serve to illustrate both tables.[14]

A basic distinction running through each of these
tabulations is that between, on the one hand, doing something which either directly or indirectly brings about the
state of affairs in question (as in a,c,e, a',c',e', a",c",
e") and, on the other hand, failing to do either what will
directly bring about the non-occurrence of the state of affairs or what could indirectly contribute to its non-occurrence (as in b,d,f, b',d',f', b",d", and f"). A further distinction can be found which also divides the varieties of
"doing" in each table into two classes, but classes which
are different from those just delineated. It is the distinction between (1) doing something which directly brings
about the state of affairs in question, either through

some positive action which immediately effects its occurrence or through failure to do something which would immediately effect its non-occurrence (as in a,b,a',b',a", and
b") and (2) doing something which only indirectly brings
about the state of affairs in question, either by doing
something else which then brings about its occurrence, or
by failure to do something else which might have effected
its non-occurrence (as in c,d,e,f, c',d',e',f', c",d",e", and
f"). The first distinction is the same as that between acts
of commission and acts of omission, whereas the second is
the same as that between proximate and remote causes. It
will be noticed that it is only in the cases of a and a'
(and a") that something is done both through an act of commission and as a proximate (and sufficient) cause. And it
is only when a person does something in this way that he
can be said to have done something *per se*.[15] It is only in
this case, therefore, that one is speaking with strictly
correct signification when he says that "X does so that p"
or "X does so that not-q". In every one of the other five
modes, to say "X does so that p" or "X does so that not-q"
is to speak improperly, for to use "X does so that p" (or
"X brings about p" or "X causes p") to report what occurs
in any of these five cases is to use a description whose
strict meaning is that X is the proximate and active sufficient cause of p when really it is something else. In some
of these cases X's action or failure to act may even be a
necessary condition of the occurrence of p, but if it is not
the proximate and sufficient cause it cannot properly be
said to bring about p. To be sure, in ordinary language we
often say (so Anselm believes) "X causes p" to describe
situations recorded in the five other modes, in which some
other agent is the proximate and active sufficient cause.
But this merely underlines the split between the essential
meaning and the ordinary use of some of our language. To
describe properly, i.e., with direct signification, a person's

action in any given event, what he does must be matched up
with the mode which describes it exactly. Thus, in giving
an exegesis of Romans 9:18—"*Quem vult [deus], indurat*"—
Anselm interprets it in the fourth mode. "God is said to
harden a man's heart when he does nothing to soften it."[16]

The four senses of "*velle*" are correlated with the
modes of "*facere*" as follows. Efficient willing is an instance of the strictly proper sense of "*facere,*" namely "X
does so that p."[17] Efficient willing, then, is willing in
the strictest and proper sense. The other senses of willing
are found in ordinary usage, but they are not strictly correct. The approving sense is correlated with the second
sense of "*facere,*" "X does so that not-p" and with the
fourth, "X does not so that other-than-p." The permitting
sense of willing also corresponds with these two modes.

Anselm illustrates these uses of "*velle*" by pointing
to various ways in which God is said to will, and it is with
respect to the will of God that these distinctions are most
important for him. He tells us, "When it is said of God,
'He hath done whatsoever he hath willed', and 'Therefore, he
hath mercy on whom he will', here 'to will' is used in the
efficient sense."[17] The acts of divine will that these
Scripture verses refer to, then, are instances of willing
in the strictly proper sense, that in which God directly
brings about what he wills. Of course, since God is omni-
potent, the qualification that is made in the definition of
the efficient sense of willing, namely, that it includes
willing something in such a way that if one cannot bring
about what he wills he would bring it about if he could,
does not apply to God. Thus, anything that God wills in the
efficient sense he actually brings about and does so directly.

Anselm goes on, "When, however, we read, 'And whom he
wills, he hardenth,' here the permitting sense of 'to will'
is in question...for God is said to will that a man's heart

be hard because he does not will efficiently that it not be
hard."[18] In other words, X is being said to will so that p
because he does not will so that not-p. Or, this passage
could be given an alternative interpretation. "If we say
that God wills to harden because he does not will to soften,
the sense will be the same and we will be referring to the
permitting sense of 'to will.'"[19] Here the passage is being
interpreted in line with the fourth mode of "*facere*": X is
said to do so that p when X does not do so that other-than-p

    Anselm also illustrates the approving sense of "*velle*"
in terms of God's will. "When we hear that 'God wills that
all men should be saved,' here the approving will is being
spoken of." Like the previous text, which spoke of God's
willing someone's heart to be hardened, this can be interpreted in either the second or the fourth mode of "*facere*."
That is to say, it may be understood to mean either "that
God does not efficiently will to make every man not to be
saved," or "that he does not efficiently will to damn all
men."[20]

    Anselm does not explicitly correlate the conceding
will with any of the modes of "*facere*." But Imelda Choquette
observes, "This conceding will differs from the permitting
will in that the latter does not approve or concede what it
is said to will, for it is concerned with evil, whereas the
conceding will is concerned with the lesser of two goods."[21]
Anselm does, however, furnish us with an example of this
kind of willing drawn from what God wills. "God wills according to the conceding will when he he wills that a man,
who has not set a better course for himself, should get
married, i.e., he concedes that he should get married."[22]

    This brings us to the end of our investigation of An-
selm's concept of the nature of the will. At the outset of
the investigation in chapter two we noted that Anselm considered that the three senses of "*voluntas*" which he distinguishes are used "equivocally." At that time it was said

that this must not be taken to mean that there is nothing
in common between the three senses, for they are all related to the process of willing. Now we may be more specific about this. The three senses in which "will" is used
all indicate conditions which are necessary, not just for
actually willing, but more importantly, for the achievement
of the ultimate end and purpose which God gave to man when
he created him. The basic requirement is to will what is
just in our actual volitions, but in order to do this we
must have the capacity to will and this capacity must be
marked by an affection for justice and an affection for
happiness.

CHAPTER FIVE

FREEDOM

I. VOLUNTAS AND ARBITRIUM

Before we begin our examination of Anselm's concept of
freedom, we need to consider a preliminary question, that
of the relation between *arbitrium* and *voluntas* in his thinking. When Anselm poses the major questions concerning freedom that he wishes to investigate, he connects freedom with
arbitrium and refers to it as *"libertas arbitrii."*[1] Ordinarily, freedom is thought to be a property of the will,
and when Anselm is exploring the nature of the will, the
term he uses for it is *"voluntas."* The relation, then, of
volantas and *arbitrium* is closely tied to the relation of
freedom and the will.

It is clear that Anselm saw a close relation between
arbitrium and *voluntas*.   Though he uses *"libertas arbitrii"*
in posing the major questions of freedom, in other contexts
liber and *libertas* are spoken of in relation to *voluntas* as
well as *arbitrium*.[2] In some places, *"liberum arbitrium"*
and *"libera voluntas"* are used interchangeably.[3] It might
seem, then, that these terms are synonyms and that Anselm
varies his usage merely for stylistic reasons. But he also
speaks of the free choice *of* the will (*libertas arbitrii
voluntatis*),[4] he speaks of the will as enjoying free
choice,[5] and he tells us that God created the will with

free choice.[6] These statements seem to indicate that free
choice belongs to or is part of the will.

At this point the original meaning of *"arbitrium"* may
be of help to us. Originally, *arbitrium* meant the judgment
or decision of an arbitrator or judge, and thus came generally to mean judgment, opinion, or decision.[7] Anselm himself expressly acknowledges this usage, and seems to endorse
it.[8] Accordingly, an *arbitrium* of the will is a determination or choice of what to do in a given circumstance. It
would, in short, be a volition. One of the features of a
volition noted earlier is that it involves conscious thought
or deliberation. *"Arbitrium,"* indicating the judgment or
choice or determination of the will, draws attention to this
rational element in volition.[9] Thus, the relation between
voluntas and *arbitrium* which Anselm has in mind when he
speaks of *arbitrium* as belonging to *voluntas* is the same as
the relation between the will-as-instrument and the will-as-
use. This is shown further by the fact that Anselm can
speak of the *voluntas* as operating through free choice (*per
liberum arbitrium*).[10]

This, however, is not all that he uses *"arbitrium"* to
mean, for he also thinks of it as a kind of power. This is
seen most clearly in his definition of free choice (*liberum
arbitrium*) as the power to keep rectitude for its own sake.[11]
It is also indicated in other passages. In one place he
states that Scripture repeatedly exhorts *liberum arbitrium*
to good works and reproaches it when it fails to heed those
exhortations.[12] In another he refers to Scripture as urging free choice to will and to work uprightly.[13] He also
thinks *liberum arbitrium* can be assailed by temptation.[14]
These are characteristics which can only belong to some kind
of underlying and enduring entity. They are not the sort we
would normally associate with episodic volitions. It seems
clear, therefore, that Anselm thinks of *arbitrium* not only
as volition, but also as the basic power to perform volitions

Thus, *"arbitrium"* has some of the same range of meaning found in the word *"voluntas."* It can be used to refer either to the will-as-instrument or to the will-as-use. It does not, however, contain the whole range of meaning found in *"voluntas,"* for nowhere does Anselm use the term to suggest the affections. Though there is this partial similarity in his use of these two terms, he does not devote the serious attention to analyzing *"arbitrium"* that he does to *"voluntas."* *"Arbitrium"* is a term which is used more informally. One could even say that the term itself is not important to Anselm. The only reason there is any question about it at all is that it is the term which is linked with freedom when he states the basic questions of freedom. What is important in these questions is not *arbitrium,* but rather freedom.

II. THE SEARCH FOR DEFINITION

Anselm's earliest investigation of freedom is found in the dialogue *De Libertate Arbitrii.* This is the middle dialogue of three that he requested be bound together in a particular order. The first is *De Veritate* and the third is *De Casu Diaboli.* Since they were written in the order in which he requested they be bound, he had already completed his dialogue on truth by the time he came to his investigation of freedom. In the dialogue on truth he secured the basic principles of his ontology, which is dominated by the concepts of truth and justice. His analysis of freedom is conducted within the context of this ontology and presupposes it. It is also conducted in accordance with the same basic method of procedure, which was outlined in chapter one, that he uses in his inquiries into truth and justice.

A major objective of his investigation of truth and justice on the one hand and of freedom on the other is to find adequate definitions of these terms. In the case

of freedom, we should note carefully that Anselm is not primarily concerned to analyze or elucidate *human* freedom. He
seeks a general definition of freedom that will apply to all
beings who are free. In searching for a definition, then,
he considers human freedom insofar as establishing and defending a general definition either requires this or results
in it.

As pointed out in chapter one, once it is seen how Anselm approaches the investigation of freedom and goes about
developing a definition, it becomes evident how misconceived
is the complaint that has been made against him that he
fails to offer proof of his doctrines. A number of writers
have reproached him for offering no proof that man has free
will.[15] The charge, of course, is true: he never does offer proof that man is free. But offered as a criticism of
Anselm's work, it is wrong-headed, for Anselm's type of investigation is such that there is neither place nor need
for proof. The type of procedure which makes proof necessary is one which comes to the data with a definition or explanation already in hand. In such a situation there may
be no apparent connection between the definition and the
data. Consequently, some kind of proof is required to show
that they correspond. Anselm's method avoids that problem.
He simply accepts it that man has freedom, because "freedom" (with its cognates and synonyms) is used to refer
inter alia to certain features of our common experience.
It is the nature of these features which Anselm seeks to
get at in his definition. Freedom, then, is a part of the
data. So it does not require proof; it calls instead for
elucidation. Anselm's inquiries and his definition are attempts at providing such elucidation.

Once the definition of freedom is secured to Anselm's
satisfaction, he is then faced with the problem of how human freedom is to be reconciled with God's sovereignty as
reflected in his foreknowledge, predestination, and grace.

He seeks to resolve these problems through a close and careful analysis of the concepts of foreknowledge, predestination, and grace; of the language that is used to describe
the way God acts in foreknowledge, predestination and grace;
and of the way the will operates in making free choices.
What he does, in short, in addressing these problems is to
give analyses of the logical relations that hold among various concepts and among various claims that are made employ-
ing these concepts.

In the rest of this chapter we will concern ourselves
with what Anselm says in seeking to establish and defend his
definition of freedom. In the next chapter we will explore
his treatment of one of the problems just mentioned, the
problem of grace and freedom. This problem is selected from
among the three because a knowledge of Anselm's view of the
relation of grace and freedom is crucial for understanding
the precise meaning of his definition of freedom and of certain claims he makes about freedom in *DLA*. His treatment of
the other two problems, those concerning the relations of
human freedom with the foreknowledge and the predestination
of God, includes some shrewd logical and conceptual points
about foreknowledge and predestination and other notions,
but it does not add anything to an understanding of the nature of freedom itself. While this chapter deals with Anselm's reasoning in *DLA* in establishing his definition of
freedom and in dealing with some of the major questions it
suggests, we will not be in a position to gain a full understanding of his conception of freedom until we have completed our study in the next chapter of his teaching concerning the relation of freedom and grace.

III.   FREEDOM DEFINED

DLA addresses itself to two major questions: (1) What
is free choice (*liberum arbitrium*)? and (2) do men always

possess free choice? Consideration of the first question
launches Anselm on his search for an adequate definition of
freedom.

In beginning this search he considers the definition
most commonly accepted in his day, namely, that freedom is
the ability both to sin and not to sin [*posse peccare et non
peccare*]. This is a definition found in the earlier Augustine.[16] Anselm immediately rejects it since this kind of
ability is not possessed by either God or the angels, and
"to say that they have no free choice is blasphemous."[17]
Christian faith, then, rules out this definition. But while
the definition is rejected, an understanding of the reason
why it is unacceptable helps to show what is needed of a
correct definition. Christian doctrine teaches that all rational beings possess freedom. The definition of freedom,
then, should be one that applies not only to man but also
to God and the angels. Anselm is thus looking for a single
defining formula that can be applied univocally to all beings—God, men, and angels—to whom freedom is ascribed.

It should be emphasized that in criticizing the commonly accepted definition, Anselm is not denying that a person who has the ability to sin or not to sin is on that account free. In fact, he believes that such a person *is*
on that account free. He is merely saying that freedom as
such cannot be wholly identical with the ability-either-to-
sin-or-not-to-sin and hence cannot be defined by this ability.[18]

Anselm finds a second reason for rejecting the commonly accepted definition. He raises the question, directed
to the student in the dialogue, "Which will seems the more
free to you: the one which wills without being able to sin,
so that in no way can it be turned away from the rectitude
of not sinning; or the will which can in some way be turned
to sinning?"[19] Anselm believes that the former will is the
freer, but the student answers that the latter is, apparentl

believing that the greater the range of alternative choices
open to a person the freer he is. To show that the student's
opinion is incorrect Anselm argues that as a property of a
rational will freedom cannot be thought of abstractly but
must be considered in relation to the whole nature and purpose of the being who is said to possess it.[20] As we have
seen, his view is that man's essential nature and purpose are
to conform to the moral standard of rectitude or justice
which God imposed in creating him.[21] Consequently, a person
whose choices and actions fulfill this end is freer than one
whose choices and actions do not, for the choices and actions of the former are more in accord with what a human being really is and essentially desires. "Don't you see that
someone who possesses what is fitting and advantageous in
such a way that he cannot lose it is more free than someone
else who possesses the same thing in such a way that he can
lose it and be drawn toward what is unfitting and disadvan-
tageous?"[22] Freedom, Anselm seems to be saying, is most
basically the ability to fulfill one's ultimate end, i.e.,
to do what is right or just.

This, however, gives rise to a problem. Christian
doctrine has always asserted that when men and the evil
angels sinned they did so freely. But Anselm's doctrine
here seems to imply that the only way people can act freely
is by doing what is right. A corollary is that when people
do what is wrong they do not do so freely, for surely one
does not do what is wrong through one's ability to do what
is right, i.e., one's ability not to do what is wrong. This
in turn seems to imply that people are morally responsible
only for the good they do, and not for the sin or evil they
commit.

Anselm's answer to this series of objections is that
even though the ability to sin is not included in any way
in freedom, nevertheless sin occurred through free choice.

They [Satan and Adam] sinned through their

> own free choice, which was free, but not
> through that by which it was free, namely,
> the ability not to sin and not to serve sin.
> Rather, they sinned by the ability they had
> for sinning, which neither helped them to-
> ward the freedom of not sinning nor com-
> pelled them into the service of sin. [23]

The key to this explanation is the statement that "they
sinned through their own free choice, which was free, but
not through that by which it was free." This may seem paradoxical at first, but I think some sense can be made of it.
Anselm is maintaining that the sin in question was committed
by a will which had a certain property, i.e., a certain
ability, and that this ability—the ability not to sin—is
what constituted its freedom. Hence the sin was committed
by a free will. But it was not committed by that will
through the particular ability which constituted its freedom
In Satan and Adam the ability which constitutes freedom is
accompanied by a second ability which is different from it,
namely, the ability to sin; and, Anselm says, this second
ability neither enhances nor detracts from the first.

One might infer from this that the connection between
Satan's and Adam's possession of freedom and their performance of an unjust act is an accidental one like the connection, say, between a person's possession of freedom and his
stomach growling. [24] Taking one's cue from Anselm, we might
say that since the growling of my stomach occurs in an
agent who has free will, therefore, the growling is something done through free choice and something for which I am
morally responsible. On the face of it Anselm's reasoning
seems to warrant this kind of inference. But there is a
crucial difference between Anselm's case and this one. For
an unjust act that Satan and Adam are guilty of occurs as a
direct result of the exercise of free choice on their part,
whereas the growling of the stomach does not come about as a
result of an exercise of free choice. The reason Anselm can
maintain this is that even though in his view freedom is not

to be *defined* as the power either to sin or not to sin,
nevertheless the form that freedom takes under the conditions of human existence is the ability either to sin or
not to sin. Hence anything, even sin, which occurs as a
result of the ability to sin or not to sin occurs as a result of freedom.

The point Anselm makes here can also be stated in
terms of the doctrine of the affections. This doctrine was
not fully developed till many years after the completion of
DLA, but when we look back at *DLA* from the vantage point of
this later doctrine, we see that it casts light on the
earlier work. In our examination of the doctrine of the
affections, we saw what makes it possible for temptation to
arise and hence for sin to occur is the possession by the
will of a second affection along with the affection for
justice. We also saw that sin actually occurs when in a
situation in which the two affections conflict, a person
elects happiness rather than justice. In such a situation
the person has the affection for justice, and it is inclin-
ing him to do what is right. But he does not do it. He
elects instead to reach for an inferior good and thereby
sins. When this happens the person obviously is not acting
through, i.e., under the aegis or impulse of, the affection
for justice; he is acting through the affection for happiness. Thus, if freedom is the ability to do what is just,
then when Satan and Adam sinned they did so with a will
which had the affection for justice, and which was therefore free, but their actual sin was committed through the
affection for happiness. They sinned through "their own
free choice, which was free, but not through that by which
it was free."

Anselm's answer, then, to what seems a troublesome
problem for his view of freedom makes sense even though it
initially appears paradoxical. Nevertheless, it follows
from his answer that strictly speaking it would be incor-

rect to say that a person sins freely. It is admissible
only to say that a person sins through free choice, not
that he sins freely. For the adverbial form (*libre*) would
imply that the person who sins does so through the ability
by which freedom is defined. But that would clearly be absurd, for it would amount to saying that a person sins
through his ability not to sin. Anselm seems to recognize
this quite clearly, for though he does not hesitate to
speak of a person sinning through free choice, he never
speaks of a person sinning freely. Whenever he has occasion to use an adverbial form to indicate the manner in
which a man sins freely, he uses *sponte* ("of one's own accord") rather than *libre*.[25]

Two consequences follow from Anselm's answer that we
have been considering. The first is that even though
strictly it is incorrect to say that sin occurs freely,
nevertheless the one who commits it is blameworthy and responsible for it. As we have seen, his doctrine is that
the necessary and sufficient condition of a person being
responsible for his action is that it be self-determined.[26]
Now when Satan and Adam sinned, their action was self-determined in the sense that they could have chosen and done
what was right instead of what was wrong, but they simply
did not do so. There was nothing compelling them to do
what they did or preventing them from doing otherwise.

The second consequence is that even though freedom
is not *defined* as the ability to make self-determined
choices between moral alternatives, nevertheless determinism
is incompatible with freedom, at least with the form of
freedom found in Satan and Adam. The reason for this is
found in Anselm's understanding of justice. We saw earlier
that for an agent to be fully just in performing a right
act, that act must be one which is self-determined. Self-
determination in a creature (as opposed to self-determination in God) is possible only if there are alternatives

from which he can choose, thus making his choice the decisive factor in bringing about the act which he elects to
do. Again, the situation seems paradoxical: freedom in man
requires that he have the ability to sin but at the same
time it is impossible for him to sin through his freedom.
But when seen in the light of the nature and end of man and
the make-up of the human will, it is fully coherent.

The way is now clear for Anselm to give a precise
formulation of the definition of freedom. Freedom, he tells
us, is "the ability to keep the rectitude of the will for
its own sake."[27] Anselm never deviates from this definition
and never modifies it though he comes back to the subject in
a number of his later treatises right up to the end of his
life. This is the definition which is designed to apply not
only to all creaturely freedom, the freedom of man and the
angels, but also to God's.

IV. THE PERMANENCE OF FREEDOM

So far we have followed Anselm as he presents the
line of reasoning which leads him to his definition of freedom. His conception of freedom is further clarified when
he considers the second major question *DLA* addresses: does
a person always possess freedom? There seems to be an obvious problem standing in the way of an affirmative answer.
To define freedom as the ability to keep rectitude seems to
imply that in order to have freedom, one must also have
rectitude. After all, how could a person keep something if
he did not have it in his possession? The problem, however,
is that a man who chooses what is wrong loses his rectitude.
Once that happens, he cannot regain it apart from the grace
of God. A sinner, then, does not have rectitude and so
cannot keep it. It seems to follow that when a person sins
he loses freedom. If this is so, a negative answer to the
question whether a person always has freedom is unavoidable.

Anselm, however, insists that a man retains his freedom even when he loses his rectitude. The argument for this
is that the successful or effective use of any given power
or ability does not depend solely upon the mere possession
of a subjective capacity. Obviously, the possession of a
subjective capacity for doing something is a necessary condition for a person doing it, but it is not the only necessary condition. He illustrates the point by an analysis of
visual perception. In order for a person to be able to see
a mountain, several conditions must be jointly met. First,
the person must have sound eyes. Second, there must be a
mountain within his field of vision. Third, there must be
enough light present to make the mountain visible. And
finally, there must be nothing in the intervening space between the person and the mountain, such as smog or even his
own shut eyelids, that would block vision. The point that
Anselm is making is one that has become commonplace in philosophy today, namely, that when it is said that a person
can do something, this "can" may be taken in any of several
different senses. Sometimes it is used to indicate subjective ability, at other times it is used to indicate that
one or more of the conditions that provide the opportunity
for doing something is present, and on still other occasions
it may be used in an inclusive sense to indicate both of
these.[28] It follows, then, that a person may well have the
subjective ability to do something even when, because of
the absence of other necessary conditions, it is quite impossible for him actually to do that thing. The application
of all this to the student's objection is, thinks Anselm,
fairly obvious. "What prevents our also having the ability
to keep the rectitude of the will for its own sake—even in
the absence of this rectitude—so long as we have the reason
by which to recognize it and the will by which to hold it
fast?"[29] Anselm thus thinks of freedom as a subjective capacity the possession of which is unaffected by whether or

not there is opportunity for its exercise. In short, a
person remains free even though he may never be able to use
his freedom.

The distinctions that Anselm draws here are valid and
important. But the use he makes of them raises very serious questions. One of these is that the distinction he
makes between the possession of a capacity and the actual
exercise of it seems inconsistent with the view that freedom in created beings requires the capacity for choice between moral alternatives, between right and wrong, between
justice and a happiness that is not just. If a person is
unable to will what is just because one of the necessary
conditions for doing so (namely that he possess justice) is
lacking, then it seems he does not have the ability to
choose either what is right or what is wrong, and consequently, the choices that he makes under these circumstances
are not self-determined and hence not something for which he
is morally responsible.

A second question is whether the distinction he draws
here is consistent with his doctrine of the affections. The
part of this doctrine that raises difficulties for the
teaching of DLA concerning the permanence of freedom is
that concerning the differences between the two affections.
As one will recall, Anselm teaches that there are two important differences between them. One is that while the
affection for happiness is something that is inseparable
from the will, the affection for justice is not. The will
can lose its affection for justice, and it does so when an
individual sins, but the affection for happiness belongs to
the will permanently. The other is that while the affection for happiness is distinct from the actual choices that
we make in seeking to achieve happiness, there is not a
similar distinction in the case of the affection for justice and the actual just choices that we make.[30] The affection for justice and the actual acts of choosing what is

just are two aspects of the same thing, which, though logically distinguishable, cannot exist apart from each other.

    A consequence of these differences seems to be the
collapse of the crucial distinction employed in *DLA* between
the subjective capacity for willing what is right and actual
just volitions. Generally, one is on sound ground in drawing a distinction between the possession of a capacity and
the actual exercise of it, but in the special case of the
capacity for justice it seems that Anselm's use of the distinction is faulty. For in *DC* he so links the disposition
for willing what is just with actually making just volitions
that if one stops making such volitions one also loses the
disposition. As we have seen, he explicitly states that
when a person sins he loses not only the ability to will
what is right, he loses the affection for justice.[31] And,
according to what he teaches concerning the function of the
affections, if a person has no affection for something then
he has no subjective capacity for it either. The defense
in *DLA*, then, of the proposition that sinners continue to
have free will after they have sinned seems to break down
when viewed in light of the teaching of *DC*.

    This brings us to a question of central importance
for understanding Anselm's thought on free will: Is there
any way of making sense of his claim that sinful men are
free? At this point we will not be able to pursue this
question or the question raised just prior to this one. For
a full treatment of these questions is possible only after
we see what role grace plays in the lives of human beings,
especially sinners. We will thus drop these questions for
now and return to them in the next chapter.

    There is a third issue which arises in connection
with the distinctions Anselm draws in defending the claim
that the sinner continues to have free choice. The way he
applies these distinctions to the case of the sinner shows
that he is hypostatizing rectitude, regarding it as an

object which it is possible to keep or to lose or to abandon.
He thinks of it as something that is apart from a person's
acts or choices rather than a property of them. This is
seen most clearly in the analogy that is drawn between
rectitude as an object to be kept and the mountain as an object to be seen. In most other passages Anselm does not
think of rectitude in this way. He thinks of it rather as
a relation—a relation of conformity of a person's acts
with the moral standards governing those acts. This latter
is the only way the idea of rectitude, as it appears in Anselm's definition of freedom, can make sense. The error
that Anselm makes when he distinguishes between freedom as
a subjective capacity-to-keep and rectitude as something
that can be kept is equivalent to the error that a person
would be making if he thought that the phrase "keeping the
law" implies that the law is some object like a coin that
can be either retained in one's possession or lost. The
error provides Anselm a handy means for answering a difficult problem, but there may have been other factors also
which led him to it. He was perhaps misled into thinking
that because "rectitude" is a noun it must therefore name
some thing. Furthermore, the fact that "keep" (*servare*) has
several different uses lends itself to this kind of confusion, and
so perhaps also played a part in his making the mistake.
When "keep" is used in a sentence, its direct object can be
any of a fairly large variety of words denoting different
types of entities, and it is easy to overlook some of the
critical differences between them.

The confusion here is not one that is damaging to Anselm's definition of freedom, for the soundness or useful-
ness of the definition does not depend on the hypostatiza-
tion of rectitude. Whether it is damaging to the claim
that men always have freedom will depend on the results of
our inquiry into the two previous questions after we have
examined the question of the compatibility of divine grace

and human freedom in the next chapter. If those questions
can be answered without hypostatizing justice, then we may
regard Anselm's error here as harmless to his major doctrines.

V. THE STRENGTH OF FREEDOM

The next problem is whether it makes sense to say that
the will has the power to keep rectitude when it can be con-
quered by sin. It must be borne in mind that in posing this
and the other major questions of *DLA*, Anselm is thinking of
the will as it was created by God, i.e., before sin. After
it sins the will can be restored to its original state, but
this takes a special work of divine grace. But even before
sin (and in the state of grace) it is *possible* for the will
to act unjustly. This is what leads to the present problem:
"How, then, was the nature of men and angels created free,
or what kind of free choice did men and angels have, if sin
could be its master?"[32] If sin can overpower the will, it
would seem that the will does not have the power to keep
justice.

Anselm solves the problem through an analysis and
critique of the language in terms of which it is cast.[33]
When someone says that sin can conquer the will, the language employed makes it appear that the power to subjugate
the righteous will belongs to sin. A careful analysis of
what actually takes place, however, shows that the power belongs not to sin but rather to the will itself. "Can" is
being used improperly when it is said that sin can overpower
the will. Sin has no ability to conquer the will. The
power of enslavement lies with the will itself. It can
yield to sin if it so chooses and thereby enslave itself.
There is nothing in the sin or the temptation that forces
the will into its choice. One can think of the possibility
of sin as being detrimental to freedom only if one is taken

in by the misleading features of some of the statements commonly but loosely made about sin.

The student, however, is not yet convinced. He notes
that temptations can be very strong and suggests that sometimes people yield to them unwillingly.[34]   The teacher's
answer is that a person cannot will something evil without
willing it and therefore cannot will it unwillingly.[35]
Against this the student points out that there are certainly
occasions when we say that a person has willed something
against his will. "Why do we sometimes say that a man who
lies in order not to be killed lies against his will, if, as
you say, he can only do this willingly? For if he lies
against his will, he wills to lie against his will. And
whoever wills to lie against his will, unwillingly wills to
lie."[36]

The teacher responds by making a distinction. There
is a sense in which this person lies willingly and a sense
in which he lies unwillingly. He lies willingly in that he
chooses to lie in order to save his life. He lies unwillingly in that it is against his will that he is faced with
the necessity of making this painful choice. But this kind
of unwillingness is not contrary to free choice.[37]   The fact
that a man is forced to choose between alternatives he would
not face if it were up to him does not mean that he does not
freely select the particular alternative he takes when he
does face that choice. The conclusion Anselm comes to, then,
is, "Temptation is not at all able to overcome an upright
will; and when we say that it can we are speaking improperly.
For it makes sense to say only that the will is able to subject itself to temptation."[38]

An interesting feature of this argument is that it
shows not only that freedom cannot be overpowered by sin but
also that freedom, while not defined as the ability to sin
or not to sin, is a necessary condition for sin. In order
for a person's act to be unjust in the sense that he is

blameworthy for it, it must be chosen from a set of alternatives that make it possible for him to choose something just
instead. Hence, while the ability to sin is not included in
the definition of freedom, nevertheless, no being can sin
unless free.

        The student still has problems with Anselm's claim.
He is not sure that it is consistent with common personal
experience. "I cannot refrain from mentioning that particular powerlessness of the will which we usually experience
when we are overcome by the force of violent temptation.
Therefore, unless you can show that the power of the will,
which you are establishing, is consistent with this powerlessness of the will which we all feel, my mind cannot be
at rest."[39] The student believes that on some occasions
"temptation, by its own force, compels the will to will what
it is suggesting."[40] The answer to this is very much the
same as the answer to the student's earlier objections:
temptations do not "so oppress us that we are utterly unable
to resist willing what they urge."[41] On the contrary, the
most that temptation can do is place us in a situation, like
the lie or die circumstance, in which doing what is right
leads to seriously harmful consequences for us. The feeling
of powerlessness that we face in certain temptations is the
inability to control the circumstances of choice, it is not
the inability to choose between the alternatives before us.
To be sure, it is very difficult to do what is right when
the consequences are death, but we have the ability to do it
whether or not we actually use it.

        Anselm's argument on the strength of the will against
the force of temptation has been subjected to vigorous criti
cal attack at the hands of Jasper Hopkins and Herbert
Richardson. After briefly expounding Anselm's argument,
they write,

                But the argument begs the question. For
                it really assumes what was supposed to be

> proved. In other words, (1) the 'argument'
> construes 'something's compelling the will'
> as meaning 'something's moving the will
> against one's will.' (2) This construal is
> then shown to be self-contradictory. (3)
> From this it immediately follows that nothing
> can compel the will. But this immediate in-
> ference might be taken as a sign of faulty
> analysis of the notion of 'compelling the
> will.' Anselm 'defines' compulsion in such
> a way that it is self-contradictory. Thus
> on the basis of a tendentious definition he
> establishes that no will is ever compelled.
> This is scarcely an argument and is handled
> best by questioning the plausibility of the
> definition.[42]

A careful reading of Anselm's argument will show, I believe, that this criticism is unfair to him. He does not make his doctrine true by definition. His argument is an effort to establish that *in fact* one always has a choice even when faced with the strongest temptation. And he submits this claim to the test of experience. He asks the student how he feels the force of temptation: is it such as to close off all the alternatives to the temptation and thus make it impossible to will anything other than the choice to which the temptation impels? The very fact he raises this question suggests he is willing to admit that if the answer to this question is no, then there would be no freedom—rational beings would not have the power to keep rectitude. He accepts the test of factual falsifiability; he believes, however, that his claim is not in fact falsified.

A fundamental defect of the Hopkins-Richardson criticism is that its account of Anselm's conception of compulsion is mistaken. He does not think of compulsion as a force which moves the will against its will, but as a force which makes it impossible for the will ever to will anything other than what it does will. This is clearly evident in his explanation of why temptation cannot turn the upright will to sin against its will. It is not because the notion of compulsion is self-contradictory. It is because the up-

right will, even in the most vexatious temptation, has before it two possible courses of action, one right, the other
wrong, and it can choose either. Thus, when Anselm says
that temptation cannot compel the will against its will, he
means that the will is in a situation in which it alone
finally determines which direction it will take.

The student, however, has yet another question to
raise. In those cases where the will yields to temptation,
it would seem that by the very fact that the temptation wins
out it is stronger than the will.

> If the will for keeping rectitude were
> stronger than the force of temptation,
> then whenever temptation urged the will
> to desert its rectitude, it would resist
> the insistence of temptation by willing
> its rectitude still more strongly....
> Therefore, when I will what I ought to
> do less strongly than a temptation urges
> me to do what I should not, I don't see
> why the temptation is not stronger than
> my will.[43]

The answer to this objection is provided by distinguishing the will as instrument from its actual volitions.
The basic strength of the will lies in the instrument. The
claim that an upright will is always stronger than any temptation that may assail it means that the instrument always
has the power to resist temptation. On any given occasion,
however, one may not use that strength to the full. This is
exactly what happens when a person succumbs to temptation.
He does not use the strength he has; his will is strong
enough, but his volition in this case is weak.

Anselm illustrates the distinction he is making by
posing the following question.

> Suppose you know a man so strong that when
> he is holding a wild bull, the bull cannot
> get away. What if you should see the same
> man holding a ram, and see the ram shake
> itself loose from the man's hands: would
> you think the man less strong when he is
> holding a ram than when he is holding a
> bull?[44]

And the student's answer is,

> I should think that his strength is the
> same in both cases, but that he didn't
> use his strength equally, for to hold a
> bull is harder than to hold a ram. The
> man is strong because he has strength,
> but his action is said to be strong because
> it is done in a strong way.[45]

There is a sense, then, in which it is correct to say
that the temptation is stronger than the will when the latter succumbs to it, for it is stronger than the will-use.
But this is quite irrelevant to the question of the strength
of freedom, for freedom is the power or capacity to keep
rectitude, not the specific acts in which it is kept. The
locus of such power, of course, is the will-instrument.

Anselm's distinction of ability and use as the means
by which to turn aside this objection is another point which
has been negatively criticized by Hopkins and Richardson.
They contend that the distinction between ability and use
does not make sense in concrete cases.

> If a man has strength enough to hold down
> a given animal, then in general he has
> strength enough to hold down a weaker
> animal. In the exceptional circumstance,
> his failure to master the weaker animal
> must be accounted for by pointing to
> some unusual occurrence. If he were sick
> that day, then he was unable to use his
> full strength, so to speak. But now the
> distinction between ability and the use
> of that ability collapses, for to say that
> he was unable to use his strength is the
> same as saying on that particular day his
> strength was gone, i.e., on that day, he
> had an inability.... A man's yielding to
> temptation in a specific circumstance is
> precisely the kind of case where the dis-
> tinction between having an ability and
> using that ability is in danger of col-
> lapsing. For to say that A had the ability
> to resist but did not use it may be the same
> as saying that in that situation he was un-
> able to resist.[46]

The exact thrust of this objection is not clear. It

seems to be saying that any time a man fails to use fully
the basic ability he normally possesses, an explanation in
terms of something other than the internal processes of the
will is required to account for it. If a man can hold down a
bull but fails on some particular occasion to hold down a
ram, the failure "must be accounted for by pointing to some
unusual occurrence." If we say that he could have held down
the ram even though he did not, then "if the 'could have'
ascription is to make sense here, it must be filled out by
adding conditions: 'He could have, if he hadn't slipped,'
'He could have if he had had a good night's sleep,' etc."[47]
The indictment against Anselm apparently is that he fails to
realize this. In describing the case of the man who falls
to temptation, he fails to provide the added conditions
which fill out the explanation.

It is not immediately clear why we should accept this
criticism, since the claim on which it is based is not argued but simply proclaimed as something which "must be" the
case.[48] Nevertheless, it does raise the question as to what
considerations could be brought on behalf of the distinction
which Anselm makes and the use to which he puts it. The
most important consideration would be common experience.
Anselm's doctrine implies that there are situations where
the degree of power or exertion that a person puts into the
performance of a given act or task is not explainable solely in terms of external circumstances, but requires reference to the act of will itself. If the Hopkins-Richardson
view is correct, it follows that a person always uses the
full power which he possesses. It would make no sense,
then, to suggest that on some occasion, without the external
circumstances being altered, a person could have simply decided to increase his effort and done so. One is always
acting with the maximum strength that he possesses at the
time in question.

Anselm's doctrine, however, seems much more in keeping

with common experience than this one. We would all, I
think, admit that there are occasions on which we do not
exert the maximum effort that we could, occasions where we
could, without the external circumstances being altered in
any way, increase our effort simply by setting our minds
(or wills) to it. If this is so, then Anselm's distinction
between ability and use does not collapse as charged.

This is the sort of consideration which not only *can*
be brought on behalf of Anselm's doctrine, it is suggested
by his own appeals to experience. He appeals to experience
in seeking to determine whether temptation compels the will.
And his reference to the man who fails to hold down a ram
though he is able to hold down a bull is also an appeal to
experience. Anselm thus does not, as Hopkins and Richardson
charge, simply "lay it down as part of the general definition of human nature that it always possesses this power"[49]
(the power to keep rectitude), and then merely draw conclusions analytically from this definition. He means his
doctrine to be an account of the human situation as it is
experienced, and his examination convinces him that experience supports his doctrine.

In order to avoid possible misconception, we should
perhaps note here that Anselm's discussion of ability and
use is related to the willing of an act rather than the doing of it. There are, of course, important similarities
between willing and doing, but there are also important differences. External circumstances, for example, which directly affect the amount of strength that is effectively
channeled into doing something often have little bearing on
the strength that is put into willing it. If a man slips
on wet ground when trying to subdue a ram, the force that
he effectively exerts on the ram will be diminished. Anselm
really has no interest in something like this. He introduces the example of the man and the ram merely to illustrate the general distinction of ability and use. His con-

cern is with the struggle internal to the will, the struggle involved in choosing what is right in the face of strong
temptation not to. The reason for this restriction of interest is that the primary locus of moral choice and responsibility is the will. We are responsible for what we
do only to the degree that this is subject to the choices
of the will. In the case of the will facing a difficult
moral choice there is nothing analogous to the accidental
slip of the man struggling to bring down the ram. Nothing
external to the will can transform its power to keep rectitude into a weakness or an inability. There are no accidental slips in the will. So, while weakness of deeds may
be due either to weakness of effort or to some special en-
vironmental circumstance, weakness of will is due solely to
weakness of effort.

As soon as one admits that there is a valid distinction to be made between ability and use, a further question
arises: what are the criteria by which we are to distinguish
the case where someone fails to do something because he does
not use the ability he has to do it from the case where he
fails to do it because he does not have the ability. This,
too, is a question which Hopkins and Richardson raise and
which they charge Anselm with failing to answer. They claim
that he "does not furnish criteria for determining occasions
when a person 'really could have done X' and occasions when
he 'really could not have done X,'" and add, "Without these
criteria the notion of 'having been able' is in danger of
becoming obscure."[50] This charge is simply incorrect, for
Anselm is quite clear in stating the conditions under which
it is correct to say that a person has the ability to keep
rectitude but does not use it, and distinguishing these from
the conditions under which a person does not have the ability
to keep rectitude. A person has this ability before he has
sinned, that is, when he still has an upright will and therefore has the rectitude he can keep if he simply chooses to

do so. A person has such an ability when there is open to
him more than merely one possible choice, and when, therefore, it is ultimately up to him to determine whether he
will do the just or the unjust act. Any being for whom
these conditions do not hold does not have such an ability.
Accordingly, if a being of the latter kind were to fail to
do the just thing, the failure would be due to an inability
to do what is just. If, however, a being of the former kind
were to fail to do the just thing, then the failure would be
a failure of willing rather than a lack of ability. The
criteria, then, for distinguishing the two cases are quite
clear.

It may be true, of course, that as observers we may
not be able to discern whether or not the conditions in
question are present. But that is a different question
from whether there are such conditions or what they are.

Even if, as I have tried to show, the foregoing crit-
icisms of Anselm are unsound, there are other questions
connected with his distinction of ability and use. In *DLA*,
the distinction is introduced to help explain how upright
will succumbs to temptation and sins. The problem with
the way Anselm uses the distinction in his explanation is
that it seems to entail a different account of how sin
occurs from that which he gives before he introduces the
distinction. And the explanations seem inconsistent.

The explanations agree in holding that the strength
required by the will to keep justice has to be measured
against a counterforce which the will must overcome. They
disagree on the character and the locus of this counterforce. In explicating the ability-use distinction Anselm
gives the impression that the counterforce is independent
of the will and has an intrinsic strength of its own. This
is suggested by the example of the man and the ram. The
man with his power to subdue the ram represents the will

with its power to keep rectitude, while the ram represents
temptation exerting its pull upon the will. This picture
suggests that when the will succumbs to temptation, it actually wills justice but temptation wins out because the
will, though choosing justice, does so weakly.

     The other explanation is the one that Anselm uses in
DLA before he comes to make the ability-use distinction. In
this account, sin occurs not because temptation, with a basic
strength of its own, wins out when the volition for justice
is weak.   It occurs when the just will gives itself to
sin by willing the unjust thing it was tempted to will.
There is no suggestion in this account that when the will
succumbs to temptation a person wills justice at all, either
strongly or weakly. The struggle involved is not between
the will and something whose reality and strength are independent of the choices the will makes. The struggle is
wholly one of the will with itself, and the counterforce
against which the will struggles is within. The difference
between these two explanations is that in the former sin
(or temptation) is conceived as having a strength of its
own and as playing an active role, though not the only or
even the decisive role, in a person's turning away from
justice; while in the latter all the strength belongs to
the will, and it alone plays an active role in turning away
from justice.

     For the sake of convenience, in the discussion that
follows I will call the former explanation the first explanation and the latter the second explanation. Our problem
at this point is to see if there is any way of reconciling
these two accounts.

     In the course of explicating the ability-use distinc-
tion and its implications, Anselm has a passage that includes elements of both these explanations. This might
provide us clues to how the explanations might be reconciled.

> So now you can see that the will which I
> call the instrument for willing has a
> strength which is both inseparable and
> not able to be overcome by any alien force.
> But when this instrument for willing is
> actually willing, it sometimes uses more
> of its strength, and sometimes less of it.
> So it follows that the will, when offered
> something, never abandons what it wills
> more for what it wills less. But when it
> is offered something that it wills more
> than what it already has, it immediately
> leaves the thing that it does not will as
> much. Therefore, the will which we call
> the actual using of the instrument, because
> it does the work whenever the will wills
> anything, is said to be more or less strong
> since it does things more or less strongly.[51]

This passage has it in common with the second explanation that the counterforce against which the upright will
must struggle in temptation is something which is internal
to the will. It is one of its own inclinations, which becomes a temptation in those situations in which it conflicts
with the demands of justice. It also has in common with the
second explanation the view that when the will succumbs to
temptation, the volition is not one which wills justice,
even weakly, but is rather one which wills what is unjust.

This passage also makes a point that is a major part
of the first explanation. It asserts that when sin occurs,
though the will's volition is for what is unjust rather than
what is just, nevertheless the will for justice is significantly involved in the process. For the struggle is an internal conflict between a will to do what is just and a will
to do what is unjust. This immediately brings to mind Anselm's doctrine of the affections, according to which the
conflict of wills which occurs when one is tempted is a conflict between the affections. The affection for justice inclines the person to do what is just; the affection for happiness inclines him for the sake of some other good toward something unjust. In the lie or die case, the affection for

justice draws the individual to tell the truth, the affection for happiness inclines him to save his life by lying.
But it is hard to make the doctrine of the affections fit
other parts of this passage. The passage tells us, "The
will, when offered something, never abandons what it wills
more for what it wills less," and it also asserts that when
the will "is offered something that it wills more than what
it already has, it immediately leaves the thing it does not
will as much." If the sense of "will" used here in talking
about the will willing more of something and less of another
is that of the affections, we run into serious difficulties.
For it is hard to see how we are to understand differences
in strength between the affections in a way that is coherent with self-determination in the will and freedom from
necessitation. For, if the reason a person chooses justice
or self-preservation is that the affection for one is
stronger than the affection for the other, then the person
really has no choice in the matter but is compelled to do
what he does by the affections he has been given.[52]

Are we to say, then, if we want to retain the notion
that the human will has the power of moral self-determination, that no sense can be made of Anselm's talk about
what the will wills more and what it wills less in the situation of temptation? I think not. There is a definite
sense in which the will does will happiness more than justice, or vice versa, *when it makes its choice*. It is not
that a stronger affection determines the choice we make;
rather the choice determines which affection is the stronger. A person's affection for justice is stronger than his
affection for happiness (or vice versa) when and because he
chooses what is just over self-preservation (or vice versa).
The variation, then, in the comparative strength of our affections when we choose justice or injustice is a *result* of
the choice we make, not a *cause* of it. It emerges from the
choice, it does not pre-exist it.

This, I believe, is the key to understanding the passage we are discussing. In it Anselm is not talking about the affections; he is talking about the actual choices, or volitions, of the will. When he says that "the will, when offered something, never abandons what it wills more for what it wills less," he means that as long as the will continues in its volitions to cling steadfastly to justice (i.e., as long as it wills justice more than anything else), it will never blunder into sin. When he says, "But when it is offered something that it wills more than what it already has, it immediately leaves the thing it does not will as much," this means that when the just will opts in its volition for something contrary to justice (i.e., when it wills something more than what it already has), it then forsakes justice, which now it does not want as much as something else. This interpretation is confirmed by the conclusion Anselm draws from these comments, which makes it clear that he is talking about the actual volitions of the will rather than its affections: "Therefore, the will which we call the actual using of the instrument, because it does the work whenever the will wills anything, is said to be more or less strong since it does things more or less strongly."

But if we accept this interpretation, another question arises. If the choice that is made is in accordance with only one of the affections, is there any sense in saying that in that choice the person willed the other alternative, the one he is drawn to by the other affection? In the passage we have been looking at, Anselm says the person does will the other alternative, though he wills it less than the one he chose. In one sense, of course, the man who elects to tell the truth does not will self-preservation at all. He simply chooses in favor of telling the truth and against saving his life. If one wished to be strictly correct, this is all that one could say. But in a looser sense, it is legitimate to say that he did will self-preservation

though not as strongly as telling the truth. For he certainly desires it and he values it very highly. It is
therefore something he would actually choose on a great
many occasions. But in this very unusual circumstance
something else gets higher priority. Though Anselm himself
does not say so, this is a point at which his distinction
between proper and improper linguistic usage would be helpful

     What then are we to say concerning the two explana-
tions delineated above of how a just man can fall into sin?
Our discussion up to now shows that there is considerably
more in Anselm to support the second explanation than the
first. The first explanation, the one which sees the counterforce against which the will struggles as having a reality and strength independent of the choices of the will, is
supported mainly by two points. One is the illustration of
the man and the ram. If this were its only support it would
be easy to deal with. We could simply note that this illustration was introduced to make a single point and then warn
against the danger of overdrawing analogies. The ram example, we could say, was brought in merely to illustrate the
distinction between ability and use; further inferences
therefore are unwarranted. But there is another point sup-
porting the first interpretation, and it is more troublesome. Anselm maintains that when the will sins it does so
because it does not will justice strongly enough. Apparently he believes that the will for justice is susceptible to
degree. If my analysis so far has been correct, this claim
has to be interpreted as referring to the volition, not the
affection, for justice. But talk about variability in
strength of the volition for justice is very puzzling; it
seems to make no sense. One might say that it makes the
kind of loose sense delineated above in terms of the value
one places on justice and its alternatives. But that will
not help here, for such a scale of values is a consequence
of the choices one makes, not some pre-existing condition to

which one yields or against which one must struggle. It
simply makes no sense to talk about degrees of power needed
to accomplish tasks when the very ease or difficulty of the
tasks themselves depend solely on whether we decide to do
them. It would make sense to say that a certain degree of
strength is needed for a task and anything less is inadequate only if there is a pre-existing counterforce that has
to be overcome in performing that task, a counterforce whose
strength is independent of the doing of the task. So Anselm's claims suggesting that just volitions can vary in
strength and that some can be too weak to do their job thus
supports the first interpretation.

The support for this interpretation is not extensive.
It is much less than that for the second interpretation.
But it is unmistakably there. Unfortunately so, for finding
textual support for it is quite a different thing from
making sense of it, and there seems no way of rendering it
coherent with other parts of Anselm's doctrine of the will
and freedom. In the ram example, it is possible for the man
to do the right sort of thing for getting the job done but
fail to accomplish it because he does not do it strongly
enough. But this cannot happen in the case of the just will
facing temptation. For its own acts determine the relative
strength of the counterforce, i.e., temptation. But even
this is deeply misleading, for there is no counterforce to
the just volition. Consider the lie or die case again.
Here there are clearly alternative choices from which the
man must choose: he may do what is just by telling the
truth or he may save his life by telling a lie. There are
also contrary inclinations in his will—the two affections.
Many would be inclined to say that what we have here is a
desperately difficult choice because the inclination for
self-preservation is usually so strong and the inclination
for telling the truth much weaker. But because of his fear
of determinism Anselm refrains from taking that view. He

holds instead that a person's inclination for self-preservation is stronger than his inclination for justice only if he
has already decided to save his life. So if he wants to
save his life more than to tell the truth, he has already
decided for self-preservation. About all that can be said,
then, to describe the way this person acts (and this would be
true of anyone facing a choice between what is right and
what is not) is that either he does what is right or he does
not. If he does what is right, then as a consequence of
this his affection for justice is stronger; if he does not,
then as a consequence of this, his affection for happiness
is stronger. If he does what is wrong, it is because he
chose (this was his volition) to do so. It is not because
in his volition he willed justice but failed to will it
strongly enough; he just did not will it at all.[53] If he
does what is wrong he could have done what is right instead.

     We see here the importance of the distinction between
ability and use. It is possible to have the capacity to do
what is right and not use it. But in this picture, no sense
can be made of the notion of varying degrees of strength in
the way one performs just volitions. For in the very nature
of the case, the existence of a counterforce *to the volition*
is excluded. Hence it makes no sense to think of a just
volition which is actually made but not made strongly enough

     Anselm's distinction between ability and use has been
the focus of our attention for some time now. What we have
found is that the distinction withstands the assaults made
on it by Hopkins and Richardson, but nevertheless, some of
what Anselm says in using it to explain the way in which the
just will sins creates serious difficulties. These are difficulties, it seems to me, which Anselm could have avoided,
for he really does not need the notion of varying degrees of
strength in just volitions to answer the objection that he
seeks to answer. The objection is summarized in the following words of the student: "When I will what I ought to

do less strongly than a temptation urges me to do what I
should not, I don't see that temptation is not stronger than
my will."[54] Before this objection comes up Anselm had already established that temptation has no power to overcome
an upright will, and that when an upright will sins it does
so solely through its own power, which it can use either to
do what is right or to do what is wrong. But having established this, he goes back on himself and implicitly acknowledges that temptation does have some power but not as much
as the will. This is incompatible with what he said before.
He could have answered, in keeping with his earlier claim,
that to say, "I will what I ought to do less strongly than a
temptation urges me to do what I should not," is an improper
usage, and that the logically correct way of putting the
point would be to say, "I chose to do what I should not do
and thereby I subjected myself to the sin toward which I
was tempted."[55] Period. By failing to say this Anselm be-
trays some of the most basic principles in his theory of
the will and freedom.

     While there is this inconsistency, I believe that the
basic thrust of Anselm's teaching on how an upright will
sins is quite clear and that his explanation in terms of
degrees of strength in willing justice is a lapse from his
more basic thought. The fundamental points in his theory of
the strength of the will are these. Freedom gives man the
power of choice, or self-determination between alternatives,
which means that the upright will has the power to keep
justice, even in the face of grievous temptation. The upright will, moreover, always has this power and is thus always free. The fact that it sometimes uses its power to
choose something unjust is no evidence against its freedom,
for even when it chooses something unjust, it could choose
what is just, since there is nothing preventing it from
doing so.

VI. THE SIGNIFICANCE OF ANSELM'S
DEFINITION OF FREEDOM

In the intellectual tradition that he received, Anselm inherited two distinct notions of freedom. In one, freedom is thought of as the state in which a person is exempt from all possibility of sin or corruption—the state of sinless perfection. Here freedom is the ability to fulfill completely the will of God. The only way to possess this freedom is to attain it or merit it (which, of course, cannot be done without the grace of God). In this notion, while "freedom" designates a state or condition, it also designates a subjective power or capacity. Freedom is the state of sinless perfection and the power to maintain that state. The antithesis of this kind of freedom is sin or the ability to sin.

The second kind of freedom is the property of will by which it is able to choose any one of a set of two or more alternatives. This kind of freedom does not have to be attained; it is a natural property of the human will. Having this kind of freedom entails having the ability to sin along with the ability not to sin. The antithesis of this kind of freedom is determinism—any kind of compulsion or necessity that so conditions a person's choices that he cannot do otherwise than he actually does.

In order to simplify reference to these two notions of freedom, I will call the first notion explained above the freedom of self-perfection and the second the freedom of choice.[56] Both these notions of freedom are found in Augustine's later writings, where they are generally, though not invariably, referred to respectively by the terms *"libertas"* and *"liberum arbitrium."*[57] Contrary to the practice of Augustine and many others throughout the Middle Ages, Anselm does not make this distinction between *liberum arbitrium* and *liberatas,* for his single definition encompasses both these types of freedom.

To understand how the single definition can be made
to stand for such diverse realities as the freedom of self-
perfection and the freedom of choice, we must realize that
freedom as Anselm defines it (the ability to keep justice)
is not as such exactly identical with either of these but
will under certain circumstances assume the form of one
while under other circumstances it will assume the form of
the other. In other words, freedom as Anselm defines it is
a determinable which will under different circumstances assume different determinate forms. In any determinate form
of freedom there are elements which are not essential to
freedom as such though they are essential to that determinate form of freedom.

The word in Anselm's definition which is the key to
its significance as a single formula covering both kinds of
freedom is "ability" (*potestas*). The freedom of self-perfection is a determinate form of generic freedom in that it
is the ability never to do anything unjust; that is to say,
it is the ability to do what is just but under certain conditions—conditions where it is impossible to do anything
unjust. Similarly, the freedom of self-determination is
also a determinate form of generic freedom because it too
is the ability to do what is just, but here it is found under conditions where it must be possible also to do what is
unjust instead.

Hence neither the state of self-perfection as such
nor the power of choice as such is essential to freedom as
such as Anselm conceives it. Freedom, therefore, is not
definable as the state of perfection or the power of choice.
One might infer from this that there could conceivably be
individuals who have neither attained the state of self-
perfection nor possess the power of choice but who are
nevertheless free. Such people, it might be thought, would
possess the ability to do what is just but under conditions
which are different from those characteristic of the free-

dom of self-perfection and the freedom of choice. But this
would be a mistake. For the respective defining conditions
of the freedom of self-perfection and the freedom of choice
are mutually exclusive and exhaustive. If a person has the
ability to do what is just, then either he is able to do
what is unjust instead or he is not. There is no other possibility.

The simplicity of Anselm's definition tends to hide
its remarkable richness. A number of major factors are
brought together coherently in a single conception: the
ultimate end of rational life, self-determination, moral
responsibility, sinless perfection, and choice between moral
alternatives. The definition makes explicit the orientation
of free will to the ultimate end of rational life, namely,
justice. A person can be just in performing an act only if
he is self-determined in doing so. Freedom, then, entails
self-determination. Self-determination, in turn, is both
necessary and sufficient for moral responsibility. Self-
determination, therefore, is found in every being that has
the obligation to be just, i.e., every being that is free.
The power of choice between alternatives, however, is present only in some of the beings who are free, namely, created beings. But it is found in all created beings who are
free, for it is the only form which self-determination can
take, and the only power by which justice can be achieved,
under the conditions of creaturehood. A created being cannot choose what is just in a self-determined way if he cannot also choose what is unjust instead. Hence, while freedom as such is not to be defined in terms of the power of
choice between moral alternatives, in human beings the only
form which freedom can take is the ability to choose between
moral alternatives. Similarly for God: while freedom as
such is not to be defined in terms of the inability to do
anything not just, the only form which freedom can take in
God is the inability to do anything not just.

Probably the greatest significance of Anselm's definition is that it enables him to do something which has not
been successfully done by any other major Christian thinker,
namely, to unify under a single concept the two major ideas
of freedom in the Christian tradition—ideas that had hereto-
fore been held distinct and had appeared so divergent. What
appears at first glance, then, to be a rather narrow definition of freedom turns out upon examination to be remarkably
inclusive in its compass.

The two traditions of freedom have often been recognized and noted.[58] But I have nowhere found a full appreci-
ation of the manner in which Anselm combines them in his
single conception of freedom. Most of his commentators have
interpreted his doctrine as a freedom of self-perfection,[59]
though there are some who have recognized elements of the
freedom of choice in his thinking.[60] There are some even
who criticize him for making no room in his theory for moral
choice.[61] And finally, there are some who think that he
fails to see clearly the distinction between the two major
kinds of freedom.[62]

The only one that I have been able to find who sees
something of the way in which Anselm incorporates both traditions in his theory is Mortimer Adler. He writes that
"Anselm does not sharply distinguish between the two free-
doms but instead distinguishes diverse modes of the will's
freedom by reference *in this life* to its possession or lack
of rectitude accompanied by the constant power to retain or
lose rectitude when possessed, but not to regain it when
lost."[63] Adler thus sees that Anselm brings together both
notions, but he is unclear on the way they are brought together. For he speaks of the freedom of self-perfection
and the freedom of choice as two "aspects" of one freedom.
This is a mistaken account of the relation between the generic freedom of Anselm's definition and the two determinate
forms. Self-perfection and choice are not aspects of free-

dom, but freedom actually is self-perfection when an individual possesses rectitude and cannot lose it, and freedom
actually is the power to keep rectitude as a matter of moral
choice when an individual possesses rectitude and can lose
it. Rather than being aspects of the same power, self-perfection and the power of choice are forms that this power
takes under different circumstances.

VII. FREEDOM AND THE WILL

The results of our investigations into the will in the
last chapter and into freedom in the present one seem to
show that there are a number of important similarities between Anselm's concept of the will and his concept of freedom. Both will and freedom have the same *raison d'être,*
namely, to make it possible for rational beings to achieve
their ultimate end. As such, both require that rational
creatures have the ability to defect from the goals or purposes imposed on them by God. Thus both require that such
creatures have the power of choice. All this raises the
question as to whether there is really any significant difference in Anselm's thought between the will and freedom.

The answer to this, I think, is clear. Freedom is
conceived by Anselm more narrowly than the will. While
freedom in rational creatures makes it necessary for them
to have the ability to will what is unjust as well as what
is just, freedom is not to be straightforwardly identified
with the power of choice, whereas the will is (in creatures)
Freedom, under whatever form it is found, is essentially and
only the power to keep justice.

This means that freedom in these created beings can be
identified with the affection for justice, and with the instrument and its acts insofar as they are governed by the af
fection for justice, but whatever else is found in the will—
the affection for happiness, and the instrument and its acts

insofar as they are governed by it——is not a part of freedom.
This holds even in those who have achieved confirmation in
rectitude. For even though their affection for happiness
has been brought into perfect subjection to the affection
for justice, the two affections are still different and
still directed toward different formal objects. Consequently,
freedom does not include the ability to will happiness or
beneficial things.

This distinction between freedom and will breaks down
when we come to the case of God, but then every distinction
breaks down in the case of God, since he is a simple unity
without any real diversity of parts or attributes.[64]   The
case of God, then, cannot be taken as indicating the relation between will and freedom on any lower level.

It may be thought that the conclusion here, that freedom is not identical with the power to choose as such, contradicts the earlier conclusion that in rational creatures
freedom takes the form of the power of choice. There is no
inconsistency, however, for the statement that freedom
takes the form of the ability to choose means that freedom
is the ability to keep justice as a matter of choice. As
such, it is still the power to keep justice, and it is only
that. In this it is like freedom generally. The way it
differs from the other form of freedom is that in this form
justice can be kept only by being willed *as a matter of
choice*. The power of choice includes the ability to will
something sinful as well as what is just, but the ability
to will justice through this kind of choice does not.

Here again the doctrine of the affections illumines
the issue. Justice can be willed only through the affection for justice, whether or not there is some other choice
which can be made instead. If there is another choice
which can be made, it must be willed through another affection. The power of choice, then, is the ability to choose
whether one shall will in accordance with the affection for

justice when one could have chosen in accordance with the
other affection instead.

In other words, when there is a possibility of moral
choice, the capacity of the will for willing justice exists
alongside of another capacity, the capacity for willing happiness. But this does not mean that the capacity for willing justice is or includes the capacity for willing happiness. The will includes both, but the affection or capacity
for willing justice does not.

If this is correct, then V. J. Bourke is mistaken when
he says that in Anselm's view the will is "in the genus of
libertas."[65] What this phrase means is not entirely clear,
but at the very least it must mean that freedom is the wider
and more encompassing concept than will. Besides the argu-
ments just given, Anselm's dictum, "All power follows the
will,"[66] also seems inconsistent with this account. Since
freedom is a particular kind of power, it then follows, or
depends upon, the will. Moreover, Anselm's doctrine that
the animals are endowed with will but do not have freedom
also militates against Bourke's view. The cumulative force
of all this evidence is hard to resist. It is difficult to
deny that Anselm held that the will is the general power of
willing, while freedom is one specific kind of power of
willing, namely the power of willing justice.

CHAPTER SIX

FREEDOM AND GRACE

Though *DLA* is the treatise Anselm devotes to the explication and defense of his definition of freedom, it is
not possible to get a complete understanding of his view of
either freedom in general or human freedom in particular
without knowing what he says about the relation of grace and
freedom in human life. This issue is examined most fully
and systematically in *DC*. In the present chapter we will
investigate what Anselm says about the relation of grace and
freedom, concentrating primarily on the teaching of *DC*, and
we will draw out the implications of this for understanding
man's freedom and freedom generally.

Though *DLA* and *DC* were written about thirty years
apart, and though the development of his theory of the affections occurs during that time, the two treatises form a
unity in his thinking. Both are prompted by the same problem, namely the seeming incompatibility between the foreknowledge, the predestination, and the grace of God on the
one hand and the free will of man on the other.[1] *DLA*, however, while prompted by this problem, never advances to the
point of actually attempting to solve it. The major questions it deals with, having to do with the nature and extent
of free will, are preliminary to a direct treatment of it.
But once the nature and extent of free will are understood,
one can go on to examine the relation of freedom to the var-

ious aspects of divine sovereignty, which is what Anselm
does, though not till many years later, in DC.

As noted earlier, we will concentrate our attention
in this chapter on the relation of grace and freedom. Anselm has some subtle and important things to say about the
relation of freedom to God's foreknowledge and predestination, but his teaching on these latter questions turns primarily on logical and conceptual points concerning foreknowledge and predestination, not on points concerning free will.
So, while these questions are important for one interested
in doctrines of God, his attributes, and his relation to the
world, they add nothing new to an understanding of freedom
and the will. The treatment of grace and free will, on the
other hand, sheds important new light on free will. It is
for this reason we focus on it in this chapter.

I.   THE PROBLEM OF GRACE AND FREEDOM

The problem of grace and free will has to do with the
relation of grace and *human* freedom (or that of rational
creatures, including the angels). There is, of course, no
problem of possible conflict between grace and divine freedom.

The basic problem is twofold: on the one hand, how to
give God the credit that is due him for the justice that men
have without undercutting moral responsibility and self-determination on the part of human beings, and on the other
hand, how to maintain human free will without jeopardizing
divine grace. To exaggerate the role of either divine grace
or human freedom would be a serious error.[2]

The general principle that Anselm offers for solving
this problem is that both grace and free will must be involved in anyone's doing what is just.[3] Difficulties immediately arise when we seek to work out this principle in
specific cases. One case where it seems particularly hard
to see how grace and freedom can both be involved, and

where consequently a solution to the difficulties may be
particularly significant, is the case of fallen man. We
must therefore examine this case with care. It is to this
case that Anselm devotes most of his discussion of grace and
freedom in DC.

There is no problem seeing why fallen man needs grace
if he is to do what is just. He has lost his justice through
sin and is therefore powerless to regain it on his own. But
there is great difficulty discerning how sinful man can be
said to have free choice, so it is hard to see how free choice
can have any role at all to play in his recovering justice.
Even if, contrary to what seems to be the plain implication
of Anselm's doctrine, we think of sinful man's unavoidable
practice of perpetually choosing evil as an exercise of free
choice, it is certainly not the sort of exercise of free
choice that could possibly aid in the recovery of justice.
So the role of free choice in the recovery of rectitude will
have to consist in somehow willing what is right. But how?

To recover rectitude is, of course, to recover *possession* of it. But, as Anselm expressly teaches, the only way
to possess rectitude is to will it in specific choices that
we make.[4] It is just at this point, however, that the doctrine of the affections seems to pose an insurmountable difficulty, for an unmistakable part of that doctrine is that
a person cannot will justly unless he is already just and
already possesses justice.[5] The sinner, then, who would cooperate with divine grace to recover justice seems caught in
a vicious bind: he needs to will justice before he can get
it back, but he cannot will it unless he already possesses
it. It seems, therefore, that there is no way of willing
rectitude and therefore no way of freely participating with
grace in the recovery of justice as long as one is in the
state of sin without rectitude.

Some of what Anselm writes in elaborating his claim
that grace and free will must cooperate in the recovery of

justice, instead of alleviating the problem seems only to
get him deeper into difficulty. He states at one point that
"grace always helps the natural free choice by giving to the
will the rectitude which it can keep through free choice."[6]
A natural way of reading this passage is as indicating that
grace restores the affection for justice to the will, and
then the will, provided with this necessary condition for
willing justly, brings about specific just volitions. Grace
restores the lost affection but the *use* of that affection
actually to will justly is accomplished through free choice.
This, however, will not work—for two reasons. First, it is
inconsistent with Anselm's teaching on the relation of the
affection for justice with specific just acts of the will.
His view, as we have seen, is that there can be no real
separation of the affection for justice from actual just
volitions. It is plain, then, that bestowing the affection
for justice on someone who does not have it cannot be accomplished without at the same time also bringing about the
just volitions that go along with it. The second reason
this interpretation will not work is that Anselm directly
contradicts it. He flatly asserts that the making of actual
just volitions must be ascribed fully and directly to God
every bit as much as the recovery of the affection for justice.[7] This is a radical doctrine for a theologian who
maintains that free choice plays an indispensable role in
making just volitions. Moreover, he asserts it as pertain-
ing not only to the first just volition or set of volitions
that an individual makes with, or after recovery of, the affection for justice but to all of them.[8] There is thus no
just act of will that any creature ever performs which is
directly brought about by the creature himself. All such
acts are directly brought about by God. Could one go any
further than this in exalting the role of divine grace and
diminishing the role of human freedom? Indeed, is there any
room at all left for the operation of free will?

Another point which leads Anselm into difficulties is
his teaching that whether or not a sinner receives divine
grace when it is offered is something for which the sinner
is responsible. No doubt one reason he insists that sinners
are free in receiving or rejecting divine grace is to support the attribution of moral responsibility to them. But
this, of course, does not answer any of the problems we have
just noted; if anything, it seems to get him into deeper
trouble. The sinner is, of course, responsible for the condition in which he finds himself as a sinner, without justice and thus unable to will anything just. But Anselm goes
beyond this and thinks that if a sinner refuses to receive
divine grace when it is offered to him, he is responsible
for a further transgression against rectitude.[9] His refusal
is blameworthy not solely because it is a product of a sinful choice made earlier; it is another sinful choice in its
own right and thus involves an added measure of culpability.
If this teaching is to be consistent with the doctrine of
moral responsibility which we have seen that Anselm holds,
the sinner's refusal of divine grace must occur as a choice
between moral alternatives. But what kind of moral alternatives are available for an individual who has no ability to
will anything that is right? Seemingly the only way in
which a person could have a choice of moral alternatives is
to have a choice between willing something that is right and
willing something that is wrong. But in Anselm's doctrine
a man in the state of sin has no ability to will anything
that is right.

The clue to the answers we are seeking is found in Anselm's explanation of the distribution of responsibility between God and men for the just actions which human beings
perform. He states that when a person wills what is just,
"everything should be attributed to grace."[10] This is precisely what we would expect after learning that he thinks
God actually brings about the just volitions that men

perform. The assertion that everything should be attributed
to God might seem to preclude there being any credit coming
to men, but Anselm denies that there is no credit due to
men for their just volitions. It is in explaining what
credit is due to men when they perform just volitions that
he provides us with the key to understanding the role that
free will plays in sinners in bringing about just volitions.

        Free choice has a role to play by virtue of the fact
that while God is the one who actually performs the just volitions in human beings, he does not force them to occur.
The individual involved can, so to speak, exercise a veto
over God's performance in his will of just acts. He exercises this veto power by willing to do something that is
unjust instead of allowing God to do what is just in his
will.[11]   The idea of a sinful man making an evil or unjust
choice poses no problem. But what kind of an act is the
sinner's act of allowing God to do what is just through
one's will and one's actions?

        The answer to this can be gathered from the following
statement that Anselm makes. "When a man does good, he is
responsible for the fact that his deeds are not evil. He
is responsible because when able to desert justice, he did
not desert, but kept rectitude through free choice with the
aid of grace."[12]   In this statement Anselm is speaking of
the just choices that the righteous make in keeping rectitude. What they do in keeping rectitude is to refrain from
willing anything that is unjust. But the basic principle
can be extended to apply also to the case of sinners who
recover rectitude. When a sinner recovers rectitude what
he does is not a positive act of doing something; rather it
is an act of refraining from doing something—from doing
anything that is unjust. The role, then, that the human
free will plays in the making of just volitions, in the recovery of rectitude or at any other time, is that of not
willing something unjust when it could will something unjust.

This very simple idea of the role that man plays in
performing just volitions gets Anselm out of all the difficulties so far noted that arise around his understanding of
the freedom of fallen man. For a fallen man's role in the
production of his just volitions and the restoration of his
rectitude has all the following features. (1) It is indispensable and necessary to the production of these volitions,
and is thus a role that is indeed required along with the
role of grace. (2) It is essentially a negative role, because it involves not doing something that one could do.
This has two important consequences. (a) It makes it legitimate to attribute everything in the production of just volitions to God, for everything positive, i.e., everything that
involves a doing rather than a refraining from doing, is
done by God. (b) It also makes it legitimate to hold that
one cannot do anything that is just unless one is already
just and possesses the affection for justice. The only one
who actually and directly does anything just is God, and
God is always fully just. If a man's just acts had to be
directly executed by himself, then it would be impossible
for a person in the state of sin ever to regain rectitude or
ever again to do anything just. There would be no escape
for him from the bind described earlier. (3) It is an exercise of choice between moral alternatives, because under the
circumstances in question one is not forced to choose something that is unjust and one is not forced to refrain from
choosing something unjust; one may do either as one chooses.
There is, then, genuine choice here. Furthermore, it is a
choice between moral alternatives and not between alternatives that make no moral difference, for one choice is the
right one to make and the other the wrong one. And like
every choice between right and wrong, its consequences are
momentous, involving the difference between staying in the
state of sin and entering the state of grace, between so
acting as to frustrate the purpose of God in one's life and

so acting as to make possible the fulfillment of God's purpose. (4) The fact that the role of human free will involves such a choice renders it coherent to hold that, if
the sinner fails to respond favorably to divine grace when
it is extended, he commits a new sin that carries with it an
additional measure of culpability and is not merely operating under the incubus of the disability resulting from an
earlier sin. And (5), while it is an exercise of choice between moral alternatives, the kind of choice involved is
fully compatible with one's being in the sinful state,
marked by an inability positively to do what is right. In
the sinful state one is not capable of doing anything positive that is just; thus whenever a person in the state of
sin positively does anything it will be something unjust.
But this is not incompatible with there being occasions
when he does not do anything and so does not do something
unjust. The kind of choice that human beings make in carrying out their role in the production of just volitions does
not presuppose a capacity positively to do anything just.
It is merely the capacity to do either what is unjust or
not to do anything at all. The traditional formula that
goes back at least to Augustine, that freedom is the ability
to sin or not to sin, is apt here, just so long as one is
careful not to take the ability not to do what is unjust in
the traditional way, as equivalent to the ability to do what
is just.

We are now in a position to see how it is possible to
resolve the difficulties raised in the previous chapter concerning the coherence of Anselm's claim in *DLA* that a sinner
who has lost rectitude nevertheless continues to possess a
subjective capacity for keeping rectitude. The first difficulty was that the possession of a subjective capacity for
justice in circumstances in which one never gets the opportunity actually to exercise it is incompatible with self-
determination, and hence with moral responsibility, on the

part of the sinner when he acts. It is clear now that there
is an assumption behind the statement of this difficulty
which, if our analysis has been correct, Anselm would reject. It is that self-determination must always take the
form of choosing between doing something that is just and
doing something that is unjust. If one makes this assumption, two consequences, which together would be very damaging to Anselm's position, do indeed follow. First, when
a person who has a native power of self-determination (understood as the ability either to do what is just or to do
what is unjust) loses the ability to do what is just, the
only thing left that he can do is something unjust. And
secondly, when under such circumstances he does will something unjust his act is not self-determined. But, as we
have seen, there is another form which self-determination
can take: choosing between doing something unjust and not
doing anything at all. This is a form of self-determination
which, in Anselm's view, a person in the state of sin, without justice, can (and does) possess. It is, moreover, a
form of self-determination which, if exercised correctly by
the sinner, can cooperate with divine grace to bring about
the restoration of rectitude. The fact that the sinner possesses this power makes it fully appropriate to hold him
morally responsible for exercising it in the right way.

The second difficulty raised in the previous chapter
was that Anselm's claim in *DLA* that a sinner who loses rectitude nevertheless continues to possess a subjective capacity
for keeping rectitude is inconsistent with his doctrine of the
affections. In his doctrine of the affections he teaches
that there is no real distinction between the basic capacity
for willing and the affections of the will, and no real distinction between the affection for justice and actual acts
of choosing what is just. The logical consequence of these
claims is that anyone who loses the ability to make actual
just volitions has lost all subjective capacity for doing

so. This seems directly contrary to the claim of DLA. Once
again, however, there is an assumption underlying the objection that one does not have to accept. This time the assumption is that the affection for justice and the accompanying
just volitions are things that a human being can fully possess and exercise in his own right. If this assumption were
correct, then it would be flatly impossible for any being
who was ever devoid of rectitude to do anything that would
effect the restoration of rectitude to him. It would even
be impossible for God to restore rectitude to him, for an
act must be self-determined to be just, and if God performed
the act in the will of the sinner, it would not be an act
that had been self-determined by the sinner. But, while Anselm never says so in so many words, his view implies that
just volitions and the affection for justice are not things
that human beings can fully possess and exercise in their
own right.[13] Everything just, whether the affection for
justice or actual just volitions, belongs fully and solely
to God. If a human being has an affection for justice, it
is really God's affection being manifested in him by grace.
So, strictly speaking, there is never a problem of restoring
rectitude, for the only one who ever really possesses rectitude as fully his own is God, and he, of course, never loses
it.

A problem that does arise is in whose lives and on
what occasions will God's rectitude be manifested. The general answer that we can draw from Anselm's teachings is that
it will be manifested in the lives of those persons, and
only those persons, who do not block it by willing what is
unjust. Those who wish to do what is unjust, preferring
that to manifesting God's justice, will in fact do what is
unjust and thereby prevent divine justice from being manifested in their lives. Those, on the other hand, who are
willing to manifest divine justice will refrain from willing anything unjust, thus keeping their lives an open chan-

nel for the working of divine justice. The sinner has a
role to play in the restoration of justice to himself, but
since strictly speaking he never himself actually does anything just and never himself actually possesses the affection for justice, it is not a role that puts him in the impossible situation of having actually to possess something
(the affection for justice) which he does not have before
he can get it back. Understood in this way, then, the role
the sinner plays in the recovering of rectitude is consistent with what Anselm teaches concerning the affections.

An objection of a different sort might be launched at
this point. If Anselm believes that just volitions and the
affection for justice always belong to God and never to any
of his creatures, is it not misleading for him to speak, as
he clearly does on numerous occasions, as if human beings
can and sometimes do possess the affection for justice and
execute just volitions? Some of what is said below is per-
tinent to this objection.[14] At this point, let it suffice
to say that though it *can* be misleading to speak this way,
there is justification for doing so. To be sure, if my interpretation has been correct, then in the strictest and
most literal sense the affection for justice belongs to God
and all just volitions are executed by him. But in a sense
that is less strictly literal a human being in the state of
grace can be said to possess an affection for justice and
to execute just volitions. For, even though the affection
and the volitions are, strictly speaking, God's, they are
manifested in *his* (the human being's) life and through *his*
will. *He* has the power to prevent their manifestation in
this way, and *his* choices determine whether they will continue to characterize his life or not. It thus makes sense,
when a person is living in grace, to speak of the affection
for justice and the just volitions involved as his.[15]

II. THE IMPLICATIONS FOR UNDERSTANDING
THE DEFINITION OF FREEDOM

We need now to trace out the leading implications of
the conception of the freedom of fallen man which we have
just found for an understanding of (a) Anselm's notion of
human freedom generally and (b) his overall definition of
freedom, the definition designed to apply not only to human
beings but also to God and the angels.

The conclusion just reached is that the freedom of
fallen man consists in the ability either to do or not to
do what is unjust. One of the most striking things about
the textual evidence that supports this conclusion is that
it applies not only to the freedom of fallen men but to that
of all men, whether fallen or in grace, whether in the present life or in the next. The assertion, for example, that
the just volitions performed by human beings are brought
about directly by God with man's only role being that of
refraining from doing anything unjust applies to all human
beings.[16] The startling consequence of this is that the
freedom of all men takes the form of having the ability
either to do or not to do what is unjust.

This, it seems to me, is exactly how Anselm's doctrine
must be interpreted. But before we can regard this interpretation as secure, we need to consider some objections
that might be raised against it. Doing so will throw added
light on his understanding both of human freedom and of
freedom in general.

After reading Anselm's writings on freedom, one might
think that there is a class of people to whom this interpretation cannot be made to apply, namely, those who have died
in their sins and have been confirmed in their unjust ways.
These people, according to Anselm, have no more opportunity
to enter the state of grace, so one might think they are not
free because they have no ability to do what is just. But
if the capacity either to do or not to do what is unjust is

he characteristic form of human freedom, it is clear that
these people need not be viewed as exceptions to the interpretation of Anselm's doctrine that I am offering. For even
the wicked who are confirmed in injustice possess this capacity. They are able, at least on some occasions, to refrain
from doing anything at all, in which case, of course, they
are not doing anything unjust. All that is needed in addition to this to make sense of the claim that sinners who
have died in sin are confirmed in their unjust ways and
therefore will never again do anything just (or more precisely, will never again have divine justice manifested in
their lives) is the further claim that they will never again
be offered the aid of grace. In this, and in this alone, do
they differ from sinners still living in the present life.
Sinners who have died in their sin are fully and finally excluded from the offer of grace whereas sinners in this life
are not. The former, therefore, never get the opportunity
to cooperate with divine grace to bring about just acts or
to recover justice, while the latter sometimes do get such
opportunity.

With respect, then, to subjective capacity of will,
the sinner who is confirmed in injustice does not differ
from the sinner in this life who may still receive grace.
But what is perhaps more surprising is that in this respect
neither does the sinner differ from a person in the state
of grace. All men (sinners and righteous) have the ability
either to do or not to do what is unjust—and this is all
their freedom consists in as far as subjective capacity of
will is concerned. Furthermore, both sinners and righteous
can actually exercise that capacity (at least on occasion)
to refrain from doing anything unjust. In this sense, then,
sinners, even confirmed sinners, have the capacity to keep
rectitude: they have all that is subjectively needed on
their part to do what is just. What is lacking in the case
of confirmed sinners is the aid of divine grace. Without

this they can do nothing to effect the actual production of
just acts in their lives. The righteous, on the other hand,
can do something to effect the production of just acts in
their lives, for they have divine grace in their wills.
Consequently, they can refrain from doing something unjust
and this *will* bring about just volitions and ensure the
preservation of rectitude in their wills.

While the conception of freedom as the ability either
to do or not to do something unjust resolves the difficulties we have looked at so far in Anselm's teachings concerning the will and its affections and concerning grace and
freedom, it may be thought that there is still a problem
that stands in the way of accepting it as Anselm's own doctrine. As we saw earlier, at the outset of *DLA* he considers
the view that freedom is the ability to sin or not to sin
(which, of course, is merely an alternative phrasing for the
ability either to do or not to do what is unjust) only to
reject it out of hand. One might object, then, that there
is clear textual evidence against ascribing this conception
of human freedom to him.

The objection, I think, fails. The key to seeing this
is to recognize that our conclusion that in Anselm's thinking human freedom takes the form of an ability either to do
or not to do what is unjust is a conclusion about *human*
freedom, whereas Anselm's search in *DLA* is for a *general*
definition of freedom, one that applies not only to human
beings but also to God and the angels. The fact that Anselm
rejects the proposal that freedom in general is the ability
either to sin or not to sin does not show that he thinks
that human freedom does not involve the ability to sin or
not to sin. By itself, of course, this does not show that
Anselm does think that human freedom involves the ability
to sin or not to sin. But in the course of this chapter we
have found such strong reasons for thinking that in his view
the form which freedom in general (i.e., the ability to keep

rectitude or justice) takes in human beings is the ability
either to do or not to do what is unjust that there can be
little doubt that this conception of human freedom is Anselm's own.

But if this is the case, a problem of a different order arises. Anselm seeks a single defining formula for
freedom that will apply to all beings who are said to be
free, i.e., to God, men, and angels. He believes he finds
such a formula in "the ability to keep rectitude for its
own sake." But when it turns out that the form which this
ability takes in human beings is the ability either to do
or not to do what is unjust, it appears that his general
definition fails to do what it was designed to do. For, in
a strict and literal sense, it applies only to God and not
to men or angels. Of God alone is it strictly correct to
say that he has the ability to keep rectitude. Strictly
speaking, men and angels do not have the ability to keep
rectitude. They have a role to play in keeping rectitude,
but it is the severely limited one of refraining from doing
something that would prevent God from executing just volitions in their lives. It would seem, then, that the reason
Anselm gives for rejecting the formula that freedom is the
ability to sin or not to sin (namely, that it does not apply to all the beings who, he believes, are free) applies
just as much to his own definition and requires him, therefore, to reject it also.

The difficulty, I believe, can be overcome by making
use of Anselm's distinction between proper and improper linguistic usage. The definition of freedom applies to God in
a strictly proper sense: God has the power to keep rectitude
because he can (and does) directly will what is just. It
applies to creatures, on the other hand, in an improper
sense: they have the power to keep rectitude, but not by directly willing what is just; rather they can keep rectitude
by refraining from directly doing something (namely com-

miting an unjust act) that would prevent God from acting
justly in them. This conforms to one of the modes of improper usage that Anselm lists in his classification of the
various uses of verbs.[17] All free beings thus have the capacity to do something that either directly or indirectly
produces just acts and maintains rectitude. So it is fair
to say that freedom is the power to keep rectitude, even
though the mechanism or operation involved in the case of
creatures differs greatly from that involved in the case of
God.

It is not clear, however, that what has been said so far
succeeds in avoiding all the difficulties. If we accept
this use of the distinction between proper and improper
ways of speaking, then we do not have the problem that it
is false to assert freedom of men and angels. It is a mistake, Anselm maintains, to confuse statements that employ
improper modes of speaking with statements that are false.
Improper uses are found frequently in ordinary discourse,
and they occasion no great difficulty if they are understood
correctly, as they usually are. Even Scripture, as he notes
frequently uses language that in his carefully defined sense
is improper; but none of the claims of Scripture is false.
But we seem to have another problem that is very serious,
namely, equivocation in the meaning of the term "freedom."
For, in using the distinction to clarify the concept of
freedom, we are perforce acknowledging that the subjective
power that constitutes God's freedom is quite different
from the subjective power that constitutes the freedom of
created beings. In itself this might not be seriously ob-
jectionable. But in the context of Anselm's investigation
it causes trouble, for it seems to clash with a primary objective of DLA, to find a definition that identifies the
freedom of all free beings with a property they share in
common. DLA proposes that this property is the power to
keep rectitude. But our analysis seems to drive us to the

conclusion that there is no single specific property or capacity shared in common by all free beings that constitutes
their freedom. The program of *DLA* thus seems defeated.

Is there a way out of this problem? One might be
tempted to think that the fundamental source of the trouble
here is Anselm's unusual definition of freedom and the turn
of mind which leads him to it. His definition reflects an
insistence on relating freedom to an external goal—rectitude—that is to be achieved through the use of free will
rather than relating it to the internal operations of the
will through which freedom is exercised. This, it might be
said, is a mistake. In seeking to identify the defining
characteristic of freedom Anselm should have focused on the
internal workings of free choice. He does give us considerable information about the internal operations of the free
will, but he refuses to define freedom in terms of them. It
is this refusal ultimately which leads him, a critic might
say, into proposing an equivocal definition. The remedy
would be to abandon the definition he offers and substitute
one that is formulated in terms of internal operations of
the will. Anselm could easily have done this, the critic
might continue, by defining freedom as the power of moral
self-determination. Not only does this formula focus on
the operation in the will by which freedom is exercised,
but the capacity to perform this operation is coextensive
with free will as Anselm understands it. Of course, the
conditions under which self-determination operates in God
differ from the conditions under which it works in men and
angels, but in all of them self-determination takes the
form of acting or choosing *a se*. One could say, therefore,
that this is the property that Anselm is looking for, the
specific capacity that is shared by God and his rational
creatures which constitutes the freedom they all possess.
This definition, then, provides us a formula which, even
given Anselm's views on the difference between God and his

creatures, applies univocally to God, to the angels, and to
human beings. Moreover, it picks out a property, the capacity for self-determination, which not only is coextensive
with free will but is in Anselm's view essential to the power
to keep rectitude wherever this is found. And, of course, it
is less idiosyncratic and more in line with the mainstream
tradition in western speculation concerning freedom than Anselm's own definition.

    But will it work? Does the substitute definition im-
prove matters for Anselm or does it worsen them? The answer,
of course, depends on how well the new definition, compared
with Anselm's, coheres with the rest of his thinking. One
point at which the new definition may not be as adequate as
Anselm's is in making sense of the freedom of the men and
angels who have been confirmed in righteousness. These beings have the capacity to keep justice, but there is serious
question whether they have the power of self-determination.
The *state* that they are in, marked as it is by an inability
any longer to sin, is self-determined, but is it correct to
say that the choices they make in that state are self-determined? It is not clear how this question should be answered.
Anselm's concept of self-determination, i.e., of acting *a se,*
is a subtle one, and perhaps further analysis would show
that it fits the situation of these beings (though perhaps
it would show that it does not).

    But we need not enter upon that question, because it
is a minor issue compared with a much more fundamental problem for the substitute definition. Even if there is nothing
amiss in saying that the actions of beings who are unable to
do anything wrong come about nonetheless through moral self-
determination, Anselm would be profoundly dissatisfied with
the substitute definition. This is not because he thinks
that sometimes the power to keep justice is present when the
power of moral self-determination is not or vice versa, for
he does not think that. It is that even though self-deter-

mination is necessary and sufficient for freedom, to define
freedom in terms of self-determination is to omit from the
definition a factor that in Anselm's outlook is of para-
mount importance, namely, the goal or purpose for which self-
determination exists. As we have seen, the notion of purpose is fundamental to Anselm's ontology and his entire
philosophical perspective. What a thing is is inseparable
from what it is for.[18] The case of freedom is just a specific instance of this general truth. The virtue of Anselm's
definition is that it makes explicit what freedom, or self-
determination, is for. And identifying what it is for is
the only way, within the framework of Anselm's ontology, of
making clear what it essentially is. At the most fundamental level, to be free is not to have the ability to choose;
it is rather to be under a particular kind of obligation and
to have the power to fulfill it. It is impossible to know
the real nature or the significance of the psychic or voli-
tional makeup of rational beings until we can see clearly
the fact and the character of this obligation. For these
reasons Anselm develops his theory of the human will and
his account of its structure and its capacities, including
its capacity for self-determination, out of an analysis of
the divine purpose for man and the obligation laid by God
upon man. The substitution of the new definition, then, far
from representing merely a minor change of focus in his understanding of freedom while leaving the rest of his thinking intact, strikes at the very foundations of his entire
metaphysical system and thus at the roots of his understanding of the nature of God, of man, and of the world.

Very well, then. We cannot substitute the proposed
definition for Anselm's and still be faithful to doctrines
that are at the very heart of his thinking. But does not
his fundamental orientation toward purpose betray him into
presenting a definition of freedom that is equivocal? It
does only if what is most important about freedom is the

operation in the will through which freedom is exercised.
For clearly the operation by which God acts to keep rectitude is quite different from the operation by which man acts
to keep rectitude. But the wording of Anselm's definition
and the general orientation of his thinking make it clear
that in his judgment this is not what is most important
about freedom. Much more significant are two facts which
the definition brings out that are universally true of everyone who is free. First, everyone who is free is so because
he has a duty to act justly. Secondly, because it is a
necessary condition of acting justly, one who is free has
the ability to exercise one's will in a self-determined and
morally responsible way. To the extent that Anselm's definition emphasizes these facts, it applies univocally to all
beings who are free, whether God or his rational creatures.

     Anselm's definition appears equivocal only when we al-
low modern interests and emphases in the philosophic and
scientific study of free action to make us blind to the
concerns that dominated his thinking. It appears equivocal,
that is, only when we interpret him anachronistically.
Present-day investigations of freedom focus on the structures, capacities, and functions of mind and body and even
of society as the significant factors for understanding what
freedom is. Concomitantly, modern thinkers show a strong
tendency to think that the mere exercise of freedom, apart
from any purpose to which it is put, has intrinsic value,
even great intrinsic value. Emphasis, accordingly, is frequently laid on the autonomy of the individual human being
as a moral legislator, or on personal authenticity in our
choices. The value of freedom, in such an outlook, is not
that it gives persons the ability to fulfill some pre-estab-
lished purpose; it is that it allows people to determine
their own purposes and their own means of attaining them.

     Such ideas and emphases are wholly absent from An-
selm's system of thought. His account of freedom incorpo-

rates a very different outlook and vastly different values.
He believes that the structures and capacities of freedom
can be known and understood only in light of the ultimate
purpose for which freedom exists. As for the value of self-
determination, the mere exercise of self-determination has
no value at all. Self-determination is valuable only when
it is exercised justly; and when it is exercised justly, its
entire value derives from the value of the life of rectitude
of which it is a part. Similarly, moral autonomy is not a
thing to be prized for its own sake, and no man enjoys the
status of independent moral legislator. Man exists under
responsibility to God and to the standard of rectitude imposed by God. Even God is not autonomous in the sense of
being free to legislate at will. Like human beings, God too
is under obligation to fulfill the requirements of rectitude.
Unlike human beings, however, he is not bound to the requirements of rectitude as to something independent of himself,
and for this reason the operation by which God exercises
free will and self-determination differs from that by which
man exercises it. In Anselm's view, the two most important,
the two most far-reaching, and the two most noble characteristics any rational being can have are the obligation to
keep rectitude and the ability to do so. And, as his definition of freedom brings out, he believes that having these
characteristics, a feature shared by all rational beings, is
what it means to be free. His definition cannot be significantly altered without losing sight of this. And when one
keeps this clearly in view, it is evident that his definition is not equivocal.

CHAPTER SEVEN

THE HISTORICAL SIGNIFICANCE OF ANSELM'S DOCTRINE

When we look at Anselm's doctrine of freedom from a historical perspective, one of the most striking things about it is that, even with the innovations it introduces, it manifests a solid Catholic orthodoxy. Christian doctrine had always held that the highest freedom, true freedom, is the liberty of the redeemed man, marked by emancipation from sin and adherence to God. And ever since the time of the Apostle Paul, the Western Church had maintained, in its teaching concerning the operations of the human will in which this liberty is shown in practice, both the primacy of grace bestowed by God and the indispensability of free choice on the part of man. Anselm's doctrine firmly embraces all these elements, as he builds his theory of the nature of freedom and his account of the life of the human will with these points as major foci. But more than this, his doctrine is noteworthy because his explanations make perhaps better sense of the orthodox Catholic position than those of any other medieval thinker.

The orthodox Catholic position on the roles of grace and free will was given conciliar statement at the Council of Orange in A.D. 529. This Council endorsed what was basically Augustine's point of view against both the Pelagians and the more moderate so-called Semi-Pelagians. Pelagius

had taught that Adam's sin did not at all impair the natural
freedom of the human will, while John Cassian, a major representative of the view that came to be labelled Semi-Pelagian-
ism, argued that sin had seriously weakened man's natural
power of free choice but had not wholly obliterated it. Augustine's doctrine was at odds with both these views. He
held that in the state of sin man has no power whatever to
do what is right or to move toward God. The condition of
sinful man is that of *non posse non peccare,* being unable
not to sin. Hence any redemption experienced by man is
wholly a work of divine grace. On the views of these three
men N. P. Williams has observed, "It has been well said that
Augustine regards human nature, prior to grace, as dead,
Pelagius as sound and healthy, and Cassian as sick."[1] The
Council of Orange denounced the view that after sin man retains any power of his own to seek God or to strive for righteousness. It also condemned the correlative claim that
grace is sometimes given in response to strivings and stir-
rings on the part of man, affirming instead that any stir-
ring toward God and righteousness by the sinner is itself a
work of grace.[2] Nevertheless, as Williams notes, the canons
of the Council reserve to man "a certain undefined share in
the work of his own salvation."[3] All of this is in line
with Augustine's teachings. The Council, however, did not
go all the way with Augustine. Augustine held to the irresistibility of grace and may also have believed in double
predestination—predestination of both the elect to redemption and unregenerate sinners to reprobation. On the question of double predestination there is some disagreement
among Augustine's interpreters about his position.[4] The
Council strongly condemned the doctrine of double predestination and refrained from endorsing the irresistibility of
grace. So, while the Council's position is fundamentally
Augustinian, it is a toned-down Augustinianism.

A toned-down Augustinianism of precisely this type is

what we find in Anselm's work. As we have seen, Anselm
staunchly maintains the utter impotence of the sinner's will
to do anything just by its own power, for the will of the
sinner has no affection for justice and no power to recover
this affection. The will can recover justice only if justice—and the affection for justice—is restored to it by
grace. Grace, thus, is given wholly freely, not in any way
because it is earned or deserved. The will, however, does
have a necessary part to play in the process: it must not
block the work of grace by choosing something inimical to
justice in preference to receiving from God the restoration
of justice. Though sinful man can do nothing of a positive
nature to bring justice back into his will, and though everything done positively is the work of grace, grace is not ir-
resistible. A sinner can refuse the gift of divine grace by
choosing to continue acting unjustly.

Anselm is thus less anti-Pelagian than Augustine without, however, diminishing Augustine's insistence on the
necessity, the unmerited character, and the completeness of
the work of divine grace. He is less anti-Pelagian because
even with his strong doctrine of grace he reserves for the
human will, even that of the sinner, a genuinely non-deterministic freedom of choice, the ability, in the special
sense defined earlier, to sin or not to sin. This is a part
of Anselm's doctrine that has not been fully appreciated.
Jasper Hopkins, for example, has recently stated, "Both Anselm and Augustine are anti-Pelagian. But Anselm, by invoking his special definition [of freedom] and by simultaneously proclaiming that every man has free choice, fos-
ters the illusion of being less anti-Pelagian than Augustine.
Only his statements on the relation of grace to free choice
make his theological kinship to Augustine perfectly clear.
For here, like Augustine, he emphasizes the *inability* of human nature to perfect itself without divine assistance."[5]
It is true that Anselm stands at one with Augustine on the

inability of human nature to perfect itself without divine
assistance, but even the semi-Pelagians did that, and it is
clear that their doctrines are very different from Augustine's. Anselm, too, rejects the views of the Semi-Pelagians, but this does not mean that there do not remain important differences between him and Augustine. For Anselm's
doctrine that every man has free choice is, as we have seen,
fully consistent with his special definition of freedom and
with the primacy of grace.

We must, of course, acknowledge that Augustine too
states, indeed insists, that sinful men continue to possess
free choice and that grace works in harmony with free choice
rather than overpowering it.[6] A major problem, however, for
anyone seeking to understand the mind of Augustine on the
relation of grace and free choice is that he also makes some
very strong assertions about the operation of grace which
seem incompatible with these statements. Some interpreters
have argued forcefully that there is no incompatibility here
Probably the most subtle of these, and certainly one of the
most influential, is Eugène Portalié.[7] But even if what
Portalié says is correct there is still a significant difference between Augustine and Anselm on the role that free
choice plays vis-à-vis grace when a sinner comes to God. According to Portalié, grace is always effective even though
free will is preserved, because for everyone God knows the
circumstances, primarily cognitive and psychological, in
which he or she will freely accept the gift of grace, and so
if God wishes a person to be saved he does not offer grace
without also engineering the occurrence of those circumstances in which the offer will be accepted.[8] The corollary
is that if God does not wish a person to be saved, he may
still make the offer of grace but neglect to bring about the
circumstances that will elicit the favorable response.
Portalié does not emphasize this corollary, but Augustine
does not shrink from it.[9] The upshot of all this is that

God not only foresees but also foreordains which men will be
saved and which will be lost.

Whether this way of construing grace and free choice is
coherent, and it certainly bristles with problems that cry
out for attention, it is quite a different view from Anselm's.
The difference can be seen most clearly by looking at two
points in Anselm's teaching: his analysis of the logic of
claims about gift-giving and his explanation of predestination. He examines the logic of claims about gift-giving in
the course of dealing with the objection that "if the good
angel received perseverance because God gave it, then the evil
angel did not receive it because God did not give it."[10] He
believes this inference is mistaken because it fails to see
that a successful act of giving requires appropriate action
on the part not only of a would-be donor but also of the in-
tended beneficiary. I cannot give something to you unless you
accept it. I can, of course, offer it to you without your accepting it, but if you do not take it, I have not succeeded in
giving it to you. With respect solely to what the would-be
donor does, then, the act of offering and the act of giving
are one and the same. Whether it is completed as an act of
giving or is aborted so that it is a mere act of offering depends on the response of the other person. For this reason
Anselm thinks it is a mistake to say that Satan did not receive the grace of perseverance because God did not give it,
for God did offer it to Satan but Satan refused it. So though
God failed to give the grace of perseverance to Satan, this
was because Satan did not accept it.[11] And, as Anselm goes on
to argue, this is the only reason God failed to give this gift.[12]

Here Anselm is discussing the original situation of
Satan and his first sin. But his doctrine of grace and freedom in general follows the account here. Unlike Augustine, who
taught that the actual imparting of grace depends not only on
the offer by God and the free acceptance of it by men but al-
also on the circumstances in which the offer and the choice
are made, Anselm teaches that the imparting of grace depends

solely on the offer by God and the free response of men. In
his view, once the offer of grace is made, the only further
thing needed for it to become effective in one's life is for
it to be accepted. The circumstances of choice have neither
a telling nor a determining effect on the choice itself. God
does not manipulate events to insure that we choose either
favorably or unfavorably.

      Anselm's explanation of predestination supports this
position. Predestination, he insists, is not foreordination
or predetermination.[13] Nevertheless, everything that occurs,
even the free choices of men, is predestined by God. How
can this be? Because predestination of evil choices occurs
through God's permissive will, not his efficient will.[14] God
predestines these choices in the same way he causes them,
i.e., by doing nothing to prevent them from occurring. "God
is said to harden a man's heart when he does not soften it,
and he is said to lead a man into temptation when he does
not deliver him from it. So, then, it is the same sort of
thing to say that God predestines evil men and their evil
works when he does not correct these men and their evil
works."[15] This is very different in both tone and substance
from Augustine: "And if the divine record be looked into
carefully, it shows that not only men's good wills...but
also those which follow the world are so entirely at the disposal of God, that he turns them whithersoever he wills, and
whensoever he wills—to bestow kindness on some, and to heap
punishment on others."[16] In Augustine the predestination of
evil deeds is active, even if it should be allowed that it is
not incompatible with free choice, for God hardens the hearts
of certain men by manipulating the circumstances of their
choices. In Anselm, however, the predestination of evil
deeds is more passive. There is no manipulation of circumstances to ensure the occurrence of evil choices that God
has foreordained. These choices are not foreordained, and
God merely refrains from preventing people from making evil

choices if that is what they decide to do. If, on the other
hand, a person decides not to reject God, then God works his
grace in his life.[17]

Not only is Anselm's outlook significantly different
from Augustine's, it is also quite different from that of
Thomas Aquinas. Thomas is closer to Augustine than he is to
Anselm on the question of divine control over the human will.
In his treatise on grace he writes, "Man is master of his
acts, both of his willing and not willing, because of the
deliberation of reason, which can be bent to one side or another. And although he is master of his deliberating, yet
this can only be by a previous deliberation: and since this
cannot go on to infinity, we must come at length to this,
that man's free choice is moved by an extrinsic principle,
which is above the human mind, namely, by God."[18] Thomas,
it is clear, holds to a compatibilist theory of free will
and determinism. Compatibilism accepts determinism and then
seeks to define freedom and moral responsibility in a way
that is consistent with it. Augustine may also be a compatibilist; but with the diversity of things he says about the
will and freedom, it is more difficult to be sure.[19] There
are both theological and secular versions of compatibilism.
Whether any version will work is still a widely debated issue. It is not my intention to enter that debate; I wish
instead to point out that in Anselm's view the fundamental
form of human freedom, a form that man never loses while he
is here on earth, is a non-deterministic one and one, therefore, which keeps him clear of compatibilism.

Anselm's theory, then, is his own. It owes much to
Augustine, but it introduces into the Augustinian framework
important clarifications and modifications. His theory is
not, as many have held, a mere echo of Augustine. Nor is it,
as others have thought, simply a way station in the development of medieval thought from the Christian Platonism of
Augustine to the Christian Aristotelianism of Thomas Aquinas.

Even with its distinctive features, Anselm's doctrine stays
fully within the bounds of Christian orthodoxy—as one would
expect from the careful and programmatic way he follows the
method of *fides quaerens intellectum*. And he avoids the
polemical, and perhaps theological, excesses of Augustine.
In its conciseness, its clarity, and the forcefulness of its
treatment of man's life in God's world, his theory is an out-
standing contribution of medieval thought.

        Anselm's doctrine is noteworthy not only in the con-
text of medieval concerns but also in a more general way.
For it is a particularly clear expression of the traditional
Christian understanding of man and freedom in contrast to
views found in secular humanism. Secular humanism considers
man the highest order of being, and offers us the picture of
autonomous man creating his own purposes and formulating his
own standards of value in a world that is otherwise governed
by mindless, impersonal causal law. In this view the independent self is the center of creative power which brings
new forms and new values into being in our personal and so-
cial lives and in our world. Autonomous man is thus independent, self-sufficient, self-creating. He is the primary
agent or actor in the world. He relies solely on his own
resources and those he can bring under his control. The
freedom of autonomous man is the ability to act at will as
he chooses for his own purposes. His fundamental enterprise
in the world is to extend his control over things and to
establish his order and his meaning in an otherwise meaning-
less world.

        In contrast to this, Anselm's doctrine, and the out-
look of Christianity generally, are grounded on the fundamental conviction that God is the creator of both man and
the world. God is thus the principal agent in the general
scheme of things. Not only did he create the world, but at
every instant he sustains and guides it for the fulfillment
of his good purpose. This purpose is not in conflict with

the good of man, it encompasses it; for God has made men not
only for himself but also for their own happiness and well-
being. Man's true self and true good, therefore, are gained
only in the fulfillment of God's purpose. In this outlook,
freedom is the freedom to respond, not the freedom to act in
one's own power as an independent being. Freedom is not
found in the self that establishes its own purposes and
values, but in the will that responds to God as he works out
the divine purpose in the world. Liberty, the highest kind
of freedom, belongs to those whose responses put them in harmony with God, which also puts them in harmony with their
own innermost beings. This is a theonomous rather than an
autonomous freedom. Its postulation implies the rejection
of the distinction which secular humanists draw between autonomy and heteronomy as a false dichotomy that overlooks a
third possibility, the possibility that an act or style of
life can be both grounded in the will of God and fully in
accord with one's own being.[20] In the Christian view that
Anselm upholds, autonomous freedom is antithetical to true
freedom, theonomous freedom, responsible freedom. Acting
autonomously, independently, self-sufficiently impedes the
work of God in one's life and in the world, for it substi-
tutes man's limited purposes for God's all-encompassing purpose. It thus isolates human beings from God, but it also
disconnects them from their own highest impulses and their
own true selves and works against their own greatest good.
In the traditional language, autonomous man is sinful man,
man in need of grace, who cannot by his own efforts—by
acting autonomously—do anything to restore the lost connection with God or to bring healing and fullness of life and
purpose to himself. Though theonomous man depends on the
working of God, he is nevertheless genuinely free. He has
the power to respond either favorably or unfavorably to God.
And his responses and his choices are decisive in determining
the character of his life and, to a degree, the state of his

world. He is not merely a passive recipient of an irresisti-
ble grace. Divine action in the world, then, is not contrary
to human freedom but supports it and depends on it.[21]

        When Anselm's definition of freedom as the ability to
preserve rectitude for its own sake is properly understood,
all this and much more is implicit in it. Anselm had a gift
for trenchant formulations. Just as the concept of the
greatest conceivable being provides him with a single lumi-
nous formula from which to derive a great deal of the Christian doctrine of God, so also the concept of freedom as the
ability to preserve rectitude for its own sake provides him
with a single simple formula that enables him to organize a
great deal of the Christian understanding of man and his
place in the world.

CHAPTER ONE: INTRODUCTION

[1]Cf. G. Stanley Kane, *"Fides Quaerens Intellectum* in Anselm's Thought," *Scottish Journal of Theology,* XXVI, 1 (Feb., 1973), pp. 40-62.

[2]*CDH,* I, 1.

[3]*St. Anselm and His Critics.*   Edinburgh: Oliver & Boyd, 1954, p. 2.

[4]Jasper Hopkins and Herbert Richardson (eds. & trs.), *Anselm of Canterbury.*   Three volumes.   Toronto and New York: The Edwin Mellen Press, 1974-76.

[5]F. S. Schmitt (ed.), *Sancti Anselmi Opera Omnia.* Six volumes.   Edinburgh: Thomas Nelson & Sons, 1946-61.

[6]Jasper Hopkins, *A Companion to the Study of Saint Anselm.*   Minneapolis: University of Minnesota Press, 1972.

[7]G. R. Evans, *Anselm and Talking about God.*   Oxford: Clarendon Press, 1978.

[8]R. W. Southern, *Saint Anselm and His Biographer.* Cambridge: Cambridge University Press, 1963.

[9]E.g., *Commentary on De Grammatico.*   Dodrecht & Boston: D. Reidel Publishing Co., 1974; *The De Grammatico of Saint Anselm: The Theory of Paronymy.*   Notre Dame, Indiana: University of Notre Dame Press, 1964; *The Logic of Saint Anselm.* Oxford: Clarendon Press, 1967.

[10]Frankfurt: Minerva.

[11]Franz Baeumker, *Die Lehre Anselms von Canterbury über den Willen und seine Wahlfreiheit.*   Band 10, Heft 6 of *Beiträge zur Geschichte der Philosophie des Mittelalters.* Munster: Aschendorff, 1912; Ernst Lohmeyer, *Die Lehre vom Willen bei Anselm von Canterbury.*   Lucka: Reinhold Berger, 1914.   In addition to these two books, Hopkins and Richard-

son (eds. & trs.) *Truth, Freedom and Evil: Three Philosophica Dialogues by Anselm of Canterbury* (New York: Harper Torchbooks, 1967) lists (p. 84) a work by G. Ottina, *La dottrina della libertà in sant' Anselmo*, which it indicates was published in Milano in 1962. I have, however, been unable to locate it. It is not listed in catalogs of the Library of Congress or the British Library, nor is it included in a bibliography of Italian books printed during 1960-64. I am indebted to Bill Wortman of Miami University Libraries for this bibliographic information.

[12]Johannes Verweyen, *Das Problem der Willenfreiheit in der Scholastik*. Heidelberg: Carl Winters' Universitatsbuchhandlung, 1909, p. 50.

[13]E.g. Howard A. Redmond, *The Omnipotence of God*. Philadelphia: Westminster Press, 1964; Charles de Rémusat, *Anselme de Cantorbéry*. Second edition. Paris: Libraire Académique, 1868, p. 393; J. F. Nourrisson, *La Philosophie de saint Augustin*. Second edition. Paris, 1866, Vol. II, p. 167; J. Fischer, *Die Erkenntnislehre Anselms von Canterbury*. Munster: Aschendorff, 1911, p. 46.

[14]Lohmeyer uses this phrase on p. 53, *op. cit.*, in connection with a particular point of Anselm's doctrine, but it aptly sums up what he is seeking throughout his study.

[15]*Op. cit.*, p. 26f.

[16]Kane, *art. cit.*

[17]See chapter two, section III below.

[18]Cf. *De Processione Spiritus Sancti*.

[19]I elaborate each of these points further in subsequent chapters.

[20]*DV*, Preface.

[21]Cf. *DV*, VI & VIII.

[22]This is the term Jasper Hopkins aptly uses to refer to *NUW*.

CHAPTER TWO: WILL: THE BASIC FACULTY

[1]Baeumker, *op. cit.*, p. 1.

[2]There has been some question concerning whether Anselm himself actually wrote this work as we have it in its

present form. G. Gerberon, the seventeenth-century editor
of Anselm's work, whose edition is used in Migne's *Patrologia
Latina* (vols. 158-159), thought that he did; cf. Gerberon's
"Censura Tractatus de Voluntate," *Patrologia Latina*, vol.
158, col. 23C. Agreeing with Gerberon is Franz Baeumker; *op.
cit.*, p. 6. Imelda Choquette, "Voluntas, Affectio and
Potestas in the Liber de Voluntate of Saint Anselm," *Medieval
Studies*, IV (1942), p. 62n, mentions A. Levasti (*Sant' Anselmo, Vita e Pensiero*, pp. 112-4) as also agreeing with this
view. F. S. Schmitt, however, editor of the critical edition
of Anselm's writings, thinks that its present structure cannot be traced directly to Anselm, but he grants that the
thought is thoroughly Anselmian and hypothesizes that it is
based on an original source; cf. *NUW*, p. 19. Imelda Choquette does not directly enter this controversy, but concludes simply that "the doctrine of the treatise is undeniably Anselmian"; *art. cit.*, p. 62. One who might wish to
dispute this point is Lohmeyer; cf. *op. cit.*, p. 16f. He
thinks that while some of the basic distinctions in this
work are Anselm's, not all of them are, for he thinks that
the logical fine points in some of the distinctions are too
subtle for Anselm and can only have been added in by a later
medieval hand. Anselm, however, was much more sophisticated
in logical matters than Lohmeyer realizes. Moreover, virtually all the distinctions which are given in *Liber de
Voluntate* are reflected in other, undeniably authentic writings of Anselm, so it is safe to hold that the doctrine of
this little work is Anselm's.

[3] *NUW*, pp. 37-39.

[4] *CDH*, I, i.

[5] Cf. *DV*, passim.

[6] *DLA*, III; *DV*, XIII.

[7] *DC*, III, xi.

[8] *Ibid.*; cf. *Liber de Voluntate, Patrologia Latina,* Vol.
158, col. 487A.

[9] *Ibid.*

[10] *Ibid.*

[11] *Ibid.*

[12] *Ibid.*

[13] *Ibid.*

[14]*Ibid.*

[15]*Ibid.*

[16]*Ibid.*

[17]*Ibid.*

[18]*Ibid.*

[19]*Ibid.*

[20]*Ibid.*

[21]*Ibid.*

[22]*Ibid.*

[23]The precise character of the two affections and the manner in which they are related to the instrument as its dispositions are examined in detail in the following chapter.

[24]*Categories,* Ia, 1-6.   This is J. L. Ackrill's translation, except "equivocal" has been substituted for "hononymous."   Cf. Boethius, *In Categorias Aristotelis,* I, *Patrologia Latina,* vol. 64, col. 163D.

[25]Not only is this true of Anselm's use of the term "equivocal," it is also explicitly recognized to be the case by Aristotle; cf. *Topics,* I, 107b, 6-13; *Metaphysics,* IV, 2, 1003a34-b5; XI, 3, 1060b36-1061a7.   For a discussion of Aristotle's theory of equivocals, see J. Owens, *The Doctrine of Being in the Aristotelian Metaphysics,* pp. 107-137.

[26]*NUW,* p. 44; *Liber de Voluntate, Patrologia Latina,* vol. 158, col. 488b.

[27]This is a point that Etienne Gilson fails to grasp. He writes, "'Power,' for him [Anselm], is the aptitude to do what one wills."   *The Spirit of Medieval Philosophy,* p. 317. Cf. *A History of Christian Philosophy in the Middle Ages,* p. 137, where Gilson, in view of Anselm's definition of *"potestas"* as *"aptitudo ad faciendum,"* characterizes the will as a "power of execution."   Anselm's definition of *potestas,* as opposed to his understanding of the *potestas volendi,* makes no reference whatsoever to the will or to willing.   This is a significant point, for Gilson's account of Anselm's definition allows him to consider Anselm's doctrine of freedom not only as the ability to will but also as the ability to *do* what one wills.   This, however, is false to Anselm, for whom the only form of doing (in general) with which freedom is concerned is willing.

[28]Cf. Gilbert Ryle, *The Concept of Mind*, ch. 3: "The Will."

[29]*CDH*, I, xi.

[30]Cf. *DV*, XII.

[31]*DV*, XII.

[32]*Ibid.*

[33]*Ibid.*

[34]*DV*, V.

[35]*DV*, XII.

[36]*Ibid.*; cf. *DCV*, III: *DC*, I, vii; *DCD*, XIX.

[37]*La Rectitudo chez saint Anselme*, p. 76.

[38]*La philosophie de saint Anselme*, p. 77.

[39]*Art. cit.*, pp. 40-62.

[40]*DC*, III, xi.

[41]*Ibid.*

[42]*Ibid.*

[43]*Ibid.*

[44]*Ibid.*, cf. *DLA*, VIII.

[45]*DCD*, VIII.

[46]*De Grammatico*, XII. The translation is D. P. Henry's, from *The De Grammatico of Saint Anselm*, p. 64.

[47]*DC*, III, xi; *DCV*, IV.

[48]*DC*, III, xi; *DCV*, IV.

[49]A point which Anselm makes; *DCD*, XII.

[50]*Die Erkenntnislehre Anselms von Canterbury*, pp. 7-8.

[51]*DC*, III, xi.

[52]E.g., Filliatre, *op. cit.*, pp. 77-78.

[53]Anselm's attitude is similar to one expressed by
C.S. Lewis: "Revelation appears to me to be purely practical,
to be addressed to the particular animal, Fallen Man, to the
relief of his urgent necessities—not to the spirit of inquiry in man for the gratification of his liberal curiosity."
"Dogma and the Universe," in *God in the Dock*. Grand Rapids:
William B. Eerdmans Co., 1970, p. 43.

[54]*CDH*, II, vii; cf. *Monologion*, XVII; *De Grammatico*,
XIII.

[55]*CDH*, II, iii.

[56]*DCV*, IV.

[57]*De Moribus Ecclesiae*, I, 27, 52.

[58]*A History of Christian Philosophy in the Middle Ages*
p. 74.

[59]*DC*, III, xi; cf. *DCV*, V.

[60]Anselm never explicitly states this, but it is en-
tailed by what he does state. He tells us that reason is an
instrument of the soul which the soul uses for reasoning. If
the soul uses it, it is obviously under the control of the
soul. But the will is the instrument by which the soul exercises this control. It follows, therefore, that reason is
governed by the will. Anselm also asserts, as we shall
presently see, that the exercise of every power (*potestas*)
in man depends upon the will. Since reason is one of man's
powers, the power of discernment ("*potestatem discernendi*"
[*CDH*, II, i]), it is clear that the exercise of one's rational powers is under the control of the will.

[61]*DCV*,   IV.

[62]*Ibid.*

[63]*CDH*, II, x.

[64]*The Logic of Saint Anselm*, p. 167.

[65]*CDH*, II, x.

[66]*Ibid.*

[67]*Ibid.*

[68]He argues that insofar as each person is human, he
is responsible for the guilt of original sin, for it was

through the will in Adam, which in him belonged to human nature as a whole, that the original sin was committed. Because all humans share this nature, they are responsible for
the sin of this nature, which acted as a whole through Adam's
will. Cf. *DCV*, XXIII & XXVII.

[69] *DV*, XII.

[70] *DCV*, III.

[71] Cf. *DCV*, III; *DV*, XII.

[72] *De Spiritu et Littera*, XXXI, liii (tr. Peter Holmes).

[73] *Confessions*, VIII, viii (tr. J. G. Pilkington).

[74] Romans 7:18.

[75] Cf., e.g., *De Spiritu et Littera*, XXXIII, lix.

[76] *Confessions*, VIII, viii & ix.

[77] *Confessions*, VIII, vii.

[78] See, for instance, what he says about the moral
standing of the Christian virgins who were violated by ma-
rauding   soldiers: "Let this, therefore, in the first
place be laid down as an unassailable position, that the
virtue which makes the life good has its throne in the soul,
and thence rules the members of the body, which becomes holy
in virtue of the holiness of the will; and that while the
will remains firm and unshaken, nothing that another person
does with the body, or upon the body, is any fault of the
person who suffers it, so long as he cannot escape it without sin." *De Civitate Dei*, I, xvi. And: "Since no one,
however magnanimous and pure, has always the disposal of his
own body, but can control only the consent and refusal of
his will, what sane man can suppose that, if his body be
seized and forcibly made use of to satisfy the lust of another, he thereby loses his purity?" *Ibid.*, I, xviii (tr.
M. Dods).

[79] *DC*, III, xi.

[80] Cf. Schmitt, *Sancti Anselmi Opera Omnia*, volume VI.
On pages 3-18 Schmitt lists all the Scripture references
which are found in Anselm's writings.

[81] *DLA*, V; *DC*, I, vi.

[82] *DLA*, III.

[83]*Ibid.*

[84]*DC*, III, xi.

[85]*DLA*, V.

[86]*Ibid.*

[87]*DCD*, XXVII.

[88]*DCD*, III.

[89]*DLA*, V.

[90]This is one more indication of Anselm's inability, noted earlier, to sense any ambiguity in the process of will

[91]*DCD*, XII.

[92]*DC*, III, xi.

[93]*CDH*, I, xvi.

[94]*DCD*, V.

[95]This makes it quite legitimate to use Anselm's claim about Satan's will and that of the angels as a source for understanding his doctrine of the human will—something I have been doing and will continue to do.

[96]Cf. Kane, *art. cit.*

[97]*CDH*, I, i; cf. *DC*, III, xiii.

[98]*CDH*, I, xvi.

[99]*CDH*, "Commendation of the Work to Pope Urban II."

[100]*DLA*, VIII.

[101]*DC*, III, vi.

[102]*DCD*, IX & XVI.

[103]*DC*, III, iii & xiii.

[104]*DC*, III, iii.

[105]*CDH*, II, i.

[106]*Ibid.*

[107]*Ibid.*

[108]*Ibid.* (The emphasis is mine.)

[109]*CDH,* I, xvi.

[110]In *CDH,* II, i, Anselm uses this phrase three times.

[111]*CDH,* II, i.

[112]*Liber de Voluntate, Patrologia Latina,* vol. 158, col. 488A-B.

[113]*CDH,* I, xi.

[114]*DCV,* XII.

[115]*DC,* III, iii & iv.

[116]*DCD,* XIV & XXV.

[117]*DC,* III, iv & xiii.

[118]*DC,* III, vi.

[119]*Ibid.* Cf. also *DC,* III, vii; *DCV,* II & VIII.

[120]This question of the relation of reason and will is directly relevant to the question of the relation of faith and reason. For a study of Anselm's doctrine of faith and reason, see my *art. cit.*

[121]*DCD,* XXIII; *DLA,* IX.

[122]*DLA,* XIV.

[123]Filliatre, *op. cit.,* p. 413.

[124]*Ibid.,* pp. 448-9.

[125]Pouchet, *op. cit.,* pp. 21, 75.

[126]J. Bayart, "The Concept of Mystery according to St. Anselm of Canterbury," *Recherches de théologie ancienne et médiévale,* IX (1937), pp. 142-3, 145-6. Bayart completely overlooks a mass of relevant material. He states that "Saint Anselm's remarks on the influence of sin on our spiritual faculties are limited to a few passages of the *Proslogion*" (p. 142).

[127]Mandonnet, *Siger de Brabant et l'averroisme latin au XIIIe siècle,* vol. I, p. lxiv.

[128]Gilson, *The Spirit of Medieval Philosophy*, p. 309.

[129]Fischer, *op. cit.*, pp. 13-15; see p. 46 for Fischer's remarks on Anselm's views of mysticism and contemplation.

[130]Cf. Thomas Aquinas's treatment of this question, *Summa Theologiae*, I, 82, 3.

[131]This is the way Paul Vignaux understands the problem. He says that the intellectualism-voluntarism dispute centers around the question "by what power of the intellect or the will the soul enters into the possession of the absoluate Good, into the enjoyment of the divine Trinity." *Philosophy in the Middle Ages*, p. 204.

[132]Gilson develops the question in these terms; cf. *The Spirit of Medieval Philosophy*, pp. 310-12.

CHAPTER THREE: THE AFFECTIONS OF THE WILL

[1]*DC*, III, xi.

[2]*Commodum* is a word that is impossible to translate into a single English word. Probably the best translation is that given by V. J. Bourke, who renders it by a phrase, "what is naturally suitable" ("Human Tendencies, Will and Freedom," in *L'Homme et son destin: Actes du premier congrès internationale de philosophie médiévale*, p. 82). A *commodum* for some being is a good or a value which is fitting or suitable for that kind of being. A good sign of the difficulty in translating the term is the wide variety of translations that have been given. Besides Bourke's translation, it has been translated as "pleasure" (by Jasper Hopkins and Herbert Richardson, in the Harvard Divinity School Library edition of their translation of *De casu diaboli*, in *Anselm of Canterbury, Theological Treatises*, Vol. I, pp. 108-109); "what is pleasing" (also by Hopkins and Richardson, *ibid.*, p. 89); "the useful" (by Imelda Choquette, "Voluntas, Affectio and Potestas in the *Liber de Voluntate* of Saint Anselm," *Medieval Studies*, IV (1942), p. 66; by Robert Pouchet, *La Rectitudo chez Saint Anselme*, p. 193; and by Etienne Gilson, *A History of Christian Philosophy in the Middle Ages*, p. 137); "well-being" (by J. Rohmer, *La Finalité morale chez les théologiens de saint Augustin à Duns Scotus*, p. 163); and as "the beneficial" (by G. Stanley Kane and Charles Waldrop, in their translation of *DC* in Hopkins and Richardson's edition of *Anselm of Canterbury, Theological Treatises*, Vol. II, 92; and by Hopkins and Richardson in the Harper Torchbook edition of their translation of *DC* in *Anselm of Canterbury, Truth, Freedom and Evil: Three Philosophical Dialogues*, p. 172). John Sheets translated the plural *commoda* as "goods"

("Justice in the Moral Thought of Saint Anselm," *Modern Schoolman*, XXV (1948), p. 138n). Because of the difficulty in providing an adequate translation of this term, I do not attempt to do so. I use the common term "happiness" except in those contexts where the thought or idiom calls for a different rendering.

[3] *DC*, III, xi.

[4] *DC*, III, xii.

[5] This is a notion which John Locke criticizes. Having argued that the will is one kind of power and that freedom is another, Locke proceeds to argue the unintelligibility of the question of the freedom of the will by saying, "...to ask whether the will has freedom is to ask whether one power has another power, one ability another ability; a question at first sight too grossly absurd to make a dispute, or need an answer. For, who is it that sees not that powers belong only to agents, and are attributes only of substances, and not of powers themselves?" *An Essay Concerning Human Understanding*, Book II, xxi, 16.

[6] *DC*, III, xi.

[7] A. C. Ewing, *The Fundamental Questions of Philosophy*. New York: Collier Books, 1962, p. 117.

[8] We will see later in this chapter a qualification on the claim that one always without exception wills in accordance with each of his affections; see section III A below. Here I am concentrating on the passage in which he defines affections and am analyzing the implications of what he says there.

[9] *DLA*, V.

[10] Cf. *DV*, XII, where "*sponte*" and "*naturaliter*" are opposed (Anselm explicitly equates "*sponte*" with what is done through the will; *DC*, I, iii: "*Opus vero voluntatis.... voluntarium sive spontaneum est...*"). In *DCV*, XXIII, the contrasting opposites are what occur "*propria voluntate*" and what "*exigit natura*." Besides these passages, in which what occurs through the will is set off from what occurs by nature, there are many passages in which what occurs through the will is opposed to what occurs through necessity. For just a small sample, see *CDH*, I, x ("*necessitate*" vs. "*libera voluntate*" and "*sponte*" vs. "*necessitate*"); *CDH*, II, xvii ("*ex voluntate*" vs. "*ex necessitate*"); *CDH*, II, XVI ("*necessitate*" vs. "*sola sua potestate*"); *DC*, I, vi ("*sola voluntas*" vs. "*vis necessitatis*"); *DC*, II, iii ("*necessitate*" vs. "*sola voluntate*").

[11]Gilbert Ryle, *op. cit.*, p. 118.

[12]*Ibid.*

[13]*DC*, III, xi.

[14]*Ibid.*

[15]*DC*, III, xiii.

[16]E.g., Jasper Hopkins and Herbert Richardson, "Editors Introduction" in *Anselm of Canterbury, Truth, Freedom and Evil: Three Philosophical Dialogues*, p. 26; Archibald Alexander, *Theories of the Will in the History of Philosophy*, p. 122.

[17]*DCD*, VII.

[18]This is true just as much of the affection for justice as it is of the affection for happiness, even though there seems to be evidence against this view in Anselm's writings. For, whenever he mentions any specific characteristic of desire and concupiscence (and also of appetite, since they are all in the same general category for Anselm), they are characteristics which could only be ascribed to the affection for happiness. He says of all three of them—desire, concupiscence and appetite—that in themselves they are not morally evil, but may become good or evil depending on the circumstances and the manner in which one consents to or gives in to them; cf. *DCV*, IV; *DCD*, VII. Thus, in Anselm's mind desire may be associated particularly with the affection for happiness. This, however, is a specialized use, which does not exclude the idea that an *affectio*, qua *affectio* and not just qua *affectio ad beatitudinem*, has features which are normally associated with desires.

[19]*DCD*, XII.

[20]*Ibid.*

[21]*Ibid.*

[22]*Ibid.*

[23]*Ibid.*

[24]*Ibid.*

[25]*DC*, III, xiii.

[26]*DC*, III, xi. Cf. *DCV*, I, X, XII, and XVII; *DCD*, IX.

²⁷Fairweather, "Truth, Justice and Moral Responsibil-
ty in the Thought of St. Anselm," *L'Homme et son destin*,
. 391.   Cf. Jean Rohmer, *La finalité morale chez les théologiens de saint Augustin à Duns Scotus*, p. 159; V. J. Bourke,
art. cit., p. 78.

²⁸Cf. *DCD*, XVI.

²⁹*DC*, I, vi.

³⁰*DCD*, XVI.

³¹*DC*, I, vi.

³²*DV*, VII.

³³Cf. *DCD*, II & III; *DC*, III, xi & xiv.

³⁴*DCV*, XXIII.

³⁵*Ibid.*

³⁶*DCD*, XIII.

³⁷*Ibid.*

³⁸*Ibid.*

³⁹*Ibid.*

⁴⁰*Ibid.*

⁴¹*DCD*, XII; *DLA*, V.

⁴²*DC*, III, xiii.

⁴³*Ibid.*

⁴⁴*Ibid.*; cf. *DCV*, V.

⁴⁵*DCD*, XIV.

⁴⁶See below, section IIIA of the present chapter.

⁴⁷See section II of chapter two, above.   Cf. *DV*, XII.

⁴⁸*CDH*, II, x; cf. *DCD*, XVIII.

⁴⁹*CDH*, II, x.

⁵⁰*DC*, III, xiii.

⁵¹*Ibid.*

[52]E.g., Robert Pouchet, *op. cit.*, pp. 146-69; E. R.
Fairweather, "'*Justitia Dei*' as the '*Ratio*' of the Incarnation," *Spicilegium Beccense,* I, pp. 327-35.

[53]Often, however, in a negative sense, as when he
speaks of sin as a "disordered" or "inordinate" willing of
beneficial things; cf. *DCD*, IV-VII.

[54]*DCD*, IV.

[55]*Ibid.*

[56]*Ibid.*

[57]*DCD*, XII.

[58]*DCD*, XXV.

[59]*CDH*, II, x.

[60]*Ibid,; DCD*, XVIII.

[61]*DC*, III, xii.

[62]*DCD*, VI.

[63]*DC*, III, xiii.

[64]*DCV*, V.

[65]*DC*, III, xiii.

[66]*DCD*, VI.

[67]*DCD*, XXV.

[68]*DC*, III, xiii.

[69]Cf. section II B of the present chapter, above, pp.
74-91.

[70]*DC*, III, xi.

[71]*DC*, III, xii.

[72]*Ibid.*

[73]*DC*, III, xiii.

[74]Filliatre, *op. cit.*, p. 389.

[75]McIntyre, *op. cit.*, p. 64 (emphasis is McIntyre's).

[76]Rohmer, *op. cit.*, pp. 158, 153.

[77]Bourke, *art. cit.*, p. 78. In view of Anselm's doctrine that man's ultimate end consists of both happiness and justice, and that the affections have been given in order to make it possible for man to achieve these ends, I cannot agree with Bourke that the affection *ad commodum* wills only an earthly and temporal happiness.

[78]Fairweather, "Truth, Justice and Moral Responsibility in the Thought of St. Anselm," *L'Homme et son destin,* pp. 388-9.

[79]*DLA*, IX.

[80]*DCD*, XXIII.

[81]*DCD*, XIX.

[82]*DC*, III, xiii.

[83]*DCD*, XXIII.

[84]*Ibid.*; *DC*, III, xi.

[85]*DC*, III, ix.

[86]A conclusion that is in accord with the findings of section IV B of chapter two, above.

[87]Cf. J. Rohmer, *op. cit.*, p. 149: "Nous croyons que son importance [the importance of Anselm's concept of rectitude] ne saurait être exagerée: elle pose pour la première fois dans la pensée médiévale la finalité morale en dohors du plan eudemoniste et utilitariste d'Aristote."

[88]*DC*, III, xiii.

CHAPTER FOUR: VOLITIONS

[1]*NUW*, p. 38. The translations from NUW in this chapter are D. P. Henry's in *The Logic of Saint Anselm*. This one is found on p. 130 of Henry's book.

[2]*Ibid.* (Henry, p. 130).

[3]*Ibid.* (Henry, p. 131).

[4]*Ibid.* (Henry, p. 131).

[5]*NUW*, pp. 38-39.

[6]*NUW*, pp. 25-37.

[7]*DCD*, XI.

[8]Henry translates *significatio per se* "precisive signification," and *significatio per aliud* as "oblique signification." Cf. *The De Grammatico of St. Anselm*, p. 64ff.
The distinction is introduced in *DG* and is used there with
respect to paronyms. But *DG* indicates that it can be extended to verbs also; *DG*, XV.

[9]*DCD*, XII.

[10]*DCD*, I.

[11]In this I am following Henry, as I also do in the
schematization of the forms of *facere*. Cf. Henry, *op. cit.*,
pp. 120-24, and "St. Anselm on Scriptural Analysis," *Sophia*
(Australia), I (October, 1962), pp. 8-15.

[12]*NUW*, pp. 29-32.

[13]*Ibid.*

[14]Henry, *The Logic of St. Anselm*, p. 126.

[15]*NUW*, p. 29.

[16]*DC*, II, ii.

[17]*NUW*, p. 39 (Henry, *Logic*, p. 132).

[18]*Ibid.*

[19]*Ibid.*

[20]*Ibid.*

[21]Choquette, *art. cit.*, p. 73.

[22]*DC*, III, xi, prior recensio; found on p. 282 of
Schmitt, *Sancti Anselmi Opera Omnia*, Vol. II. The translation is my own.

CHAPTER FIVE: FREEDOM

[1]*DLA*, I; *DC*, *Praefatio*.

[2]Cf., e.g., *DLA*, I & X; *DC*, I, iii-vi; III, iv; *CDH*,
II, xi & xvii.

[3] E.g., *DC* I, v; III, i.

[4] *DLA*, XIII.

[5] Schmitt, "Eine fruehe Rezension des Werkes *De Concordia* des hl. Anselm von Canterbury," *Revue Bénédictine*, XLVIII (1936), p. 62.

[6] *DC*, III, xiv.

[7] Cf. Charlton T. Lewis, *A Latin Dictionary*. New York & London: Harper & Brothers Publishers, 1899

[8] *DC*, I, vi.

[9] Cf. Pouchet, *op. cit.*, p. 96n; Rohmer, *op. cit.*, p. 176.

[10] *DC*, III, iii.

[11] *DLA*, III.

[12] *DC*, III, i.

[13] *DC*, III, vi.

[14] *Ibid*.

[15] E.g. Baeumker, *op. cit.*, p. 26f; Filliatre, *op. cit.*, p. 380.

[16] Cf. *De Actis cum Felice Manichaeo*, II, iii & *De Libero Arbitrio*, I, xvi, 35. I owe these references to Schmitt, *Sancti Anselmi Opera Omnia*, Vol. I, p. 207n.

[17] *DLA*, I.

[18] How Anselm can maintain all this without inconsistency will become apparent only in light of what is said in section VI of this chapter.

[19] *DLA*, I.

[20] *Ibid*.

[21] *DLA*, VIII; *CDH*, II, i; *DCV*, XII.

[22] *DLA*, I.

[23] *DLA*, II.

[24] This example was suggested to me by Kenneth Kennard.

[25] In line with this Anselm gives a slightly different definition for free will (*liberum arbitrium*) than he does for freedom of the will (*libertas arbitrii*), and the distinction between them is correlated with the distinction noted in these paragraphs. Cf. *DLA*, III: "...illa libertas arbitrii est potestas servandi rectitudinem voluntatis propter ipsam rectitudinem.... Iam ergo clarum est liberum arbitrium non esse aliud quam arbitrium potens servare rectitudinem voluntatis propter ipsam rectitudinem."

[26] See section II of chapter three, above.

[27] *DLA*, III. One should not place too great an emphasis on the fact that Anselm uses "keep" in this definition rather than "choose" or "do," for in *DV*, XII, he explains that the only way to keep rectitude is to choose it and that it is the same act by which rectitude is willed and kept.

[28] Cf. J. L. Austin, "Ifs and Cans," *Philosophical Papers*. Oxford: Clarendon Press, 1961, p. 177f. As is well known, Austin distinguished opportunity and ability as two "restricted senses" of "can" and he speaks of the inclusive sense as "the 'all-in' sense."

[29] *DLA*, IV.

[30] *DC*, III, xii.

[31] *DC*, III, xiii; cf. *DC*, III, iii.

[32] *DLA*, II.

[33] *Ibid.*; cf. *DV*, VIII.

[34] *DLA*, V.

[35] *Ibid.*

[36] *Ibid.*

[37] *Ibid.*

[38] *Ibid.*

[39] *DLA*, VI.

[40] *Ibid.*

[41] *Ibid.*

^{42}"Editors' Introduction," *Anselm of Canterbury, Truth, Freedom, and Evil,* pp. 34-35.

^{43}*DLA,* VII.

^{44}*Ibid.*

^{45}*Ibid.*

^{46}*Op. cit.,* p. 32. Hopkins develops this argument also in *A Companion to the Study of St. Anselm,* p. 147f.

^{47}*Ibid.*

^{48}Notice the use of this phrase in the two previous quotations.

^{49}*Op. cit.,* p. 31.

^{50}*Ibid.,* p. 37. This criticism occurs in a section in which the authors are comparing Anselm and J. L. Austin, and the immediate target of this criticism is actually Austin. It is clear, however, that the authors mean to include Anselm in this criticism also.

^{51}*DLA,* VII.

^{52}Cf. *DCD,* XXVII.

^{53}We see here a reflection of the point made in chapter two that Anselm, unlike Augustine, cannot conceive of an ineffective volition. In Anselm's view, one either wills something or one does not.

^{54}*DLA,* VII.

^{55}Again, cf. *DCD,* XXVII.

^{56}These designations are used by M. Adler, *The Idea of Freedom.* Garden City, N.Y.: Doubleday & Co., 1958, Vol. I, p. 167ff. and *passim.*

^{57}*Ibid.,* p. 136. Mary Clark claims that "the distinction between free will and freedom—a distinction indispensable to a correct understanding of Augustine's teaching on freedom—is taken up and utilized by Anselm." *Augustine Philosopher of Freedom.* New York and other cities: Desclée Company, 1958, p. 175. This is one more example of a scholar seeing more of Augustine in Anselm than is there.

^{58}Cf. Adler, *op. cit.,* p. 136; Gilson, *The Christian Philosophy of Saint Augustine,* pp. 157-64; and *The Spirit of*

Medieval Philosophy, pp. 315ff.

[59]E.g., R. W. Southern, *St. Anselm and His Biographer,* pp. 104-5; Pouchet, *op. cit.,* pp. 100, 110; Filliatre, *op. cit.,* p. 380.

[60]E.g., Rohmer, *op. cit.,* p. 177.

[61]E.g., Filliatre, *op. cit.,* pp. 414-418; Baeumker, *op. cit.,* pp. 24-26; Domet de Vorges, *Saint Anselme,* pp. 203-13.

[62]E.g., Dom O. Lottin, *Psychologie et Morale aux XII*[e] *et XIII*[e] *siècles,* Vol. I, p. 223.

[63]*Op. cit.,* p. 562.

[64]Cf. *DCD,* XII.

[65]"Human Tendencies, Will and Freedom," *L'Homme et son destin,* p. 82; *The Will in Western Thought,* ch. 4, especially pp. 82-83.

[66]*CDH,* II, x.

CHAPTER SIX: FREEDOM AND GRACE

[1]*DLA,* I; *DC, Praefatio.*

[2]*DC,* II, iii & III, i.

[3]*DC,* III, v.

[4]*DV,* XII.

[5]*DC,* III, iii.

[6]*Ibid.*

[7]*DC,* III, xi. Cf. *DV,* XII: "We receive justice from God, from whom we simultaneously receive the having and willing and keeping of rectitude of will. And as soon as we have and will this rectitude of will, we may be said to have justice."

[8]*Ibid.*

[9]*DC,* III, v.

[10]*DC,* III, iii; also iv & v.

[11]*DC,* III, xiv.

[12]*Ibid*.

[13]Cf. *DC*, II, ii; III, xi; III, v; *DCD*, XX.

[14]See the application below of Anselm's distinction between proper and improper modes of speaking to understanding his definition of freedom.

[15]Cf. *CDH*, II, x: "When an angel could have deprived himself of justice, and could have made himself unjust and did not, it is correct to say he gave himself justice and made himself just. In this way, then, he possesses justice from himself—since the creature cannot possess it from himself in any other way—and for that reason he is to be praised for his justice." What is said of angels here applies also to human beings, since, as we have seen, their situation with respect to freedom and justice is essentially the same as the angels'.

[16]*DC*, III, xi.

[17]See the tabulation of these modes in chapter four, above.

[18]*DV*, II and *passim*.

CHAPTER SEVEN: THE HISTORICAL SIGNIFICANCE OF
            ANSELM'S DOCTRINE

[1]N. P. Williams, *The Grace of God*. London: Hodder and Stoughton, 1966, p. 60.

[2]Cf. Henry Bettenson (ed.), *Documents of the Christian Church*. New York & London: Oxford University Press, 1943, pp. 85-87.

[3]*Op. cit.*, p. 67.

[4]For some details concerning this disagreement, see Gerald Bonner, *St. Augustine of Hippo*. Philadelphia: The Westminster Press, 1963, pp. 386-90.

[5]Hopkins, *op. cit.*, pp. 157-8 (the emphasis is Hopkins'). Hopkins notes that "In *De Libertate* 12 Anselm utilizes Augustine's very terminology in describing fallen man: *non potest non peccare*." It might be thought that this counts against my interpretation, given in chapter six, of Anselm's doctrine of human freedom as being characterized by the ability to sin or not to sin. A reading of *DLA*, XII, however, shows that this is not the case. For what

Anselm is claiming in this chapter when he says that the
sinner is unable not to sin is merely that the sinner is unable to recover rectitude on his own. And that clearly is
consistent with the understanding of human freedom that I
have ascribed to Anselm.

[6]For a host of references, see Eugène Portalié, *A
Guide to the Thought of Saint Augustine*. Chicago: Henry
Regnery Company, 1960, pp. 196-8.

[7]*Op. cit.*, pp. 198-229.

[8]Cf. *De Gratia et Libero Arbitrio*, XXXII.

[9]Cf. *De Praedestinatione Sanctorum*, XIV; *De Gratia et
Libero Arbitrio*, XLI-XLIII.

[10]*DCD*, II.

[11]*DCD*, III.

[12]*Ibid.*

[13]*DC*, II, i.

[14]Cf. ch. 4 above.

[15]*DC*, II, ii.

[16]*De Gratia et Libero Arbitrio*, XLI.

[17]Hopkins, therefore, is mistaken when he asserts that,
"Like Augustine, [Anselm] can silently leave it a mystery
why this grace, which cooperates with the act of faith by
being its necessary precondition, should be given to some
men and not to others." *Op. cit.*, p. 158.

[18]*Summa Theologiae*, II-II, q. 109, a. 2, ad 1.

[19]If Etienne Gilson's interpretation of Augustine is
correct, he is a compatibilist. Cf. *The Christian Philosophy of Saint Augustine*. New York: Random House, 1960, p.
157.

[20]Cf. Paul Tillich, *Systematic Theology*. Volume One.
Chicago: University of Chicago Press, 1951, pp. 83-86.

[21]For a contemporary discussion of responsive freedom,
see Donald Evans, "Does Religious Faith Conflict with Moral
Freedom?" in Gene Outka & John P. Reeder, Jr. (eds.), *Religion and Morality: A Collection of Essays*. Garden City,

N.Y.: Anchor Books, 1973, pp. 348-392.   At points, however,
Evans develops the notion in ways that would be disagreeable
to Anselm.

BIBLIOGRAPHY

I. TEXTS AND ENGLISH TRANSLATIONS

Anselm of Canterbury, *Opera Omnia.* Edited by G. Gerberon.
In J. P. Migne (ed.), *Patrologia Latina,* vols. 158-159.

_____, *Sancti Anselmi Opera Omnia.* Edited by F. S.
Schmitt. 6 vols. Edinburgh: Thomas Nelson & Sons,
1946-61.

_____, *St. Anselm: Basic Writings.* Second Edition.
Translated by S. N. Deane. LaSalle, Illinois: The
Open Court Publishing Company, 1962.

_____, *Truth, Freedom, and Evil: Three Philosophical Dia-
logues.* Translated and edited by Jasper Hopkins and
Herbert Richardson. New York: Harper Torchbooks,
Harper & Row, 1967.

Fairweather, Eugene R. (ed. and tr.), *A Scholastic Miscel-
lany: Anselm to Ockham.* Vol. X of *Library of Christian Classics,* edited by John Baillie, *et al.* Philadelphia: Westminster Press, 1956.

Henry, Desmond P., *The De Grammatico of St. Anselm. The
Theory of Paronymy.* Vol. XVIII of *Publications in
Medieval Studies,* edited by Philip S. Moore. Notre
Dame, Ind.: Notre Dame University Press, 1964.

_____, *The Logic of St. Anselm.* Oxford: Clarendon Press,
1967.

Hopkins, Jasper and Herbert Richardson (eds.), *Anselm of
Canterbury: Theological Treatises.* 3 vols. Cambridge,
Mass.: Harvard Divinity School Library, 1965-67.

_____ (trs. and eds.), *Anselm of Canterbury.* 4 vols.
(The first three volumes contain the complete treatises of Anselm in English translation. The fourth
volume, by Jasper Hopkins, deals with hermeneutical

and textual problems in the complete treatises, and
contains an extensive bibliography.) Toronto & New
York: The Edwin Mellen Press, 1974-76.

McKeon, Richard (ed. and tr.), *Selections from Medieval
Philosophers.* New York: Charles Scribner's Sons,
1929.

Schmitt, F. S., "Eine fruehe Rezension des Werkes *De Concordia* des hl. Anselm von Canterbury," *Revue Bénédictine,*
XLVIII (1936).

_____, *Ein neues unvollendetes Werk des hl. Anselm von
Canterbury: De Potestate et Impotentia, Possibilitate
et Impossibilitate, Necessitate et Libertate.* Band
XXXIII, Heft 3 of *Beiträge zur Geschichte der
Philosophie des Mittelalters.* Munchen: Aschendorff,
1936. A translation of this work is included under
the title of "Philosophical Fragments" in Hopkins' *A
Companion to the Study of St. Anselm* and in volume two
of Hopkins and Richardson, *Anselm of Canterbury.*

II. SECONDARY SOURCES

Adler, Mortimer J., "Freedom: A Study of the Development of
the Concept in the English and American Traditions of
Philosophy," *Review of Metaphysics,* XI (1958).

_____, *The Idea of Freedom.* 2 vols. Garden City, N.Y.:
Doubleday and Co., Inc., 1958-61.

Alexander, A., *Theories of the Will in the History of
Philosophy.* New York: Charles Scribner's Sons, 1898.

Armstrong, A. H. (ed.), *The Cambridge History of Later Greek
and Early Medieval Philosophy.* Cambridge: Cambridge
University Press, 1967.

Atkins, Anselm, "Caprice: The Myth of the Fall in Anselm
and Dostoevsky," *Journal of Religion,* 47 (October,
1967).

Auer, Johann, *Die Entwicklung der Gnadenlehre in der
Hochscholastik.* 2 vols. Frieburg: Verlag Herder,
1951.

Augustine, *The City of God.* Translated by M. Dods, G. Wil-
son, and J. J. Smith. In Whitney J. Oates (ed.),
Basic Writings of Saint Augustine. New York: Random
House, 1948.

_____, *Confessions*. Translated by J. G. Pilkington. In Whitney J. Oates (ed.), *Basic Writings of Saint Augustine*. 2 vols. New York: Random House, 1948.

_____, *De Correptione et Gratia*. Translated by Peter F. Holmes and Robert Ernest Wallis. In *A Select Library of the Nicene and Post-Nicene Fathers of the Christian Church*. First Series, Vol. V: *St. Augustin: Anti-Pelagian Writings*, ed. Philip Schaff. Grand Rapids: Wm. B. Eerdmans Company, 1956.

_____, *De Libero Arbitrio*. Translated by J. H. S. Burleigh. In Burleigh (ed), *Augustine: Earlier Writings*. Vol. VI of *Library of Christian Classics*. Philadelphia: Westminster Press, 1953.

Austin, J. L., *Philosophical Papers*. Edited by J. O. Urmson and G. J. Warnock. Oxford: Clarendon Press, 1961.

Baeumker, Franz, *Die Lehre Anselms von Canterbury über den Willen und seine Wahlfreiheit*. Band X, Heft 6 of *Beiträge zur Geschichte der Philosophie des Mittelalters*. Munster: Aschendorff, 1912.

_____, *Die Lehre des hl. Anselms von Canterbury und des Honorius Augustodunensis vom Willen und von der Gnade*. Teil I. Munster, Aschendorff, 1911.

Baillie, D. M., "Philosophers and Theologians on the Freedom of the Will," *Scottish Journal of Theology*, IV (1951). Reprinted in D. M. Baillie, *The Theology of the Sacraments and Other Papers*. New York: Charles Scribner's Sons, 1957.

Bainvel, J., "Anselme de Cantorbéry," *Dictionnaire de théologie catholique*. Vol. I. Paris: Letouzey et Ané, 1903.

Balthasar, Hans Urs von, "La *Concordantia Libertatis* chez saint Anselme," in *L'Homme devant Dieu: Mélanges offerts au P. Henri de Lubac*. Vol. II. Paris: Aubier, 1963.

Balthasar, N., "La Méthode en théodicée. Idéalisme anselmien et réalisme thomiste," *Annales de l'Institute Supérieur de Philosophie*. I (1912).

Baron, Roger, "L'idée de liberté chez S. Anselme et Hughes de Saint-Victor." *Recherches de Théologie Ancienne et Médiévale*. XXXII (1965).

Barral, Mary Rose, "Anselm and Contemporary Man," *Analecta*

Anselmiana 4:2 (1975).

Barth, Heinrich, *Die Freiheit der Entscheidung im Denken Augustins*. Basel: Helbing & Lichtenhahn, 1935.

Barth, Karl, *Anselm: Fides Quaerens Intellectum*. Translated by I. W. Robertson. London: S. C. M. Press, 1960.

Battenhouse, Roy W. (ed.), *A Companion to the Study of St. Augustine*. New York: Oxford University Press, 1955.

Baucher, Dom J., "Justice," *Dictionnaire de Théologie Catholique*. Vol. VIII. Paris: Letouzey et Ané, 1903.

Baudry, L., "La préscience divine chez saint Anselme," *Archives d'histoire doctrinale et littéraire du moyen âge*, XIII (1940-42).

Bayart, J., "The Concept of Mystery According to St. Anselm of Canterbury," *Recherches de théologie ancienne et médiévale*, IX (1937).

Becelaere, E. L. van, "Grace, Doctrine of (Roman Catholic)," *Encyclopedia of Religion and Ethics*. Vol. VI. New York: Charles Scribner's Sons, 1914.

Becker, J. B., "Der Satz des hl. Anselm: *Credo ut Intelligam*, in seiner Bedeuteng und Tragweite," *Philosophisches Jahrbuch der Görres-Gesellschaft*, XIX (1906).

Berofsky, Barnard (ed.), *Free Will and Determinism*. New York: Harper and Row, 1966.

Betzendorfer, W., "Glauben und Wissen bei Anselm von Canterbury," *Zeitschrift für Kirchengeschichte*, XLVIII (1929)

_____, *Glauben und Wissen bei grossen Denkern des Mittelalters*. Gotha, 1931.

Bird, Otto A., *The Idea of Justice*. New York: Frederick A. Praeger Publishers, 1967.

Blachere, DePaule, "Le péché originel d'après saint Anselme," *Revue Augustinienne*, VI (1905).

Bochenski, I., *Ancient Formal Logic*. Amsterdam: North-Holland Publishing Co., 1951.

Bouchitté, H., *Le rationalisme chrétien à la fin du XIe siècle*. Paris: Libraire d'Amyot, 1842.

Bourke, V. J., "Human Tendencies, Will and Freedom," *Actes du Premier Congrès Internationale de Philosophie Médiévale: L'Homme et son destin.* Louvain, 1960.

_____, *Will in Western Thought.* New York: Sheed and Ward, 1964.

Boyer, C., *L'idée de vérité dans la philosophie de saint Augustin.* Paris: Beauchesne, 1940.

Braga, G. C., "Il problema della libertà in S. Anselme," *Sophia,* III (1935).

Bréhier, E., *The Middle Ages and the Renaissance.* Part III of *The History of Philosophy.* Translated by Wade Baskin. Chicago: University of Chicago Press, 1965.

Briancesco, Eduardo, "Como Interpretar La Moral de San Anselmo?" *Revista Latinoamericana de Filosofie,* 4 (July, 1978), 119-140.

_____, "La Doctrina Moral de San Anselmo," *Ethos: Revista de filosofia Practica,* 4 (1976-77).

Broad, C. D., *Five Types of Ethical Theory.* Paterson, N.J.: Littlefield, Adams and Co., 1959.

Buetler, P. A., *Die Seinslehre des hl. Anselm von Canterbury.* Ingenbohl: Theodosius Druckerei, 1959.

Burch, George B., *Early Medieval Philosophy.* Columbia University, N.Y.: King's Crown Press, 1951.

Campbell, C. A., *On Selfhood and Godhood.* London: George Allen and Unwin, 1957.

_____, *In Defense of Free Will and other Philosophical Essays.* New York: Humanities Press, 1967.

Carr, H. Wildon, *The Free Will Problem.* London: Benn, 1928.

Cauchy, V., *Désir Naturel et Béatitude chez saint Thomas.* Montreal: Fides, 1958.

Cayré, F., *La contemplation augustinienne.* Paris: Desclée de Brouwer, 1954.

Chisholm, R. M. "The Ethics of Requirement," *American Philosophical Quarterly,* I (1964).

Choquette, Imelda, "*Voluntas, Affectio* and *Potestas* in the

Liber de Voluntate of St. Anselm," *Medieval Studies,*
IV (1942).

Church, R. W., *Saint Anselm.* London, 1888.

Clark, Mary, *Augustine Philosopher of Freedom.* New York:
Desclée Company, 1958.

Copleston, Frederick, *A History of Philosophy.* Vol. II:
Medieval Philosophy. Westminster, Md.: Newman Press,
1960.

Corvino, Francesco, "Necessità e libertà de Dio in Pier
Damiani e in Anselmo d'Aosta." *Analecta Anselmiana*
5 (1975).

Courtenay, William J., "Necessity and Freedom in Anselm's
Conception of God." *Analecta Anselmiana* 4:2 (1975).

Cousin, D. R., "Truth," *Proceedings of the Aristotelian
Society,* Supplementary Volume XXIV (1950).

Cranston, Maurice, *Freedom: A New Analysis.* London:
Longmans, Green and Co., 1953.

Crouse, Robert D., "The Augustinian Background of St. Anselm's Concept *Justitia,*" *Canadian Journal of Theology,*
IV (1958).

Davies, A. E., "The Problem of Truth and Existence as Treat-
ed by Anselm," *Proceedings of the Aristotelian Society,*
N.S. XX (1920).

Delhaye, P., "Quelques aspects de la morale de saint Anselme,"
Spicilegium Beccense, Vol. I. Paris: Libraire Philosophique J. Vrin, 1959.

Del Vecchio, G., *Die Gerechtigkeit.* Basel: Verlag für Recht
und Gesellschaft, 1940.

Dempf, Alois, *Metaphysik des Mittelalters.* Munchen & Berlin:
Druck & Verlag von R. Oldenbourg, 1930.

Domet de Vorges, E., *Saint Anselme.* Paris: Félix Alcan,
1901.

_____, "Le milieu philosophique à l'époque de s. Anselme,"
Revue de philosophie, 15 (1909).

Dondeyne, Albert, "Truth and Freedom: A Philosophical Study," in Louis deRaeymaeker, *et al*, *Truth and Freedom*. Pittsburgh: Duquesne University Press, 1954.

Duclow, Donald F., "Structure and Meaning in Anselm's *De Veritate*," *American Benedictine Review* 26 (1975).

Eadmer, *The Life of Saint Anselm Archbishop of Canterbury*. Edited with Introduction, Notes and Translation by R. W. Southern. London: Thomas Nelson and Sons, Ltd., 1962.

Endres, J. A., *Forschungen zur Geschichte der frühmittelalterlichen Philosophie*. Band XVII, Hefte 2-3 of *Beiträge zur Geschichte der Philosophie des Mittelalters*. Munster: Aschendorff, 1919.

Espenberger, Johannes N., *Die Elemente der Erbsunde nach Augustin und der Frühscholastik*. Volume V of *Forschungen zur christlichen Literatur und Dogmengeschichte*. Mainz, 1905.

Evans, G. R., *Anselm and Talking about God*. Oxford: Clarendon Press, 1978.

_____, "*Cur Deus Homo*: The Nature of St. Anselm's Appeal to Reason," *Studia Theologica: Scandinavian Journal of Theology* 31 (1977).

_____, "*Inopes Verborum sunt latini*. Technical language and Technical Terms in the Writings of St. Anselm and Some Commentators of the Mid-Twelfth Century," *Archives d'histoire doctrinale et littéraire du moyen âge*, 43 (1977).

_____, "'*Interior Homo*': Two great monastic scholars on the Soul: St. Anselm and Ailred of Rievaulx," *Studia Monastica*, 19 (1977).

_____, "St. Anselm's Analogies," *Vivarium*, 14 (1976).

_____, "St. Anselm's Definitions," *Archivum Latinitatis Medii Aevi*, Vol. 41 (1979).

_____, "Saint Anselm's Technical Terms of Rhetoric," *Latonus*, 26 (1977).

_____, "Why the 'Fall of Satan' by St. Anselm?" *Recherches de théologie ancienne et médiévale* 45 (1978).

Ewbank, W. F., "Anselm on Sin and Atonement," *Church Quarterly Review*, CXLVI (1948).

Fairweather, E. R., "'*Justitia Dei*' as the '*Ratio*' of the
    Incarnation," *Spicilegium Beccense*. Vol. I. Paris:
    Libraire Philosophique J. Vrin, 1959.

_____, "Truth, Justice and Moral Responsibility in the
    Thought of St. Anselm," *Actes du premier congrés inter-
    national de philosophie médiévale: L'Homme et son
    destin.* Louvain, Nauwelaerts, 1960.

Farrer, Austin, *The Freedom of the Will.* London: Adam and
    Charles Black, 1958.

Filliatre, Charles, *La philosophie de saint Anselme. Ses
    principes, sa nature, son influence.* Paris: Felix
    Alcan, 1920.

Fischer, Joseph, *Die Erkenntnislehre Anselms von Canterbury.*
    Band X, Heft 3 of *Beiträge zur Geschichte der Philoso-
    phie des Mittelalters.* Munster: Aschendorff, 1911.

Flasch, K., "Zum Begriff der Wahrheit bei Anselm von Canter-
    bury," *Philosophisches Jahrbuch,* 72 (1965).

Flew, A. G. N. (ed.), *Logic and Language.* First and Second
    Series. Oxford: Basil Blackwell, 1951-53.

Foley, G. C., *Anselm's Theory of the Atonement.* London:
    Longmans, Green and Co., 1909.

Folghera, J.-D., "La vérité définie par saint Anselme,"
    Revue Thomiste, VIII (1900).

Forest, A., F. VanSteenberghen, M. de Gandillac, *La Mouve-
    ment doctrinal du XIe au XIVe siècle.* Paris: Bloud
    & Gay, 1956.

Foreville, R., "L'école du Bec et le Studium de Cantorbéry
    aux XIe et XIIe siècles," *Bulletin philologique et
    historique du comité des travaux historiques et
    scientifiques.* Paris, 1957.

_____, "L'ultime *ratio* de la morale politique de saint
    Anselme: *Rectitudo voluntatis propter se servata,*"
    Spicilegium Beccense. Vol. I. Paris: Libraire
    Philosophique J. Vrin, 1959.

Franck, G. F., *Anselm von Canterbury.* Tubingen: C. F.
    Osiander, 1842.

Fuchs, Ernst, "Freiheit," *Die Religion in Geschichte und
    Gegenwart.* Third Edition. Vol. II. Tubingen: Mohr,
    1958.

Gallerand, H., "La Rédemption dans l'église latin d'Augustin à Anselme," *Revue de l'histoire des religions*, XCI (1925).

_____, "La Rédemption dans les écrits d'Anselme et d'Abélard," *Revue de l'histoire des religions*, XCI (1925).

Geiger, L. -B., "De la liberté: les conceptions fondamentales et leur retentissement dans la philosophie pratique," *Revue des sciences philosophiques et théologiques,* XLI (1957).

Ghellinck, J. de, *Le mouvement théologique du XIIe siècle.* Paris: Victor Lecoffre, 1914.

Gilson, E., *A History of Christian Philosophy in the Middle Ages.* London: Sheed and Ward, 1955.

_____, *La Doctrine Cartésienne de la Liberté et la Théologie.* Paris: Felix Alcan, 1913.

_____, *Reason and Revelation in the Middle Ages.* New York: Charles Scribner's Sons, 1938.

_____, *The Christian Philosophy of Saint Augustine.* Translated by L. E. M. Lynch. New York: Random House, 1960.

_____, *The Spirit of Medieval Philosophy.* Translated by A. H. C. Downes. New York: Charles Scribner's Sons, 1940.

Gray, Christopher B., "Freedom and Necessity in St. Anselm's Cur Deus Homo," *Franciscan Studies,* 36 (1976).

Gregoire, R., "L'utilisation de l'Écriture sainte chez Anselme de Cantorbéry," *Revue d'ascétique et de mystique,* XXXIX (1963).

Haenchen, E., "Anselm, Glaube und Vernunft," *Zeitschrift für Theologie und Kirche,* XLVIII (1951).

Hampshire, Stuart, *Freedom of the Individual.* New York: Harper and Row, 1965.

_____ (ed.), *Philosophy of Mind.* New York: Harper and Row, 1966.

Harnach, Adolf, *History of Dogma.* Vol. III. Translated by Neil Buchanan. New York: Dover Publications, Inc., 1961.

Hasse, Friedrich R., *Anselm von Canterbury*. 2 vols.
Leipzig: Wilhelm Engelmann, 1843-52. Reprinted
Frankfurt: Minerva G.M.B.H., Univeranderter Nachdruck,
1966.

Hayen, A., "La méthode théologique selon saint Anselme."
Appendix II of "Le Concile de Reims et Gilbert de la
Porrée," *Archives d'Histoire doctrinale et Littéraire
du moyen âge*, X-XI (1935-36).

Heinzmann, R., "*Veritas humanae naturae*. Ein Beiträge zur
Anthropologie Anselms von Canterbury," in Leo
Scheffczyk, et al (eds.), *Wahrheit und Verkündigung*
(Michael Schmaus zum 70. Geburttag). Munich: Paderbor
and Vienna: Schonigh, 1967.

Henry, D. P., *The De Grammatico of St. Anselm: The Theory of
Paronymy*. Notre Dame, Ind.: University of Notre Dame
Press, 1964.

_____, *The Logic of St. Anselm*. Oxford: Clarendon Press,
1967.

_____, *Commentary on De Grammatico*. Dodrecht and
Boston: D. Reidel Publishing Co., 1974.

_____, "Numerically Definite Reasoning in the *Cur Deus
Homo*," *Dominican Studies*, VI (1953).

_____, "Remarks on Saint Anselm's Treatment of Possibil-
ity," *Spicilegium Beccense*. Vol. I. Paris: Libraire
Philosophique J. Vrin, 1959.

_____, "St. Anselm's *De Grammatico*," *Philosophical Quar-
terly*, X (1960).

_____, "St. Anselm on Scriptural Analysis," *Sophia*
(Australia), I (1962).

_____, "St. Anselm on the Varieties of 'Doing,'" *Theoria*,
XIX (1953).

_____, "St. Anselm's Nonsense," *Mind*, LXXII (1963).

_____, "The Scope of the Logic of St. Anselm," *Actes du
premier congrès internationale de philosophie médiévale
L'Homme et son destin*. Louvain: Nauwelaerts, 1960.

_____, "Why '*Grammaticus*'?" *Archivum Latinatis Medii Aevi*,
XXVIII (1958).

Heyer, George S., "St. Anselm on the Harmony between God's
Mercy and God's Justice," in *The Heritage of Christian
Thought: Essays in Honor of Robert L. Calhoun*. Edited

by Robert E. Cushman and Egil Grislis. New York:
Harper and Row, 1965.

'Homme devant Dieu: mélanges offerts au P. Henri de Lubac.
3 vols. Paris: Aubier, 1963-64.

*'Homme et son destin. Actes du premier congrès interna-
tionale de philosophie médiévale.* Louvain: 1960.

Hook, Sidney (ed.), *Determinism and Freedom in the Age of
Modern Science.* New York: New York University Press,
1958.

Hopkins, Jasper, *A Companion to the Study of St. Anselm.*
Minneapolis: University of Minnesota Press, 1972.

Hopkins, Jasper and Herbert Richardson, "Editors' Introduction" to Anselm of Canterbury, *Truth, Freedom, and Evil:
Three Philosophical Dialogues.* Translated by Hopkins
and Richardson. New York: Harper Torchbooks, 1967.

Hufnagel, Alfons, "Anselm und das Naturrecht," *Analecta
Anselmiana,* 5 (1976): 133-40.

Kane, G. Stanley, "'*Fides Quaerens Intellectum*' in Anselm's
Thought," *Scottish Journal of Theology,* XXVI (1973).

_____, "Anselm's Definition of Freedom," *Religious
Studies,* IX (1973).

_____, "Elements of Ethical Theory in the Thought of
Saint Anselm," *Studies in Medieval Culture,* XII (1978).

Kemp, J., *Reason, Action and Morality.* London: Routledge
and Kegan Paul, 1964.

Kenny, Anthony, *Action, Emotion and Will.* London: Routledge
and Kegan Paul, 1963.

Kirk, K. E., *The Vision of God: The Christian Doctrine of
the Summum Bonum.* London: Longmans, Green and Co.,
1931. Reprinted in paperback edition. New York:
Harper Torchbooks, Harper and Row, 1966.

Klubertanz, George P., "St. Thomas' Treatment of the Axiom,
'*Omne Agens Agit Propter Finem,*'" in Charles J. O'Neil
(ed.), *An Etienne Gilson Tribute.* Milwaukee:
Marquette University Press, 1959.

Kohlenberger, Helmut K., *Similitudo und Ratio: Überlegungen
zur Methode bei Anselm von Canterbury.* Bonn:
H. Grundmann, 1972.

_____ (ed.), *Sola Ratione.* Stuttgart: Frommann, 1970.

Kors, J.-B., *La Justice Primitive et le Péché Originel.*
Kain: Le Saulchoir, 1922.

Laird, John, *On Human Freedom.* London: George Allen and
Unwin, 1947.

_____, "Will," *Encyclopedia of Religion and Ethics.* Vol.

XII. New York: Charles Scribner's Sons, 1922.

Landgraf, A. M., "Der Gerechitgkeitsbegriff des hl. Anselm
    von Canterbury und seine Bedeutung für die Theologie
    der Frühscholastik," *Divus Thomas*, Freiburg, 1927.

_____, *Dogmengeschichte der Frühscholastik*. 4 vols.
    Regensburg: Verlag Friedrich Pustet, 1952.

Lapierre, Michael J., "Aquinas' Interpretation of Anselm's
    Definition of Truth," *Sciences Ecclésiastiques*, XVIII
    (1966).

Leclerq, J., *The Love of Learning and the Desire for God*.
    Translated by Catharine Misrahi. New York: New Ameri-
    can Library, Mentor Omega Book, 1962.

Leff, Gordon, *Medieval Thought from Saint Augustine to
    Ockham*. Hammondsworth: Penguin Books, 1958.

Lehrer, Keith (ed.), *Freedom and Determinism*. New York:
    Random House, 1966.

Leipoldt, J., "Der Begriff *meritum* in Anselms von Canterbury
    Versönungslehre," *Theologische Studien und Kritiken*,
    LXXVII (1904).

Levi, I. and S. Morgenbesser, "Belief and Disposition,"
    American Philosophical Quarterly, I (1964).

Lohmeyer, E., *Die Lehre vom Willen bei Anselm von Canterbury*
    Lucka: Reinhold Berger, 1914.

Lottin, O., "Le concept de justice chez les théologiens du
    moyen âge avant l'introduction d'Aristote," *Revue
    Thomiste*, XLIV (1938).

_____, *Le droit naturel chez saint Thomas et ses
    prédécesseurs*. Bruges: Charles Beyaert, 1951.

_____, "Les definitions du libre arbitre au XIIe siècle,"
    Revue Thomiste, XXXII (1927).

_____, "Libre arbitre et liberté depuis saint Anselme
    jusqu'à la fin du XIIIe siècle," in Lottin's
    Psychologie et Morale aux XIIe et XIIIe siècles. Vol.
    I. Louvain: Abbaye du Mont César, 1942.

Macdonald, A. J., *Authority and Reason in the Early Middle
    Ages*. London: Oxford University Press, 1933.

McGiffert, A. C., *A History of Christian Thought*. Vol. II.

New York: Charles Scribner's Sons, 1933.

McGill, V. J., "Conflicting Theories of Freedom," *Philosophy and Phenomenological Research,* XX (1960).

McIntyre, John, "Premises and Conclusions in the System of St. Anselm's Theology," *Spicilegium Beccense.* Vol. I. Paris: Librairie philosophique J. Vrin, 1959.

_____, *St. Anselm and His Critics. A Re-interpretation of the Cur Deus Homo.* Edinburgh: Oliver and Boyd, 1954.

Mackenzie, Donald. "Free Will," *Encyclopedia of Religion and Ethics.* Vol. VI. New York: Charles Scribner's Sons, 1914.

_____, "Libertarianism and Necessitarianism," *Encyclopedia of Religion and Ethics.* Vol. VII. New York: Charles Scribner's Sons, 1915.

McKeon, Richard, *Freedom and History, the Semantics of Philosophical Controversies and Ideological Conflicts.* New York: Noonday Press, 1952.

_____, "Philosophic Differences and the Issues of Freedom," *Ethics,* LXI (1950-51).

Mackintosh, H. R., "Grace," *Encyclopedia of Religion and Ethics.* Vol. VI. New York: Charles Scribner's Sons, 1914.

Mandonnet, Pierre, *Siger de Brabant et L'averroisme latin au XIIIe siècle: Étude critique et documents inédits.* Fribourg: La Libraire de L'Université, 1899.

Marechaux, B., "A propos du *'Fides quaerens intellectum'* de saint Anselme," *Revista Storica Benedettina,* Vol. IV (1909).

Martin, A. S., "Predestination," *Encyclopedia of Religion and Ethics.* Vol. X. New York: Charles Scribner's Sons, 1919.

Mascall, E. L., "Faith and Reason: Anselm and Aquinas," *Journal of Theological Studies,* XIV (1963).

Melden, A. I., "Willing," *Philosophical Review,* LXIX (1960).

Merton, Louis, "Reflections on Some Recent Studies of St. Anselm," *Monastic Studies,* III (1965).

Michaud-Quantin, P., "Notes sur la vocabulaire psychologique de saint Anselme," *Spicilegium Beccense.* Vol. I. Paris: Libraire Philosophique J. Vrin, 1959.

Michel, A., "Justice Originelle," *Dictionnaire de Théologie Catholique*. Vol. VIII. Paris: Letouzey et Ané, 1903.

Morgenbesser, Sidney and James Walsh (eds.), *Free Will*. Englewood Cliffs, N.J.: Prentice-Hall, Inc., 1962.

Morris, H. (ed.), *Freedom and Responsibility*. Stanford: Stanford University Press, 1961.

Nédoncelle, Maurice, "La notion de personne dans l'oeuvre de saint Anselme," *Spicilegium Beccense*. Vol. I. Paris: Libraire Philosophique J. Vrin, 1959.

Nourrisson, J. F., *La philosophie de saint Augustin*. Second Edition. 2 vols. Paris: Minerva, 1866.

Oates, Whitney J., *Basic Writings of Saint Augustine*. Two vols. New York: Random House, 1948.

Ofstad, Harald, *An Inquiry into the Freedom of Decision*. Oslo: Norwegian Universities Press; London: George Allen and Unwin, Ltd., 1961.

_____, "Recent Work on the Free-Will Problem," *American Philosophical Quarterly*, IV (July, 1967).

Oppenheim, Felix E., *Dimensions of Freedom: An Analysis*. New York: St. Martin's Press, 1961.

Osborn, Robert T., *Freedom in Modern Theology*. Philadelphia Westminster Press, 1967.

Ostlender, H., *Anselm von Canterbury, der Vater der Scholastik*. Dusseldorf, 1927.

Overbeck, F., *Vorlesungen über die Frühscholastik*. Basel: B. Schwabe & Co., 1917.

Palmer, G. H., *The Problem of Freedom*. Boston: Houghton Mifflin, 1911.

Partridge, P. H., "Freedom," *Encyclopedia of Philosophy*. Edited by Paul Edwards. Vol. III. New York: The Macmillan Company and The Free Press, 1967.

Pears, D. F. (ed.), *Freedom and the Will*. London: Macmillan and Co., Ltd., 1963.

Peters, R. S., *The Concept of Motivation*. London: Routledge and Kegan Paul, 1958.

helan, Gerald B., *The Wisdom of Saint Anselm*. Latrobe, Pa.: Archabbey Press, n.d.

itcher, George (ed.), *Truth*. Englewood Cliffs, N.J.: Prentice-Hall, Inc., 1964.

ontifex, M. *The Problem of Free Choice*. (A translation with introduction and notes of Augustine's *De Libero Arbitrio*.) Vol. XXII of *Ancient Christian Writers*. Westminster, Md.: Newman Press, 1955.

_____, *Providence and Freedom*. London: Burns and Oates, 1960.

ope, R. Martin, "Liberty," *Encyclopedia of Religion and Ethics*. Vol. VII. New York: Charles Scribner's Sons, 1915.

ouchet, Robert, *La Rectitudo chez saint Anselme*. Paris: Études Augustiniennes, 1964.

rior, A. N., "The Correspondence Theory of Truth," *Encyclopedia of Philosophy*. Edited by Paul Edwards. Vol. II. New York: The Macmillan Company and The Free Press, 1967.

aab, E. F. X., *Die Wahrheit als metaphysische Problem*. Munchen: Verlagsanstalt und Kunstdruckerei Manz in Dillingen an der Donau, 1959.

agey, R. P., *Histoire de saint Anselme*. Two vols. Paris and Lyon: Delhomme et Briguet, 1890.

assam, J., "Existence et Vérité chez Anselme," *Archives de philosophie*, XXIV (1961).

émusat, Charles de, *Anselme de Cantorbéry*. Second Edition. Paris: Libraire Academique, Didier et Cie, 1868.

evue de Philosophie, XV (1909). (The entire issue is composed of articles on Anselm.)

ichard, P., "Anselme de Cantorbéry," *Dictionnaire d'histoire et de géographie ecclésiastique*. Vol. III. Paris: Letouzey et Ané, 1924.

igg, J. M., *Saint Anselm of Canterbury. A Chapter in the History of Religion*. London: Methuen and Co., 1896.

ivière, J., "'Justice' et 'droit' dans la langue de saint Augustin," *Bulletin de littérature ecclésiastique*, XXXIII (1932).

Roberts, Victor W., "The Relation of Faith and Reason in Saint Anselm of Canterbury," *American Benedictine Review*, 25 (1974).

_____, "Saint Anselm of Canterbury's Teaching on Faith," *American Benedictine Review*, 21 (1970).

Robinson, Richard, *Definition*. Oxford: Clarendon Press, 1954.

Rohmer, J., *La finalité morale chez les théologiens de saint Augustin à Duns Scotus*. Paris: Librarie Philosophique J. Vrin. 1938.

Rondet, Henri, "Grace et Péché, l'augustinisme de saint Anselme," *Spicilegium Beccense*. Vol. I. Paris: Librarie Philosophique, 1959.

Roques, R., "*Derisio, Simplicitas, Insipientia*: Remarques mineures sur la terminologie de saint Anselme," in *L'Homme devant Dieu: Mélanges offerts au P. Henri de Lubac*. Vol. II. Paris: Aubier, 1963.

Rule, M., *The Life and Times of Saint Anselm*. Two vols. London: Kegan Paul, Trench, and Co., 1883.

Ryan, Alan, "Freedom," *Philosophy*, XL (1965).

Ryle, Gilbert, *The Concept of Mind*. New York: Barnes and Noble, 1949.

Schmitt, F. S., "Anselm of Canterbury," *New Catholic Encyclopedia*, Vol. I. New York: McGraw-Hill, 1967.

_____, "Eine fruehe Rezension des Werkes *De Concordia* des hl. Anselms von Canterbury," *Revue Bénédictine*, XLVIII (1936).

_____, "Zur Chronologie der Werke des hl. Anselm von Canterbury," *Revue Bénédictine*, XLIV (1932).

Schurr, Adolf, "Vie et Réflexion selon saint Anselme" *Archives de Philosophie*, 35 (1972). (Includes a section on Anselm's notion of truth.

Séjourné, P., "Les Trois Aspects du Péché dans le *Cur Deus Homo*," *Revue des sciences religieuses*, XXIV (1950).

Sheets, John R., "Justice in the Moral Thought of Saint Anselm," *Modern Schoolman*, XXV (1948).

Sidgwick, Henry, "The Kantian Conception of Free Will,"

Mind, XIII (1888). Reprinted in Sidgwick, *The Methods of Ethics.* Seventh Edition. Chicago: University of Chicago Press, 1907; reissued 1962.

Söhngen, G., *"Rectitudo* bei Anselm von Canterbury als Ober-begriff von Wahrheit und Gerechtigkeit," in Helmut K. Kohlenberger (ed.), *Sola Ratione.* Stuttgart: Frommann, 1970.

Sontag, F., "Augustine's Metaphysics and Free Will," *Harvard Theological Review,* Vol. LX (1967).

Southern, R. W., *Saint Anselm and His Biographer. A Study of Monastic Life and Thought, 1059-c. 1130.* Cambridge: Cambridge University Press, 1963.

Spicilegium Beccense. Vol. I. Paris: Libraire Philosophique J. Vrin, 1959.

Stolz, A., *Anselm von Canterbury: Sein Leben, seine Bedeutung, seine Hauptwerke.* Munchen: Kösel-Pustet, 1937.

Strawson, P. F., "Truth," *Analysis,* IX (1949).

Taylor, Charles, *The Explanation of Behavior.* London: Routledge and Kegan Paul, 1964.

Taylor, H. O., *The Medieval Mind. A History of the Development of Thought and Emotion in the Middle Ages.* Two vols. Fourth Edition. London: Macmillan and Company, 1927.

Taylor, Richard, "Determinism," *Encyclopedia of Philosophy.* Edited by Paul Edwards. Vol. II. New York: The Macmillan Company and The Free Press, 1967.

Thieme, K., *"Fides Quaerens Intellectum,"* **Divus Thomas,** LVII (1944).

Thonnard, F.-J., "Charactères augustiniens de la méthode philosophique de saint Anselme," *Spicilegium Beccense,* Vol. I. Paris: Libraire Philosophique J. Vrin, 1959.

_____, "La personne humaine dans l'augustinisme médiéval (saint Anselme et saint Bonaventure)," *L'Homme et son destin.* Louvain: 1960.

Tielsch, Elfriede, "Anselm von Canterburys Stellung inner-halb der Geschichte des 'De Libero Arbitrio'-Problems," *Analecta Anselmiana,* 4:2 (1975).

Tomberlin, James E., "About the Problem of Truth," *Philoso-
    phy and Phenomenological Research,* XXVII (1966).

Toner, P. J., "St. Anselm's Definition of Original Sin,"
    The Irish Theological Quarterly, III (1908).

Torrance, T. F., "The Ethical Implications of Anselm's *De
    Veritate,*" *Theologische Zeitschrift,* 26 (1968).

Turmel, J., "Le dogme du péché originel d'après saint
    Augustin dans l'église latine," *Revue d'histoire et de
    littérature religieuses.* 3 parts, 1901, 1902, 1903.

Vanni Rovighi, Sofia, "Il problema del male in Anselmo
    d'Aosta," *Analecta Anselmiana,* 5 (1976).

_____, *S. Anselmo e la Filosofia del Sec. XI.* Milan:
    Fratelli Bocca, 1949.

_____, *Studi di Filosofia Medioevale* (Collected Essays).
    Vol. I: *Da sant' Agostino al XII secolo.* Milan:
    Vita e Pensiero, 1978. Includes "'Ratio' in S.
    Anselmo d'Aosta," "Libertà e libero arbitrio in S.
    Anselmo d'Aosta," "L'ètica di S. Anselmo," and "Notes
    sur l'influence de saint Anselme au XIIe siècle."

Vérité, La., *Actes du XIIe Congrès des Societés de Philoso-
    phie de Langue Française.* 2 vols. Louvain and Paris:
    Nauwelaerts, 1964-65.

Verweyen, Johannes, *Das Problem der Willensfreiheit in der
    Scholastik.* Heidelberg: Carl Winter's Universatsbuch-
    handlung, 1909.

Viglino, H., "De Mente sancti Anselmi quoad pristinum
    hominis status," *Divus Thomas,* XLII (1939).

Vuillemin, Jules, *Le Dieu d'Anselme et les apparences de la
    raison.* Paris: Editions Montaigne, 1971.

Walton, Douglas, "St. Anselm and the Logical Syntax of
    Agency," *Franciscan Studies,* 14 (1976).

Warnach, V., "Wort und Wirklichkeit bei Anselm von Canter-
    bury," *Salzburger Jahrbuch für Philosophie,* V-VI
    (1961-62).

Warnock, G. J., "Truth and Correspondence," in C. D. Rollins
    (ed.), *Knowledge and Experience.* Pittsburgh: Uni-
    versity of Pittsburgh Press, 1962.

Weber, Eduoard-Henri, "Dynamisme du bien et statut histori-
que du destin crée. Du traité sur la chute du diable
de s. Anselme aux questions sur le mal de Thomas
d'Aquin," in Albert Zimmerman (ed.), *Die Macht des
Guten und Bösen: Vorstellungen in XII und XIII
Jahrhundert über ihr Wirken in der Heilsgeschichte*.
Berlin & New York: B. de Gruyter, 1977.

Weddington, A. van, *Essai Critique sur la Philosophie de
saint Anselme de Cantorbéry*. Vol. 25 of *Memoires
couronnés et autre memoires publiés par l'Académie
Royale des Sciences, des Lettres et des Beaux-Arts
de Belgiques*. Bruxelles, 1875.

Welch, A. C., *Anselm and His Work*. New York: Charles
Scribner's Sons, 1901.

Williams, N. P., *The Grace of God*. London: Longmans, Green
and Co., 1930. Printed in paperback edition by
Hodder and Stoughton, 1966.

_____, *The Ideas of the Fall and of Original Sin. A
Historical and Critical Study*. London: Longmans,
Green and Co., 1929.

Wilmart, A., *Méditations et prières de saint Anselm*.
Paris: Maredsons, 1923.

Wolz, Henry G., "Plato's Doctrine of Truth: *Orthotes* or
Aletheia?" *Philosophy and Phenomenological Research*,
XXVII (1966).

Woozley, A. D., "Dispositions," *Mind*, LVII (1948).

Wulf, M. de, *History of Medieval Philosophy*. Translation
of the 6th French Edition by Ernest C. Messenger.
Vol. I: *From the Beginnings to the End of the Twelfth
Century*. New York: Dover Publications, 1952.

TEXTS AND STUDIES IN RELIGION